Communication, Legitimation and Morality in Modern Politics

Why? This question drives scientific inquiry, not least in the social sciences: why war, revolution, racism and inequality? Asking and debating about 'why?', however, is not the prerogative of scholars; social actors, endowed with thought, reflection and speech, do it too. While we all dance to the beat of genes, emotions, identities and habituated norms, we occasionally stop to ask 'why?' The social sciences have been long preoccupied with the ostensibly objective 'why' while sidelining the social, intersubjective 'why?' This book focuses on the latter, analysing the social actors' search for justification in their public, political sphere. Justifications, broadly understood, are answers to why-questions given and debated by social actors. The chapters focus on public justifications. While the contributors do not submit that private encounters addressing why-questions do not matter, they choose to put public encounters addressing these questions under scrutiny. Given the ongoing tele-communications revolution, and new political practices associated with it, these public encounters become increasingly pertinent in our evolving political orders.

This book originally published as a special issue of *Contemporary Politics*.

Uriel Abulof is a Senior Lecturer of Politics, teaching at Tel-Aviv University, Israel, and Princeton University, USA. He is the author of *The Mortality and Morality of Nations* (2015) and *Living on the Edge: The Existential Uncertainty of Zionism* (2016), which won Israel's best academic book award (Bahat Prize). His articles have appeared in journals such as *International Studies Quarterly*, *International Political Sociology*, *Nations and Nationalism*, *British Journal of Sociology*, *European Journal of International Relations*, *Ethnic and Racial Studies*, and *International Politics*.

Markus Kornprobst holds the Chair in International Relations at the Diplomatic Academy of Vienna, Austria. He previously taught at the School of Public Policy at University College London and Magdalen College at Oxford University, UK. His research appears in leading journals in the discipline, such as *International Organization*, *European Journal of International Relations*, *International Studies Review*, *Review of International Studies*, and *Millennium*. He is the author of *Irredentism in European Politics* and co-editor of *Metaphors of Globalization*.

Communication, Legitimation and Morality in Modern Politics

Studying Public Justification

Edited by
Uriel Abulof and Markus Kornprobst

Routledge
Taylor & Francis Group

LONDON AND NEW YORK

First published 2018 by Routledge

2 Park Square, Milton Park, Abingdon, Oxfordshire OX14 4RN
52 Vanderbilt Avenue, New York, NY 10017

Routledge is an imprint of the Taylor & Francis Group, an informa business

First issued in paperback 2019

British Library Cataloguing in Publication Data
A catalogue record for this book is available from the British Library

ISBN 13: 978-1-138-55494-8 (hbk)
ISBN 13: 978-0-367-89199-2 (pbk)

Typeset in Myriad Pro
by RefineCatch Limited, Bungay, Suffolk

Publisher's Note
The publisher accepts responsibility for any inconsistencies that may have arisen during the conversion of this book from journal articles to book chapters, namely the possible inclusion of journal terminology.

Disclaimer
Every effort has been made to contact copyright holders for their permission to reprint material in this book. The publishers would be grateful to hear from any copyright holder who is not here acknowledged and will undertake to rectify any errors or omissions in future editions of this book.

Contents

Citation Information   vii
Notes on Contributors   ix

Introduction: the politics of public justification   1
Uriel Abulof and Markus Kornprobst

1. A psychological perspective on moral reasoning, processes of decision-making,
   and moral resistance   19
   Elliot Turiel

2. Conscientious politics and Israel's moral dilemmas   34
   Uriel Abulof

3. The fusion of the private and public sectors   53
   Amitai Etzioni

4. Empirical legitimation analysis in International Relations: how to learn from
   the insights – and avoid the mistakes – of research in EU studies   63
   Achim Hurrelmann

5. The public valuation of religion in global health governance: spiritual health
   and the faith factor   81
   Tine Hanrieder

6. Arguing deep ideational change   100
   Markus Kornprobst and Martin Senn

7. Caveat: addressing public justification as an empirical phenomenon   120
   Liah Greenfeld

8. Unpacking public justification   126
   Uriel Abulof and Markus Kornprobst

Index   135

Citation Information

The chapters in this book were originally published in *Contemporary Politics*, volume 23, issue 1 (March 2017). When citing this material, please use the original page numbering for each article, as follows:

Introduction
Introduction: the politics of public justification
Uriel Abulof and Markus Kornprobst
Contemporary Politics, volume 23, issue 1 (March 2017), pp. 1–18

Chapter 1
A psychological perspective on moral reasoning, processes of decision-making, and moral resistance
Elliot Turiel
Contemporary Politics, volume 23, issue 1 (March 2017), pp. 19–33

Chapter 2
Conscientious politics and Israel's moral dilemmas
Uriel Abulof
Contemporary Politics, volume 23, issue 1 (March 2017), pp. 34–52

Chapter 3
The fusion of the private and public sectors
Amitai Etzioni
Contemporary Politics, volume 23, issue 1 (March 2017), pp. 53–62

Chapter 4
Empirical legitimation analysis in International Relations: how to learn from the insights – and avoid the mistakes – of research in EU studies
Achim Hurrelmann
Contemporary Politics, volume 23, issue 1 (March 2017), pp. 63–80

Chapter 5
The public valuation of religion in global health governance: spiritual health and the faith factor
Tine Hanrieder
Contemporary Politics, volume 23, issue 1 (March 2017), pp. 81–99

Chapter 6

Arguing deep ideational change
Markus Kornprobst and Martin Senn
Contemporary Politics, volume 23, issue 1 (March 2017), pp. 100–119

Chapter 7

Caveat: addressing public justification as an empirical phenomenon
Liah Greenfeld
Contemporary Politics, volume 23, issue 1 (March 2017), pp. 120–125

Chapter 8

Unpacking public justification
Uriel Abulof and Markus Kornprobst
Contemporary Politics, volume 23, issue 1 (March 2017), pp. 126–133

For any permission-related enquiries please visit:
http://www.tandfonline.com/page/help/permissions

Notes on Contributors

Uriel Abulof is a Senior Lecturer of Politics, teaching at Tel-Aviv University, Israel, and Princeton University, USA. He is the author of *The Mortality and Morality of Nations* (2015) and *Living on the Edge: The Existential Uncertainty of Zionism* (2016), which won Israel's best academic book award (Bahat Prize). His articles have appeared in journals such as *International Studies Quarterly*, *International Political Sociology*, *Nations and Nationalism*, *British Journal of Sociology*, *European Journal of International Relations*, *Ethnic and Racial Studies*, and *International Politics*.

Amitai Etzioni is a Professor of International Affairs at the George Washington University, USA. He previously served as a Senior Advisor at the Carter White House; taught at Columbia University, Harvard University, and the University of California at Berkeley; and served as the President of the American Sociological Association.

Liah Greenfeld is a Professor of Sociology, Political Science and Anthropology at Boston University, USA. She is the author of, among other publications, a trilogy on nationalism and modernity: *Nationalism: Five Roads to Modernity*, *The Spirit of Capitalism: Nationalism and Economic Growth*, and *Mind, Modernity, Madness: The impact of Culture on Human Experience* (1992, 2001, 2013).

Tine Hanrieder is a Senior Researcher at the WZB Berlin Social Science Center, Research Unit Global Governance, Germany. She has published articles on global health politics, international theory and institutional change in journals including *International Theory* and the *European Journal of International Relations*.

Achim Hurrelmann is Associate Professor of Political Science and Director of the Institute of European, Russian and Eurasian Studies (EURUS) at Carleton University, Ottawa, Canada. He holds the Jean Monnet Chair 'Democracy in the European Union'.

Markus Kornprobst holds the Chair in International Relations at the Diplomatic Academy of Vienna, Austria. His research appears in leading journals in the discipline, such as *International Organization*, *European Journal of International Relations*, *International Studies Review*, *Review of International Studies*, and *Millennium*.

Martin Senn is Associate Professor of International Relations at the University of Innsbruck, Austria. In his research, he focuses on ideas and international order, rhetoric, the (non) proliferation of nuclear weapons, and targeted-killing practices.

Elliot Turiel received a PhD in Psychology from Yale University and has taught at Columbia University, Harvard University, and the University of California, Santa Cruz. He is currently Professor in Education at the University of California, Berkeley, USA, where he holds the Jerome A. Hutto Chair in Education.

Notes on Contributors

Introduction: the politics of public justification

Uriel Abulof and Markus Kornprobst

ABSTRACT
Introducing the special issue, this introduction sketches a broad frame for studying public justification. Addressing the relevance of studying this phenomenon, we contend that justificatory processes are very much at the core today's politics. Defining the concept inclusively, we highlight the relevance of communicative agency and, at the same time, the salience of communicative contexts that enable this agency. Casting our net widely, we show how public justification is related to other, more thoroughly studied concepts, such as legitimacy, authority and power. Encouraging students of public justification to add to our understanding of justificatory processes, we highlight multiple fruitful methodological avenues for studying the concept.

Introduction

Why? This question drives scientific inquiry, not least in the social sciences: why war, revolution, racism and inequality? Asking and debating about 'why?', however, is not the prerogative of scholars; social actors, endowed with thought, reflection and speech, do it too (Archer, 2012; Sandel, 2005). While we all dance to the beat of genes, emotions, identities and habituated norms, we occasionally stop to ask 'why?' The social sciences have been long preoccupied with the ostensibly objective 'why' while sidelining the social, intersubjective 'why?' This special issue focuses on the latter, analysing the social actors' search for justification in their public, political, sphere.

Justifications, broadly understood, are answers to why-questions given and debated by social actors. In order to ensure that our task remains doable, we focus on public justifications. While we do not submit that private encounters addressing why-questions do not matter, we choose to put public encounters addressing these questions under scrutiny. Given the ongoing telecommunications revolution, and new political practices associated with it, these public encounters become increasingly pertinent in our evolving political orders.

This introduction is organized into four sections. First, we underline why it is important to address the social why-question. Human beings are the only justificatory animals. Thus, it is not sufficient to assume justification away. The *onus* is on the researcher to understand how this justification happens and what political repercussions failures and successes of justifications have. Second, we conceptualize public justifications as reason giving and contesting in public communicative encounters that are made possible and impossible by social context, and (re-)produce policies and even political orders. Third, we propose several research avenues for studying how social actors come to justify and how they ought to do so. We encourage multidisciplinary and multiperspectival research that criss-crosses established scholarly categories. Finally, we provide an overview of the contributions to this special issue. They demonstrate empirically that human beings are justificatory animals, trace the processes through which justification affect political outcomes, and develop normative arguments for how they ought to do so.

Human beings as justificatory animals

This collection of papers proceeds from a clearly articulated ontological micro-foundation. Human beings have evolved into justificatory animals. Practices of justification have come to be deeply woven into the political orders we inhabit (*nomization*).

Humans are the only *why*-asking animals. This capacity and proclivity did not emerge at the dawn of humanity. It has evolved gradually. This uniquely human software required certain 'hardware,' such as our advanced prefrontal cortex. It also required language – not as a mere form of communication, which most animals possess – but the ability, even the instinct, to use a finite set of elements (such as words) and rules (grammar and syntax) to create infinite combinations, each of which is comprehensible (Pinker, 1994). Only humans can communicate across mediums about intangibles. People are storytellers, contriving narratives to express and ease their anxieties and uncertainties, to justify themselves and their actions – to themselves and to others – probing alternative courses of being and doing (Bruner, 1986, 1990; Gottschall, 2012; Henriques, 2011, p. 18). Importantly, justification can transpire a priori as well as a posteriori; we may give reasons both before and after, and indeed throughout, our practical conduct.

As human civilization has evolved, so has our factual, practical and moral *Why* – our justificatory capacity – and its political impact on an increasingly universal scale. Jaspers (1953) famously designated the period from 800 to 200 BC as the Axial Age, when 'the *specifically human in man*' blossomed. Poets, prophets and sages in China (e.g. Confucius), India (Buddha), Persia (Zarathustra), Israel (Isaiah) and Greece (Plato) embarked on religious and philosophical quests that changed the course of humanity, indeed shaped it. They have critically observed their societies, and prescribed changes.

The Axial separation of the *is* from the *ought* – the real from the ideal – was transformative. Bellah (2011) ascribes it to socio-economic shifts that engendered simultaneous legitimacy crises of urbanized societies – and motivated their individualistic renouncers, and defenders. However, these 'Axial agents' generated the very idea of 'legitimation crisis' on a universal scale: they contested the given, calling into question the very existence of institutions and practices that were previously seen as self-evident.

The Axial Age cast an existential spell. *Logos* appended *mythos* to deliver *nomos* out of *chaos*; refutable reflection conjoined fictitious narration to breed a socially meaningful order in a meaningless universe. The *nomos* turned out to be a constant work-in-progress: we construct, construe and contest our social order to shield us against *anomy*, socio-moral vacuity. As Berger (1967, pp. 23–22) suggested, 'Every socially constructed nomos must face the constant possibility of its collapse, into anomy … every nomos is an area of meaning carved out of a vast mass of meaninglessness,' and thus 'the most important function of society is *nomization*,' evincing the 'human craving for meaning that appears to have the force of instinct.'

Crucially, the Axial agents conveyed their reasoning to others, justifying their claims. Nomization is communicative; ultimately, 'nomos is constructed and sustained in conversation with significant others' (Berger, 1967, p. 21). Nomization involves both reification and 'aporiation,' as some agents attempt to turn the social order into a given, while others challenge it (fostering *aporia*, cognitive puzzlement) through deliberation. Invariably, we inhabit a world of multiple *nomoi*, or *nomospheres*, a world where cooperating and competing cultures subscribe to different social orders to provide meaning and moral guidance to their life, not least in the political domain.

Since the Axial Age, legitimation has permeated the construction and maintenance of socio-political orders within and across state borders (Fukuyama, 2011, 2014; Harle, 1998). *What is*, and *why* it *ought* to, became invariably entangled. Power, practice and passion were not enough; persuasion too became part of politics. Reasons have been publicly given to convince people that certain orders are just, or at least justifiable. Importantly, however, public justification – the articulated, communicative, reasoning of politics – need not be principled. Unlike legitimation, which many see as pertaining to social order alone (see Hurrelmann, 2017), public justification can also be pragmatic, reasoning the practicalities of politics. Granted, principled and pragmatic arguments often intertwine, even coalesce, but typically still figure differently. Overall, legitimation can, but need not, involve justification. If you order, 'Obey!' and I reply 'Ok,' you have effectively legitimated your power (attaining a Weberian 'authority'), but if I ask 'why?' and you answer, for example, 'Because I was elected,' justification commences.

Public justification ascended in modernity. 'Winning hearts and minds' has become a new battle cry, as elites and publics alike fight to make their case in a world of expanding ideational contestation. 'Things fall apart; the centre cannot hold,' wrote Yeats in the wake of the First World War; nearly a century later similar signs are all around. Where some see 'the deeper logic of liberal order' still intact (Ikenberry, 2011), others behold entropy and chaos (Schweller, 2014), a transition 'from a would-be concert of nations to a cacophony of competing voices' (Bremmer & Roubini, 2011). Either way, the triumphant chants heralding 'the end of history' (Fukuyama, 2006) have been hushed – in both the West and the Rest – by acute challenges to, and doubts about, liberal, secular, capitalist democracy. The battle over ideas, subscribing to the justificatory imperative, is still with us. This divergence invites us to go beyond *political moralism*, 'the priority of the moral over the political,' to *political realism*, revealing the myriad ways publics have tried to meet 'the basic legitimation demand' (Williams, 2005, pp. 2–3) of political life.

The troubled attempts to meet this demand resonate acutely in recent years. Consider the Arab Spring, a surprising season, not least for regional experts, who did not envision a quiescent public turning against the ingrained status quo (Gause, 2011). Likewise, the unprecedented mass demonstrations in Israel, 2011, calling for 'social justice,' and in India, 2012, demanding 'gender equality,' went against the grain of the former's 'cult of security' and the latter's 'entrenched patriarchy.' Notably, in all three cases, protestors reasoned why authorities and policies should transform. We may readily doubt their proclaimed justification and criticize their suboptimal outcomes. Still, Weber's (1922/1978) *Verstehen*, once refined (Feest, 2010), persuasively suggests that sociological explanation should include an understanding of the social actors' own intersubjective reasoning, urging us to consider the activists' articulated public justification as a *complementary* account for their emergent calls. Public justification, as a form of intersubjective reasoning, thus becomes a key piece in the explanatory puzzle of our socio-political universe.

Justification in the scholarly literature

What does the literature say about the social why-question? What clues does it provide for how actors reflect upon reasons with others? This section discusses how different perspectives in Political Theory, Comparative Politics and International Relations circumvent or address this question.

Approaches that rely heavily on materialist explanations do not address the 'why' question. What drives the explanation is not the reasoning of actors but material forces. These forces determine what actors end up doing. In 1979, two path-breaking and frequently cited books on world politics were published. Kenneth Waltz's *Theory of international politics* introduced Structural Realism. It focused on the distribution of military capabilities as the determinant of state interaction (Waltz, 1979). Immanuel Wallerstein's *The capitalist world-economy* is the foundational work of world systems theory. It identified the distribution of economic capabilities as the determinant of interaction between blocs of states (Wallerstein, 1979). A number of influential works in Comparative Politics draw heavily from materialist structure to explain outcomes as well. Research on revolutions conducted in this vein, for instance, has profoundly shaped this field of study. This includes the path-breaking research conducted by Moore (1966) and Skocpol (1979).

Structuralist explanations came under increasing pressure from the mid-1980s onwards. They were charged for being too one-sided in addressing the structure-agency problem. They provided fascinating insights into structure but very little into agency. To some extent, the pendulum then swung the other way. Rational choice portrays itself as a thoroughly agential approach to human reasoning. How this reasoning proceeds is a function of scholarly assumption rather than scholarly inquiry. Being more or less constrained by material forces, actors maximize their expected utility. They do this kind of reasoning by themselves. What they want (rank-ordered preferences) in a particular encounter is unaffected by the reasoning of others. Rational choice scholars readily admit that these assumptions simplify the actual reasoning process considerably. But they hold that these assumptions amount to analytically useful simplifications of a complex world (Keohane, 1988, p. 379; Levi, 1997; Martin, 2007).[1]

Criticisms of rational choice abound. Many critics submit that these assumptions are simplistic and distort reality (Abulof, 2015a). Given the purpose at hand, DiMaggio and Powell's criticism of rational choice is particularly pertinent. They observe that some organizations survive in the midst of material pressures to maximize gain even if they are ineffective. Their answer to this puzzle is legitimacy. Organizations may be ineffective. But they survive even in a competitive economic environment if they are considered legitimate (DiMaggio & Powell, 1991). This sociological line of argumentation goes back at least to Weber's thought on legitimacy (*Legitimitätsgeltung*). Authority (*Herrschaft*) is a form of legitimated power. Weber distinguishes three kinds of legitimacy: charismatic, traditional and legal. Charismatic authority is rooted in the aura of the governor, traditional authority in customary differentiations between governors and governed, and legal authority in bureaucratic and legal proceedings of modernity (Wiener, 2008, §16). For Weber (1926/1992, p. 8), these modes of legitimation are all about reasons. He writes about 'reasons of legitimation' (*Legitimationsgründe*). But these reasons are not out in the open. They are 'inner justifications' (*innere Rechtfertigungen*).

Taken together, Weber's conceptualization of legitimacy opens up some room for understanding how actors answer a crucial 'why' question. They have reasons for subscribing to a particular mode of authority. These reasons form the very foundations of a polity. Subsequent research echoes Weber in a number of ways. Most of all, it underlines the connections between legitimacy, authority and order (Bukovansky, 2002; Clark, 2005; Hurrelmann, Schneider, & Steffek, 2007; Steffek, 2007). At the same time, it also goes beyond Weber. Two elaborations are particularly noteworthy. First, some authors provide more details on the kinds of reasons that underpin authority. Hurd (2007), for instance, writes about favourable outcomes, fairness and correct procedure. Typologies such as these broaden our understanding of legitimating reasons. Weber often seems to focus on what Hurd labels correct procedure. But the other types of reasons should not be neglected. Favourable outcomes, for instance, matter, too (Gelpi, 2003; Lake, 2009; Rogowski, 1974). Second, authors putting the process through which legitimation occurs under scrutiny identify implicit and explicit dimensions of this process. Scott (1995) was among the first authors who alluded to the latter. This prompted researchers to pay closer attention to how actors communicate about legitimacy (Banchoff & Smith, 1999; Beetham & Lord, 2014).

These two amendments of Weber are important for any kind of research on reasons. The reasons upon which actors reflect range from what is, broadly speaking, beneficial to what is appropriate. Actors debate about some of these reasons. By communicating with one another, actors contest and decontest these ideas. Research on social movements and advocacy networks provides important insights into these communicative processes. Here, the debate about reasons is no longer always linked to how reasons legitimate an order. Debates may be related to discussions of polity and policy. In the communicative process, there are senders and receivers. The former advocate ideas and provide reasons for this advocacy. This package of advocated ideas and reasons for the advocacy is often conceptualized as frame. Established reasons provide the frame for the advocated idea (Gamson, 1992; Snow, Rochford, Worden, & Benford, 1986; Williams & Kubal, 1999).

Related clusters of research include narrative theory and various rhetorical approaches. The former analyses how communicators make their case by telling stories to audiences. An advocated idea is embedded in a familiar story (Fisher, 1987; McGee & Nelson, 1985; Ringmar, 2006). There are many variations of rhetorical approaches (Bjola & Kornprobst, 2011). Many of these are, in principle, compatible with narration and framing. The key claim of rhetoric is that actors assemble compelling messages by embedding an advocated idea in what is already familiar. In ancient Greek rhetoric, these commonplaces are referred to as *topoi* (Aristotle, 1995). Roman writers translate them literally as *loci* (Cicero, 2003; Quintilian, 1953). Some rhetorical research is more agency-oriented. Authors underline the political efficacy of the interlocutor (Crosswhite, 2010; Frank, 2004; Perelman & Olbrechts-Tyteca, 1969). Other writers put more emphasis on contextual factors constituting agency. These contexts usually constitute political efficacy unevenly. There are actors who are relegated to the status of receivers and there are those who are privileged as senders. This context is sometimes conceptualized as field, for instance, as discursive field (Ellingson, 1995; Fiss & Hirsch, 2005; Hajer, 2003), argumentation field (Bird, 1961; Toulmin, 2003, p. viii; Willard, 1983, p. 136) or rhetorical field (Kornprobst & Senn, 2016).[2]

Political Theory has generated a number of important normative approaches to argumentation. They deal with the question of how communication ought to be conducted. Pragmadialectics, for instance, is about universal rules for how actors ought to assemble arguments and how they ought to exchange arguments. The former is about how to make valid inferences from premises and the latter is about the exchange of messages in argumentative encounters (Van Eemeren & Houtlosser, 1999, 2000). Deliberative approaches left more of a mark on the study of politics. Habermas's often-cited ideal speech situation dares to think of the counterfactual that communicators let the better argument to come to the fore in encounters in which everyone has equal access (Habermas, 1991, p. 132). This counterfactual has frequently been criticized as too idealistic. This criticism has given rise to deliberative arguments that allow for more social context, including context that qualifies the equal access (Benhabib, 1994; Blaug, 2000; Wellmer, 1999). These differences notwithstanding, the key argument widely shared among deliberation scholars is that today's politics – domestic and international – revolves around exchanges of public reasons. Indeed, this is even fully acknowledged by political theorists who have kept their distance from deliberative approaches (Rawls, 1999, p. 137).

For all the differences across approaches dealing with reason giving and contesting, most of them share two features in common. On the one hand, they frequently employ the term 'justification' in order to describe how actors discuss reasons. Justification, in this context, is to be understood broadly. It is not just about justice but about discussing reasons more generally.[3] On the other hand, however, they refrain from defining the term. Justification is merely a frequently used term. It is not a concept that is addressed in detail. Habermas's definition and typology of the concept (pragmatic, ethical and moral) is an exception. So is his detailed discussion of the salience of justification in our times. Habermas argues that legitimate orders in our days are no longer just grounded in the kind of rational bureaucratic procedures that Weber writes about but in reflexive justification. Thus, justification becomes ubiquitous in politics (Habermas, 1991, p. 117).

No one has argued this ubiquity of justification more forcefully than Boltanski and Thévenaut. Public justification is an 'imperative' in today's politics, as the protagonists of the so-called new pragmatism put it (Boltanski & Thévenot, 2000, p. 209). Their account of justification puts a strong emphasis on plurality. The actors are situated in the midst of 'a plurality of cognitive and evaluative formats' (Thévenot, 2007, p. 411). Communication failures are always possible in this heterogeneous constellation. But so is persuasion and compromise (Boltanski & Thévenot, 2000). Critics of the new pragmatism tend to focus on the six orders of worth that the authors outline in their often-cited 2006 book entitled *On justification*. Some critics submit that these orders (inspired, domestic, fame, civic, market and industrial) over-conceptualize the social context that actors put to use to orient themselves. The formats that actors rely upon cannot easily be squeezed into orders of worth (Blok, 2013; Honneth, 2010). Other critics charge that the authors under-conceptualize the context because they remain rather silent on power. Access to communication, constituted by the context, is usually very unequal (Bénatouïl, 1999; Wagner, 1999).

What the critics do not do, however, is dismiss Boltanski and Thévenaut's observation that gave rise to their theorizing in the first place. Today's politics revolves around public justification. This puts the onus on students of politics to make sense of the phenomenon. The following two sections sketch some conceptual work for an inclusive study of justification and politics that invites contributions from multiple perspectives. First, we define public justification. Then we propose how to study it.

Conceptualizing public justification

This section conceptualizes public justification inclusively, leaving room for philosophical, (social-)psychological and sociological interpretations of the concept. It outlines four features of public justification: giving reasons, public communication, social context and the productivity of justificatory encounters.

First, public justifications address 'why' questions. They are about giving reasons and discussing the reasons given by others. How actors come to so varies greatly. Some are believers in their messages while others twist and turn their stance to make it palatable to an audience. Actors tend to privilege certain kinds of reasons over others. Religious reasons, for example, may appeal to some actors much more than secular ones. Others may foreground pragmatic reasons as opposed to moral ones and so on. The literature is full of classifications of different kinds of reasons. Habermas's distinction of pragmatic, ethical and moral ones as well as Hurd's on reasons related to outcomes, fairness and correct procedure have been alluded to above already. To mention but a few others, Alker (2011) writes about political, ethical and religious reasons. Boltanski and Thévenaut's orders of worth identify various kinds of powerful reasons. These range from efficiency in the industrial world and the accumulation of wealth in the market world to the common good in the civic world and originality in the inspired world.

Second, justifying is communicating. Public justifications are made in public communicative encounters. In most instances, this involves verbal communication. Public justifications are made in speeches, newspaper articles, blogs, twitter, etc. But communication is not necessarily verbal. When West German and East German artists painted against one another in the 1950s, for instance, the style they used justified the one polity and dejustified the other. Abstraction and Realism, respectively, were forms of public communication. What was liberating and democratic to Western painters (Abstraction) was a signifier of exploitation by a capitalist system to those from the East. What amounted to a symbol for overcoming capitalism to Eastern painters (Realism) was a totalitarian mode of expressing oneself to those from the West (Belting, 1999; Hermand, 1991; Schmied, 1995). Political caricatures, too, contain justifications that are not verbalized (Rostbøll, 2009).

Third, public justifications are underpinned by social context. This context matters procedurally and substantially. On a procedural level, social context delineates the opportunities of actors to be heard in particular communicative encounters. In most circumstances, some actors have more authority to speak than others. They are recognized as interlocutors. Others, by contrast, lack this recognition (Bourdieu, 1991, p. 109). They find it much more difficult to assert themselves. On a substantive level, the context delineates the intelligibility of messages. Some ideas have assumed a taken-for-granted quality. Interlocutors can put them to use to string justifications together that make sense to them.

Equally important, some of these ideas are more widely shared. The audience embraces them, too. This provides opportunities for interlocutors to make their justifications resonate with this audience. These taken-for-granted procedural and substantive ideas make for a complex constellation[4] of repertoires. There is not just one. Some taken-for-granted ideas are more widely shared. Others are more idiosyncratic. Even widely shared established ideas are multivocal. They are interpreted differently by different actors (Ansell, 1997, p. 373; Beiner, 1983, p. 132).

Fourth, exchanging public justifications generates divergences and convergences on reasons. Debating justifications is always a challenge. The plurality of the social context poses challenges for communication and understanding. Actors often end up speaking past one another. If they anchor their justifications in different sets of taken-for-granted ideas, these justifications appear nonsensical or even foolish to the other. But discussing justifications does not always generate divergences. It can also generate convergences. These hardly ever amount to an all-encompassing consensus (D'Agostino, 1996; Gaus, 2003). Usually, justifications resonate with certain segments of the audience but not with the entire audience. Usually, some of the receivers with whom they resonate come to embrace these justifications more than others. But even given such a patchwork of agreements, such convergences make a difference. They support policies and even the re-making of polities. As far as the latter is concerned, public justifications come full circle. They are enabled by a context. But they also have the potential to remake this context (Kornprobst, 2011, 2014).

Studying public justification

The study of public justification is multifaceted. Some research on public justification deals with how polities are justified while others deal with policy issues. There are positive and normative research avenues. Pragmatic and moral dimensions invite different kinds of investigations. Actors ranging from public intellectuals to state leaders, from journalists to parliamentarians and from bloggers to international bureaucrats await analysis.

There is some overlap between research on public justification, on the one hand, and legitimacy, on the other. Legitimacy is, arguably, 'not merely an important topic, but the central issue in social and political theory' (Beetham, 1991, p. 41). The importance of political legitimacy, however, is matched by its elusiveness. Political philosophy equates legitimacy with appropriateness and justice (Hegtvedt & Johnson, 2009), encouraging us to observe reality to prescribe and proscribe what we believe it ought, and ought not, to become (e.g. Rawls, 2005).

Conversely, from a sociological perspective, reality itself matters most, and we must empirically examine the ways things are, not how they normatively ought to be. The trouble with turning legitimacy into an object of sociological inquiry is that it brings the normative deep into the empirical. The typical sociological solution lies in equating legitimacy with 'willing obedience' (Cromartie, 2003, p. 93), support and compliance (Booth & Seligson, 2009). Legitimacy then becomes a snapshot of the given public endorsement of certain authorities and policies. But in so doing, sociology shuns the Axial revolution: legitimacy only makes sense when there is a deep divorce between the *is* and the *ought* (whether moral or practical). When the *is* and the *ought* are equated, the very concept of legitimacy loses meaning.

Instead of imposing the *ought* on the *is* (as in philosophy), or equating the two (as in mainstream sociology), the study of public justification probes the empirical-normative gap and the social actors' attempts to bridge it. Public justification is thus less concerned with *legitimacy* per se, instead focusing on *legitimation* and delegitimation (Barker, 2001, pp. 7–9). It examines the communicative process of legitimacy-making (and unmaking) in the public sphere.

Equally important, the scope of research on public justification is greater than the one on legitimacy and even legitimation. The latter focuses heavily on political order. To give but a few examples, Majone (1999) and Englebert (2002) write about the legitimacy of the state, Moravcsik (2002) as well as Beetham and Lord (2014) address the legitimacy of the European Union (EU), and Claude (1966) and Hurd (2007) examine the legitimacy of the United Nations. Research on public justification, by contrast, has a greater breadth. Social actors justify a range of political phenomena. On the one end of the spectrum, they justify a highly specific aspect of a highly specific policy. On the other end of the spectrum, they justify the pillars of political order that enable the production of such policies in the first place. Reason giving and contesting is ubiquitous in the political orders the social actors we study inhabit. While some flows of justification focus more on the big questions of order and others more on the details of a policy, the social actors engaged in justificatory encounters often blur this line. More narrowly confined contestations about how to justify a policy can develop into broader contestations about order, and vice versa.

To study how social actors blur the lines that scholarly categories oftentimes superimpose on their interaction amounts to a difficult task. This task need not, and cannot, be accomplished through one method alone. Humility should guide our search for causality in the human sciences. No approach is perfect and only the joint efforts of scholars from various fields can bring us closer to a fuller understanding of humanity. Studying public justification can draw on behavioural, attitudinal and psychological indicators, such as protests, surveys, interviews and experiments (Kaase & Newton, 1995). Analysing, for example, the dynamics of groupthink and conformism sheds light on the forces that induce us to relinquish autonomous judgement, and seek consensus (Bond & Smith, 1996; Janis, 1983). Still, at heart, public justification takes the 'linguistic turn' seriously, drawing less on behaviour and more on discourse, tracing the language of justification as it unfolds. Language both mirrors and moulds justification. The latter is not caused, but created, and tracing the public reasoning of politics can reveal why and how.

Studying the language of public justification makes for a taxing though exciting endeavour. Social scientists who follow the lead of the natural sciences prefer to quantify observable aspects of national behaviour, posit them as dependent/independent variables and statistically test for a 'covering law' that hypothetically guides their correlation. This successful hypothetico-deductive approach has its known limitations, especially in the social sciences. No 'variable' is truly independent, and robust correlation can suggest, but never demonstrate, the reasons of agents, particularly since similar actions need not emanate from the same motivations.

Public justification research regards social science causality as intersubjective reasoning. It walks the middle way of 'explication,' between objective explanation and subjective interpretation (Larsen, 1997). Specifically, public justification research seeks to explicate the emergence of Weberian 'social actions': socially oriented and subjectively meaningful conduct, whether tangible or ideational. Perhaps surprisingly, Karl Popper effectively acknowledged the many merits of this approach in the social sciences where he proposed 'situational logic/analysis' to understand an actor's choice as driven by the interplay of his views and changing circumstances (Martin, 2000, pp. 117–136).

The daunting task of 'the interpretation of [social] action in terms of its subjective meaning' in the social actors' eyes is viable for 'one need not have been Caesar in order to understand Caesar' (Weber, 1947, pp. 87–115). We can grasp such 'social actions' through both our emotional and rational faculties. The natural language of the social actors is invaluable for explicating their cultural meaning-making, for it both reflects and shapes the multifaceted public reasoning behind their conduct (Alexander, 2003). Indeed, 'analyzing discourse offers access to the space in which collective perceptions are present' (Wiener, 2008, p. 75). While the perceptions themselves perforce remain hidden, when underpinned by ideas, understood as causal beliefs, they are often sufficiently articulated to be scholarly accessible (Beland & Cox, 2011). Grasping the actors' articulated reasoning allows us to 'accomplish something which is never attainable in the natural sciences, namely the subjective understanding of the action of the component individuals,' which can be then abstracted to the society-level explanation through ideal-types (Weber, 1922/1978, p. 15).[5] Importantly, both qualitative and quantitative methods are apt to the task (e.g. critical discourse analysis and corpus linguistics), and mixed methods research is often advisable (Abulof, 2015c, 2016).

Studying public justification requires probing both its content and context. Both pose major challenges. As for the content, utterances are not always sincere, just or accurate; they may be disingenuous, false or vile, occasionally the offshoot of manipulation (Bok, 1999; Kuran, 1995). Still, a political utterance typically indicates that the speaker believes that other people can be swayed by it. Moreover, even insincere speech may shape future sincere discourse. We need not assume that speakers and authors are sincere for us to consider their discourse valuable, since their narratives both reflect and shape beliefs and practices (Alexander, 2003; Crawford, 2002; Reyes, 2011; Van Leeuwen, 2008, pp. 105–123). The study of public justification is thus less interested in passing moral judgement on the justificatory efforts, and even less in peeling away layers of consciousness to arrive at an allegedly subconscious, mostly emotional, core; instead, it probes those deliberate, occasionally deliberative, layers – in both open and closed societies (e.g. Abulof, 2015b). It seeks to uncover evolving, and often interrelated, discursive strategies 'adopted to achieve a particular social, political, psychological or linguistic goal' (Wodak, 2011, p. 49).

Public justification is rarely monochromatic or static. It typically involves contestation as the public is challenged from within and without to answer why certain arguments provide sufficient justification. Social actors may kick the proverbial can down the road of justification – and keep on asking, 'but why?' after each stroke of reasoning. In tracing the public's use of language, we should follow the can's path through various crossroads. We should also find when the agents stop kicking the can: where they rest their reasoning – until the next round. Notably, as discussed above, the actors' justification may turn to practical or moral reasoning, or both. They may, for example, justify privatization on the ground that the government is wasteful, or that 'big government' encroaches on individual liberties, or both.

Space does not allow delving into the specific modes of discourse analysis. A note on the research strategy, however, may be due, as the discourse analysis of public justification may follow the little-known research tradition of 'abduction,' rather than the typical induction or deduction. The essence of abduction lies in tracing the lay language of the social actors and then in 'moving from lay descriptions of social life to technical descriptions of that social life' by the 'iterative process of immersion in these social worlds and reflection on what is discovered' (Blaikie, 2010, pp. 90–91). Abduction aims at optimal correspondence between actual social discourses and their academic conceptualization so that our scholarly 'constructs of the second degree' resonate sufficiently with those first-order constructs 'made by the actors on the social scene' for the social actors to recognize themselves in the scholarly accounts (Schutz, 1982, p. 59).

Contextualizing claims of justification is paramount for the study of public justification. It requires that we identify key speakers, uncover their communicative strategies, evaluate their impact and situate all within their changing socio-political universe. What was said is obviously crucial, but where, when, how, why, by who (and to whom) it was said is equally important. In particular, analysing the politics of public justification requires that we uncover its underpinning power relations, since 'language indexes power, expresses power, is involved where there is contention over and a challenge to power' (Wodak & Meyer, 2009, pp. 6, 10). Still, in charting the power matrix enveloping public justification, we must realize that while might makes right, the reverse is also true. Power can boost a speaker's capacity to persuasively justify; but doing the right thing, and arguing for it, may likewise augment an actor's power (Krebs & Jackson, 2007; Nye, 2004).[6]

Overview of contributions

The collection of papers is multidisciplinary and multiperspectival. Among its contributing authors are political scientists (Political Theory, Comparative Politics and International Relations), psychologists and sociologists. They focus on particular aspects of justification, for instance, moral and pragmatic reasoning, the private–public divide, its overlap with legitimacy and legitimation, etc., putting to use various theoretical approaches. Researching public justification requires this plurality. It is a protean phenomenon.

The special issue is organized into four parts. First, Elliot Turiel and Uriel Abulof inquire into moral reasoning. Turiel refutes the so-called people are stupid school of psychology, which regards human reasoning as an epiphenomenon used to rationalize decisions already made by our hardwired intuitions, dictated by evolution, emotion and cultures. Based on time-long investigation into the development of morality among children, adolescents and adults, Turiel concludes that morality matters, not least in politics: 'debate and argumentation commonly within and between groups are often at the root of moral and social transformations.' He distinguishes between three domains: the moral, where justifications are universalizable; the social, where conventions are seen as culture-specific; and the personal, where views are individual 'tastes.' In practice, our decisions involve situational coordination of considerations between and within these domains. Even in non-liberal and patriarchal societies, conformism to conventions and obedience to authority are often subverted by moral reasoning and resistance.

Abulof, like Turiel, focuses on the moral aspect of justification, and delineates the blurry line between its personal and public faces. Introducing the idea and practice of 'conscientious politics,' Abulof suggests that morality matters for both the individual and the collective, not least in the political domain. He suggests that conscientious politics – politics informed by moral deliberations about legitimacy – are often 'hidden in plain sight,' and the normative task of bringing them to light depends on revealing the moral dilemmas that underpin actual politics. Abulof pursues this task in theory, charting the contours of individual and public conscience, as well as in practice, showing the moral dilemmas at heart of key moves made by the Israeli public in recent years.

Second, Amitai Etzioni and Achim Hurrellmann look at patterns of justification in domestic and EU politics, respectively. Etzioni challenges the viability of the private–public divide, which has been a key foundation for the public justification of liberal, capitalist, democracy. While private–public divide was never complete to begin with, the wall between the governmental and non-governmental organizations and activities has further eroded in recent years, not least due to the cyber age's technological advancements. Undermining the imagery of the modern state as managing national security, the erosion of the public/private dichotomy challenges not only the public justification of democracy but the very notion of public justification, as the 'public' itself is losing its discrete meaning.

Hurrellmann draws from the EU literature on legitimation to arrive at lessons for the study of global governance more generally. After some conceptual clarifications, the paper presents a critical review of the literature on the EU's legitimation, focusing on six crucial aspects – the analysis of legitimation change over time, the arenas where legitimation occurs, the role of the state as a reference point in legitimacy assessments, the difference between various objects of legitimation, the interplay of top-down and bottom-up legitimation processes, as well as the relationship between legitimation and polity development. In each of these respects, the paper identifies important insights that can be gained from EU studies, but also conceptual and methodological weaknesses in the EU-related literature that researchers working on other polities should avoid. The paper closes by formulating a set of general desiderata for empirical legitimation research in International Relations.

Third, Tine Hanrieder as well as Markus Kornprobst and Martin Senn focus squarely on global governance. Hanrieder explores how the role of religion is evaluated in global health institutions, focusing on policy debates in the World Health Organization (WHO) and the World Bank. Drawing on Luc Boltanski and Laurent Thévenot's pragmatist approach to justification, she suggests that religious values are creative and worldly performances. The public value of religion is established through a two-pronged justification process, combining generalizing arguments ('thinning') with particularizing empirical tests ('thickening'). To substantiate the claim that thinning alone does not suffice to create religious values in global public health, she compares the futile attempts of the 1980s to add 'spiritual health' to the WHO's mandate with the more recent creation of a 'faith factor' in public health. While the vague reference to some 'Factor X' inhibited the acceptance of spiritual health in the first case, in the second case 'compassion' became a measurable and recognized religious value.

Kornprobst and Senn inquire into the question of how actors change deeply seated background ideas. In order to answer this question, they draw heavily from rhetorical studies and social theory. The authors conceptualize the deep background as nomos, and the more easily accessible background as doxa. Then, they proceed to identify three sets of conditions that make nomic change possible. These relate to opportunity, message and messenger. Nomic change becomes possible when the need for something new has become widely established and a supply of new nomic ideas is easily available (opportunity); new nomic ideas are 'smuggled' into more orthodox and widely resonating arguments (message); and advocates succeed in augmenting their authority to speak (messenger). A plausibility probe of nomic contestation about nuclear governance provides evidence for this framework. This article provides novel insights into the structure-agency problem. It shows how approaches to communication that heavily focus on social context can be fruitfully combined with scholarly perspectives on communication that foreground agency.

Fourth, we conclude with a friendly debate between Liah Greenfeld, and Uriel Abulof and Markus Kornprobst. Greenfeld cautions against ahistorical assumptions of public justifications and emphasizes the contexts of justification. Engaging with these *caveats*, Abulof and Kornprobst develop an agenda for further research. This debate – *in lieu* of a monolithic conclusion written by the editors – highlights again the multidisciplinary and multiperspectival nature of studying public justification.

Notes

1. More sophisticated – and less parsimonious – conceptualizations of rational choice have been around for a while, for instance, evolutionary game theory (Smith, 1972). But they continue to remain marginalized by their simpler variants.
2. Bourdieu's field theory borrows heavily from rhetorical theory as well. Concepts such as nomos and doxa are taken from classic works on rhetoric, especially Aristotle (1995) and Sophistic thought (see Sprague, 1972).
3. In French (*justifier*) and German (*rechtfertigen*), this broader meaning of the term is more established than in the English language.
4. We borrow the term 'constellations' from Bernstein (1991), who is interested in how different sets of background ideas crisscross among communities.
5. While the assumption of 'rationality' is pivotal in Weber, his conceptualization of rationality clearly goes beyond material calculation to encompass morality ('value-rationality').
6. Conducting discourse-tracing may, but need not, be driven by the attempt to uncover 'the way social power abuse, dominance, and inequality are enacted, reproduced, and resisted by text and talk in the social and political context' (Van Dijk, 2003, p. 352).

Acknowledgements

This special issue started with a weekend workshop, hosted by the Liechtenstein Institute on Self-Determination (LISD) at the Woodrow Wilson School, Princeton University. We thank the LISD Director, Professor Wolfgang Danspeckgruber and his team for their help and insights. Furthermore, we would like to thank the editors and reviewers of *Contemporary Politics* for excellent feedback.

Disclosure statement

No potential conflict of interest was reported by the authors.

Funding

Funding for this special section was provided by the Liechtenstein Institute on Self-Determination (LISD) at the Woodrow Wilson School, Princeton University, and the Vienna School of International Studies, Diplomatische Akademie Wien.

References

Abulof, U. (2015a). The malpractice of rationality in international relations. *Rationality and Society, 27* (3), 358–384.

Abulof, U. (2015b). *The mortality and morality of nations.* New York, NY: Cambridge University Press.

Abulof, U. (2015c). Normative concepts analysis: Unpacking the language of legitimation. *International Journal of Social Research Methodology, 18*(1), 73–89.

Abulof, U. (2016). We the peoples? The strange demise of self-determination. *European Journal of International Relations.* Advance online publication.

Alexander, J. C. (2003). *The meanings of social life: A cultural sociology.* New York, NY: Oxford University Press.

Alker, H. (2011). The powers and pathologies of networks: Insights from the political cybernetics of Karl W. Deutsch and Norbert Wiener. *European Journal of International Relations, 17*(2), 351–378.

Ansell, C. (1997). Symbolic networks: The realignment of the French working class 1887–1894. *American Journal of Sociology, 103*(2), 359–390.

Archer, M. S. (2012). *The reflexive imperative in late modernity.* New York, NY: Cambridge University Press.

Aristoteles. (1995). *Rhetorik* (F. G. Sieveke, Trans. and Annotated). Munich: Wilhelm Fink.

Banchoff, T., & Smith, M. P. (1999). *Legitimacy and the European Union: The contested polity.* New York, NY: Psychology Press.

Barker, R. S. (2001). *Legitimating identities: The self-presentation of rulers and subjects.* New York, NY: Cambridge University Press.

Beetham, D. (1991). *The legitimation of power.* Atlantic Highlands, NJ: Humanities Press International.

Beetham, D., & Lord, C. (2014). *Legitimacy and the European Union.* London: Routledge.

Beiner, R. (1983). *Political judgement.* Chicago, IL: University of Chicago Press.

Beland, D., & Cox, R. H. (Eds.). (2011). *Ideas and politics in social science research.* New York, NY: Oxford University Press.

Bellah, R. N. (2011). *Religion in human evolution: From the Paleolithic to the Axial Age.* Cambridge, MA: Belknap Press of Harvard University Press.

Belting, H. (1999). *Identität im Zweifel: Ansichten der deutschen Kunst.* Cologne: DuMont.

Bénatouïl, T. (1999). A tale of two sociologies: The critical and the pragmatic stance in French contemporary sociology. *European Journal of Social Theory, 2*(3), 379–396.

Benhabib, S. (1994). Deliberative rationality and models of democratic legitimacy. *Constellations, 1*(1), 26–52.

Berger, P. L. (1967). *The sacred canopy: Elements of a sociological theory of religion.* Garden City, NY: Doubleday.

Bernstein, R. (1991). *The new constellation: The ethical-political horizons of modernity/postmodernity.* Cambridge: Polity.

Bird, O. (1961). The re-discovery of the 'topics'. *Mind, LXX,* 534–539.

Bjola, C., & Kornprobst, M. (2011). Introduction: The argumentative deontology of global governance. In C. Bjola & M. Kornprobst (Eds.), *Arguing global governance* (pp. 1–16). London: Routledge.

Blaikie, N. (2010). *Designing social research: The logic of anticipation* (2nd ed.). Cambridge: Polity Press.

Blaug, R. (2000). Citizenship and political judgment: Between discourse ethics and phronesis. *Res Publica, 6,* 179–198.

Blok, A. (2013). Pragmatic sociology as political ecology: On the many worths of nature(s). *European Journal of Social Theory, 16*(4), 492–510.

Bok, S. (1999). *Lying: Moral choice in public and private life* (2nd Vintage Books ed.). New York, NY: Vintage Books.

Boltanski, L., & Thévenot, L. (2000). The reality of moral expectations: A sociology of situated judgement. *Philosophical Explorations, 3*(3), 208–231.

Boltanski, L., & Thévenot, L. (2006). *On justification: Economies of worth.* Princeton, NJ: Princeton University Press.

Bond, R., & Smith, P. B. (1996). Culture and conformity: A meta-analysis of studies using Asch's (1952b, 1956) line judgment task. *Psychological Bulletin, 119*(1), 111–137.

Booth, J. A., & Seligson, M. A. (2009). *The legitimacy puzzle in Latin America: Political support and democracy in eight nations.* New York, NY: Cambridge University Press.

Bourdieu, P. (1991). *Language and symbolic power.* Cambridge, MA: Harvard University Press.

Bremmer, I., & Roubini, N. (2011). A G-Zero world. *Foreign Affairs, 90*(2), 2–7.

Bruner, J. S. (1986). *Actual minds, possible worlds.* Cambridge, MA: Harvard University Press.

Bruner, J. S. (1990). *Acts of meaning.* Cambridge, MA: Harvard University Press.

Bukovansky, M. (2002). *Legitimacy and power politics: The American and French revolutions in international political culture.* Princeton, NJ: Princeton University Press.

Cicero, M. T. (2003). *Topica.* Oxford: Oxford University Press.

Clark, I. (2005). *Legitimacy in international society.* Oxford: Oxford University Press.

Claude, I. L. (1966). Collective legitimization as a political function of the United Nations. *International Organization, 20*(3), 367–379.

Crawford, N. C. (2002). *Argument and change in world politics: Ethics, decolonization, and humanitarian intervention.* New York, NY: Cambridge University Press.

Cromartie, A. (2003). Legitimacy. In R. Bellamy & A. Mason (Eds.), *Political concepts* (pp. 93–104). New York, NY: Palgrave.

Crosswhite, J. (2010). The new rhetoric project. *Philosophy and Rhetoric, 43*(4), 301–307.

D'Agostino, F. (1996). *Free public reason: Making it up as we go.* Oxford: Oxford University Press.

DiMaggio, P. J., & Powell, W. (Eds.). (1991). *The new institutionalism in organizational analysis.* Chicago, IL: University of Chicago Press.

Ellingson, S. (1995). Understanding the dialectic of discourse and collective action: Public debate and rioting in antebellum Cincinnati. *American Journal of Sociology, 101,* 100–144.

Englebert, P. (2002). *State legitimacy and development in Africa.* New York, NY: Lynne Rienner.

Feest, U. (2010). *Historical perspectives on erklären and verstehen.* New York, NY: Springer.

Fisher, W. R. (1987). *Human communication as narration: Toward a philosophy of reason, value, and action.* Columbia: University of South Carolina Press.

Fiss, P. C., & Hirsch, P. M. (2005). The discourse of globalization: Framing and sensemaking of an emerging concept. *American Sociological Review, 70*(1), 29–52.

Frank, D. (2004). Argumentation studies in the wake of the new rhetoric. *Argumentation and Advocacy, 40,* 267–283.

Fukuyama, F. (2006). *The end of history and the last man*. New York, NY: Free Press.

Fukuyama, F. (2011). *The origins of political order: From prehuman times to the French Revolution* (1st ed.). New York, NY: Farrar, Straus and Giroux.

Fukuyama, F. (2014). *Political order and political decay: From the industrial revolution to the globalization of democracy* (1st ed.). New York, NY: Farrar, Straus and Giroux.

Gamson, W. A. (1992). The social psychology of collective action. In A. D. Morris & C. McClurg Müller (Eds.), *Frontiers in social movement theory* (pp. 53–76). New Haven, CT: Yale University Press.

Gaus, G. F. (2003). *Contemporary theories of liberalism*. London: Sage.

Gause, F. G. (2011). Why Middle East studies missed the Arab Spring: The myth of authoritarian stability. *Foreign Affairs, 90*(4), 81–90.

Gelpi, C. (2003). *The power of legitimacy: Assessing the role of norms in crisis bargaining*. Princeton, NJ: Princeton University Press.

Gottschall, J. (2012). *The storytelling animal: How stories make us human*. Boston, MA: Houghton Mifflin Harcourt.

Hajer, M. (2003). A frame in the fields: Policymaking and the reinvention of politics. In M. Hajer & H. Wagenaar (Eds.), *Deliberative policy analysis: Understanding governance in the network society* (pp. 88–110). Cambridge: Cambridge University Press.

Harle, V. (1998). *Ideas of social order in the ancient world*. Westport, CT: Greenwood Press.

Habermas, J. (1991). *Erläuterungen zur Diskursethik*. Frankfurt am Main: Suhrkamp.

Hegtvedt, K. A., & Johnson, C. (2009). Power and justice. *American Behavioral Scientist, 53*(3), 376–399.

Henriques, G. (2011). *A new unified theory of psychology*. New York, NY: Springer.

Hermand, J. (1991). Freiheit im Kalten Krieg: Zum Siegeszug der abstrakten Malerei in Westdeutschland. In H. Boger, E. Mai, & S. Waetzoldt (Eds.), *45 und die Folgen: Kunstgeschichte eines Wiederbeginns* (pp. 135–162). Cologne: Böhlau.

Honneth, A. (2010). Dissolutions of the social: On the social theory of Luc Boltanski and Laurent Thévenot. *Constellations, 17*(3), 376–389.

Hurd, I. (2007). *After anarchy: Legitimacy and power in the United Nations Security Council*. Princeton, NJ: Princeton University Press.

Hurrelmann, A. (2017). Empirical legitimation analysis in International Relations. How to learn from the insights – and avoid the mistakes – of research in EU Studies. *Contemporary Politics, 23*(1).

Hurrelmann, A., Schneider, S., & Steffek, J. (2007). Introduction: Legitimacy in an age of global politics. In A. Hurrelmann, S. Schneider, & J. Steffek (Eds.), *Legitimacy in an age of global politics* (pp. 1–16). Basingstoke: Palgrave.

Ikenberry, G. J. (2011). *Liberal leviathan: The origins, crisis, and transformation of the American world order*. Princeton, NJ: Princeton University Press.

Janis, I. L. (1983). *Groupthink: Psychological studies of policy decisions and fiascoes* (2nd ed.). Boston, MA: Houghton Mifflin.

Jaspers, K. (1953). *The origin and goal of history*. New Haven, CT: Yale University Press.

Kaase, M., & Newton, K. (1995). *Beliefs in government*. New York, NY: Oxford University Press.

Keohane, R. O. (1988). International institutions: Two approaches. *International Studies Quarterly, 44*(1), 83–105.

Kornprobst, M. (2011). The agent's logics of action: Defining and mapping political judgement. *International Theory, 3*(1), 70–104.

Kornprobst, M. (2014). From political judgements to public justifications (and vice versa): How communities generate reasons upon which to act. *European Journal of International Relations, 20*(1), 192–216.

Kornprobst, M., & Senn, M. (2016). A rhetorical field theory: Background, communication, and change. *British Journal of Politics and International Relations, 18*(2), 300–317.

Krebs, R. R., & Jackson, P. T. (2007). Twisting tongues and twisting arms: The power of political rhetoric. *European Journal of International Relations, 13*(1), 35–66.

Kuran, T. (1995). *Private truths, public lies: The social consequences of preference falsification*. Cambridge, MA: Harvard University Press.

Lake, D. A. (2009). Relational authority and legitimacy in international relations. *American Behavioral Scientist, 53*(3), 331–353.

Larsen, H. (1997). *Foreign policy and discourse analysis: France, Britain, and Europe*. New York, NY: Routledge/LSE.

Levi, M. (1997). A model, a method, and a map: Rational choice in comparative and historical analysis. In M. I. Lichbach & A. S. Zuckerman (Eds.), *Comparative politics: Rationality, culture, and structure* (pp. 19–41). Cambridge: Cambridge University Press.

Majone, G. (1999). The regulatory state and its legitimacy problems. *West European Politics, 22*(1), 1–24.

Martin, L. (2007). Neoliberalism. In T. Dunne, M. Kurki, & S. Smith (Eds.), *International relations theories: Discipline and diversity* (pp. 109–126). Oxford: Oxford University Press.

Martin, M. (2000). *Verstehen: The uses of understanding in social science*. New Brunswick, NJ: Transaction.

McGee, M. C., & Nelson, J. S. (1985). Narrative reason in public argument. *Journal of Communication, 35*(4), 139–155.

Moore, B. (1966). *Social origins of democracy and dictatorship*. Boston, MA: Beacon.

Moravcsik, A. (2002). Reassessing legitimacy in the European Union. *Journal of Common Market Studies, 40*(4), 603–624.

Nye, J. S. (2004). *Soft power: The means to success in world politics*. New York, NY: Public Affairs.

Perelman, C., & Olbrechts-Tyteca, L. (1969). *The New Rhetoric: A treatise on argumentation* (J. Wilkinson & P. Weaver, Trans.). Notre Dame, IN: University of Notre Dame Press.

Pinker, S. (1994). *The language instinct* (1st ed.). New York, NY: W. Morrow.

Quintilian. (1953). *Institutio oratoria* (H. E. Butler, Trans.). Cambridge: Harvard University Press.

Rawls, J. (1999). *The law of peoples*. Cambridge: Harvard University Press.

Rawls, J. (2005). *Political liberalism* (Expanded ed.). New York, NY: Columbia University Press.

Reyes, A. (2011). Strategies of legitimization in political discourse: From words to actions. *Discourse & Society, 22*(6), 781–807.

Ringmar, E. (2006). Inter-textual relations: The quarrel over the Iraq War as a conflict between narrative types. *Cooperation and Conflict, 41*(4), 403–421.

Rogowski, R. (1974). *Rational legitimacy: A theory of political support*. Princeton: Princeton University Press.

Rostbøll, C. F. (2009). Autonomy, respect, and arrogance in the Danish cartoon controversy. *Political Theory, 37*(5), 623–648.

Sandel, M. J. (2005). *Public philosophy: Essays on morality in politics*. Cambridge, MA: Harvard University Press.

Schmied, W. (1995). Ausgangspunkt und Verwandlung. In C. M. Joachimides, N. Rosenthal, & W. Schmied (Eds.), *Deutsche Kunst im 20. Jahrhundert: Malerei und Plastik 1905–1985* (pp. 63–71). Munich: Prestel-Verlag.

Schutz, A. (1982). *Collected papers*. Boston, MA: Hingham.

Schweller, R. L. (2014). *Maxwell's demon and the golden apple global discord in the new millennium*. Baltimore, MD: Johns Hopkins University Press.

Scott, W. R. (1995). *Institutions and organizations*. Thousand Oaks, CA: Sage.

Skocpol, T. (1979). *States and social revolutions: A comparative analysis of France, Russia and China*. Cambridge: Cambridge University Press.

Smith, M. J. (1972). Game theory and the evolution of fighting. In *On evolution* (pp. 8–28). Edinburgh: Edinburgh University Press.

Snow, D. A., Rochford, E. B., Worden, S. K., & Benford, R. D. (1986). Frame alignment processes, micromobilization, and movement participation. *American Sociological Review, 51*, 464–481.

Sprague, R. K. (1972). *The older Sophists*. Columbia: University of South Carolina Press.

Steffek, J. (2007). Legitimacy in international relations: From state compliance to citizen consensus. In A. Hurrelmann, S. Schneider, & J. Steffek (Eds.), *Legitimacy in an age of global politics* (pp. 175–192). Basingstoke: Palgrave.

Thévenot, L. (2007). The plurality of cognitive formats and engagements moving between the familiar and the public. *European Journal of Social Theory, 10*(3), 409–423.

Toulmin, S. E. (2003). *The uses of argument*. Cambridge: Cambridge University Press.

Van Dijk, T. A. (2003). Critical discourse analysis. In D. Schiffrin, D. Tannen, & H. E. Hamilton (Eds.), *The handbook of discourse analysis* (pp. 352–370). Malden, MA: Blackwell.

Van Eemeren, F. H., & Houtlosser, P. (1999). Strategic manoeuvering in argumentative discourse. *Discourse Studies, 1*, 479–497.

Van Eemeren, F. H., & Houtlosser, P. (2000). Rhetorical analysis within a pragma-dialectical framework: The case of R. J. Reynolds. *Argumentation, 14*, 293–305.

Van Leeuwen, T. (2008). *Discourse and practice: New tools for critical discourse analysis*. New York, NY: Oxford University Press.

Wagner, P. (1999). After justification: Repertoires of evaluation and the sociology of modernity. *European Journal of Social Theory, 2*(3), 341–357.

Wallerstein, I. (1979). *The capitalist world-economy*. Cambridge: Cambridge University Press.

Waltz, K. (1979). *Theory of international politics*. Reading, MA: Addison-Webley.

Weber, M. (1922/1978). *Economy and society: An outline of interpretive sociology* (2 Vols.). Berkeley: University of California Press.

Weber, M. (1926/1992). *Politik als Beruf*. Stuttgart: Reclam.

Weber, M. (1947). *The theory of social and economic organization*. New York, NY: Free Press.

Wellmer, A. (1999). *Ethik und Dialog: Elemente des moralischen Urteils bei Kant und in der Diskursethik*. Frankfurt/Main: Suhrkamp.

Wiener, A. (2008). *The invisible constitution of politics: Contested norms and international encounters*. New York, NY: Cambridge University Press.

Willard, C. A. (1983). *Argumentation and the social grounds of knowledge*. Tuscaloosa: University Alabama Press.

Williams, B. (2005). *In the beginning was the deed: Realism and moralism in political argument*. Princeton, NJ: Princeton University Press.

Williams, R. H., & Kubal, T. J. (1999). Movement frames and the cultural environment: Resonance, failure, and the boundaries of the legitimate. *Research in Social Movements, Conflicts & Change, 21*, 225–248.

Wodak, R. (2011). Critical discourse analysis. In K. Hyland & B. Paltridge (Eds.), *Continuum companion to discourse analysis* (pp. 38–53). New York, NY: Continuum.

Wodak, R., & Meyer, M. (2009). Critical discourse analysis: History, agenda, theory and methodology. In R. Wodak & M. Meyer (Eds.), *Methods of critical discourse analysis: Introducing qualitative methods* (pp. 1–33). London: Sage.

A psychological perspective on moral reasoning, processes of decision-making, and moral resistance

Elliot Turiel

ABSTRACT
This article presents a psychological approach on the development of social and moral judgments that has relevance for the topics of public justification and world politics. In contrast with approaches assuming that morality is primarily determined by emotions and non-rational, the research discussed shows that moral development involves the construction of thinking about welfare, justice, and rights. In parallel with judgments in the moral domain, individuals construct judgments about conventions in the social system and areas of personal jurisdiction. Research documents that moral and social decisions involve processes of coordination, or weighing and balancing, moral and non-moral considerations and goals, as well as different moral goals. Processes of coordination are also involved in decisions about cultural practices that include social inequalities and relationships between those in dominant and subordinate positions in social hierarchies. Judgments about the fairness of practices entailing inequalities produce social opposition and moral resistance.

Researchers in political science who have thought long and hard about on the topics of public justification and world politics author most of the articles in this volume. These are not topics I have researched. I am a psychologist and have studied the development of social and moral judgments from childhood to adolescence and adulthood. I have also researched aspects of relations between morality and culture, with a focus on evaluations and processes of decision-making about cultural practices involving social hierarchies and social inequalities. That work has yielded findings of social opposition and moral resistance to systems of social organization and inequalities. Consequently, people's participation in cultural practices has, at least, a dual and sometimes conflictful orientation in that they are both accepting and critical of cultural practices.

I believe, however, that the body of research I discuss in this article has a bearing on politics. Certainly, the topic of morality is not unrelated to politics. Moreover, there is likely to be a connection between political thought and the research on social hierarchies, social inequalities, and moral resistance. Another feature of the approach I take that should bear on politics is the presumption that people actively think and reason about morality, social relationships, social institutions, and the norms of society.

A little background

The theoretical approach of my research on development is based on the proposition that children construct ways of thinking through varied types of interactions and social relationships in multifaceted environments. Children attempt to understand, make sense of, experiences of many kinds. This includes the formation of moral judgments and reasoning, stemming from children's interactions with other children, as well as with adults. In this perspective, moral judgments do not reflect an acceptance of or accommodation to societal norms or cultural practices nor a reflection of predetermined biological dispositions, but involve understandings of substantive issues such as welfare and harm, fairness and justice, and the rights of individuals and groups.

The proposition that morality involves the formation and application of judgments and reasoning is at odds with some past and current psychological theorizing. For a long time now – going back to behaviourism – many psychologists have rejected choice and reasoning as human attributes. They regarded thought, reasoning, and rationality as outdated ideas to be discarded in psychological explanations (except, of course, when psychologists use reasoning in generating their theories about the lack of reasoning). Although behaviourism has largely faded from the scene, the rejection of reasoning as a human attribute continues in some contemporary quarters of psychology, including social psychology and in work in psychological neuroscience (Turiel, 2010). A provocative but accurate term was coined by Kihlstrom (2004) for those contemporary formulations: the *people are stupid school of psychology* (PASSP). According to Kihlstrom, this school of psychology maintains 'as we go about the ordinary course of everyday living, we do not think very hard about anything, and simply rely on biases, heuristics, and other processes that lead us into judgmental error' (2004, p. 169). The major tenets of PASSP are: (1) that people are fundamentally non-rational; they do not engage in much reflection, are driven by emotions, and rely on shortcuts like heuristics, (2) that decisions are made on automatic pilot, which are, (3) out of awareness, of a non-conscious nature, and do not involve choice, and (4) that as a consequence decisions are often irrational. Kihlstrom (2008) also details how the evidence for these propositions is not strong. Briefly, the evidence most often comes from contrived experiments (such as those on 'priming') that entail implicit communications about the expectations of experimenters in what are unusual situations. The experiments produce temporary effects, and often are not replicable (Turiel, 2015). Another problem in the PASSP line of thinking is that errors are confused with irrationality. However, errors can often reflect efforts to comprehend events, interpret experiences, and make choices.

Two examples bearing on conservative and liberal political views serve to illustrate how the rejection of choice and reasoning as human attributes has been applied to arenas of politics. In one study (Oxley et al., 2008), participants classified as liberals (e.g. they support foreign aid, immigration, gun control, and gay marriage) or conservatives (e.g. they support defence spending, the war in Iraq, the death penalty, and school prayer) were assessed on physiological reactions to perceived threats (e.g. by showing them threatening images) indicating individuals' general levels of fear. It was reported that those with conservative views showed more fearful reactions to threat than those with liberal views.

The researchers' interpretation of the findings is that the political positions associated with levels of fearfulness entail tendencies to be either more vigilant to perceived threats and to be protective of the existing social unit or to be less vigilant and supportive of changes in the social order. Accordingly, in this reductionist position, political views are not seen as due to analyses and judgments about matters such as defence, war, violence, or many other social policies. There are also problems in the logic of some of the connections drawn between the supposed emotional dispositions and the particular positions taken by conservatives and liberals. For example, would it not be expected that more fearful people would favour gun control to avoid the risks of many carrying guns, or that less fearful people would be in favour of engaging in a war? Missing in this approach is an analysis of how people make sense of the morality of the issues they support and how they apply their moral judgments and more general conceptions about society to the issues at hand.

A second example comes from propositions put forth by Haidt et al. that also included characterizations of the moral orientations of liberals and conservatives (Haidt, 2001; Haidt & Graham, 2007). Their general proposition, in line with PASSP, is that moral decisions are largely based on what they refer to as intuitions, which are defined in their own particular way as immediate, non-reflective, non-rational reactions that are emotionally driven evolutionary adaptations partially shaped by culture (see Bruner, 1960; Shweder, Turiel, & Much, 1981 for alternative definitions of intuition). In this view, reasoning is an epiphenomenon used not to come to decisions but to rationalize decisions already made (see Jacobson, 2012 and Turiel, 2015 for critiques). A further proposition is that cultures and sub-cultures shape intuitions into the so-called moral foundations. The proposed moral foundations relevant for our purposes are those that are said to distinguish between conservatives or Republican and liberals or Democrats in the United States (Graham, Haidt, & Nosek, 2009; Haidt & Graham, 2007). They proposed that the moral orientations of Rebublicans/conservatives are based on respect for authority, social hierarchy, and sanctity, whereas the fundamentally different orientations of Democrats/liberals are to harm, fairness, individual freedoms, and a disdain for authority.

These moral foundations are seen as fixed, intuitively applied orientations of a homogeneous nature derived by individuals, in these cases, from each sub-culture's different and incommensurable morality. However, it is not at all clear that the positions of conservative and liberals divide up so neatly into these categories. A few salient examples of political and social policy positions taken in the latter part of the twentieth and early part of the twenty-first centuries serve to question the claim that these sub-groups maintain different and cohesive orientations. During these times, conservatives have championed the pronouncement in 1981 by the then President Ronald Reagan that 'Government is not a solution to our problem, government is the problem.' This has been more than a slogan for conservatives as they have voted for candidates espousing this position and attempted to enact legislation and policies aimed at shrinking the role of government for purposes of promoting free enterprise and individual freedoms (e.g. to own guns, keep their money from being taxed, make individual decisions on health care and medical insurance, and to freely contribute to political candidates). In the election cycles of 2008 and 2012, liberals have championed governmental authority and initiatives that would restrict freedoms in order to promote general welfare and community interests (including on guns, taxes, and health care). Whereas conservatives invoke respect for the *authority* of the US Constitution (the Second Amendment) in support of the freedom and right to own guns, they disparage the Constitutional ruling in *Roe versus Wade* that supports the freedom and right to abortion. Liberals invoke respect for *Roe versus Wade* to support the right to abortion, but disparage rulings regarding the Second Amendment as a basis for gun ownership, as well as rulings in *Citizens United versus Election Commission*. Conservatives have shown disdain for the authority of the Presidency of the United States (as in their attitudes towards President Barack Obama during his tenure), just as liberals showed disdain for the authority of the Presidency (as in their attitudes towards President George W. Bush during his tenure). Both groups appear to be concerned with freedoms, restrictions, the role of authority, and the welfare of people and the community. For instance, liberals/Democrats have often espoused communitarian positions that rely on the moral force of the group and they value democratic institutions without distrust of authority (Bellah, Madsen, Sullivan, Swidler, & Tipton, 1985; Putnam, 2000). In turn, on the conservative/Republican side anti-abortion positions are strongly guided by commitments to avoiding harm and the value of life – as are liberal positions on abortion (Dworkin, 1993; Turiel, Hildebrandt, & Wainryb, 1991).

Part of the characterizations of the different moral orientations is the idea that the concept of rights is part of some cultures and not others. In particular, some have theorized that cultures can be divided as representing individualistic (in many cases, Western cultures) and collectivistic (in many cases, non-Western cultures) worldviews (for examples of this position, see Markus & Kitayama, 1991; Shweder & Bourne, 1982; Triandis, 1990; for discussion of their shortcomings see Sen, 1997; Turiel, 2002; Turiel & Wainryb, 1994). One feature attributed to individualistic cultures is that morality is framed to a great extent by rights, whereas collectivistic cultures deemphasize rights – a distinction applied to conservative and liberal political positions by Haidt et al. A good example is the commentary provided by Haidt and Graham (2007) on an interchange between Rick Santorum, a Republican politician (a former Senator and presidential aspirant), and Jon Stewart, a liberal journalist. On Stewart's television programme, the two debated the validity of gay marriage, each taking opposite sides. Haidt and Graham (2007, p. 111) used the difference between them on the matter to illustrate fundamental and incommensurable differences in the morality of conservatives and liberals, asserting: 'Santorum's anti-gay-marriage views were based on concerns for traditional family structures, Biblical authority, and moral disgust for homosexual acts (which he had previously likened to incest and bestiality).' By contrast, liberal positions on gay marriage and homosexual acts presumably stem from different moral foundations oriented to harm, fairness, autonomy, and rights. In essence, Haidt and Graham treat the perspective of those who are regarded with disgust and denied worth, respect, and freedom of choice as irrelevant to morality in the conservative orientation – and as simply different from the liberal orientation.

If this type of division between cultures or between the 'culture' of political conservatism and political liberalism were accurate, it would certainly have implications for public discourse and political strategies. A significant implication is that there would be little dialogue and argumentation that would make a difference in the public sphere since groups would simply be talking in different cultural and moral frameworks.

Thought, reasoning, and emotions

Is there an alternative and what is it? An alternative is that both groups (whether seen as cultural groups or sub-cultures), as well as individuals within groups, are not unitary or homogeneous in their moral and social orientations and that variations would exist in approaches to moral issues: that by virtue of processes of reasoning individuals maintain moral judgments of welfare, justice, and rights; that such moral judgments are not solely the province of particular groups; that judgments regarding authority and social order are not solely the province of particular groups; that moral judgments can be in conflict with other social considerations and applied in different ways in different social situations; that individuals reflect upon systems of social organization and cultural practices and thereby can be critical of systems and practices perceived to be unfair. All of the above makes for dynamic social interactions with dialogue, debate, and argumentation among people within groups as well as between groups (including in political discourse). The different positions on gay rights taken by Stewart and Santorum, for example, are not simply irreconcilable differences but are more complex judgments about fairness, rights, the social order, and the preservation of traditions. (Whereas some liberals may emphasize fairness and rights in some situations more than some conservatives, in other contexts it can be the other way around.) Such debate and argumentation commonly within and between groups are often at the root of moral and social transformations. Indeed, the philosopher, Vlastos (1962, p. 31), has maintained that, 'The great historical struggles for social justice have centered about some demand for equal rights: the struggle against slavery, political absolutism, economic exploitation, the disfranchisement of the lower and middle classes and the disfranchisement of women, colonialism, racial oppression.' The point is that most individuals and groups in their social interactions and recommendations for social policies engage in consideration of issues of justice, equality, and rights.

In keeping with Vlastos' perception of historical struggles, there is a long tradition of philosophical analyses emphasizing the roles of thought, reasoning, and choices, in human endeavours. This tradition continues to contemporary times, as succinctly and pointedly stated by Nussbaum (1999, p. 71), 'human beings are above all reasoning beings, and ... the dignity of reason is the primary source of human equality' (see also Dworkin, 1977, 1993; Gewirth, 1982; Habermas, 1993; Nussbaum, 2000; Rawls, 1971, 1993; Sen, 1999, 2006, 2009). In his treatise on economic development and human freedom, Sen (1999, p. 272) maintained that a sense of justice involves judgment, thought, and inference:

> It is the power of reason that allows us to consider our obligations and ideals as well as our interests and advantages. To deny this freedom of thought would amount to a severe constraint on the reach of our rationality.

Human reasoning also implies that people make choices and reflect upon social conditions: 'Central to leading a human life ... are the responsibilities of choice and reasoning' (Sen, 2006, p. xiii).

These philosophers are in what Nussbaum refers to as the 'tradition of liberalism', not meant to refer to a political ideology, but to a tradition going back to the thought of Greek and Roman Stoics. In this tradition it is presumed (Nussbaum, 1999),

> that all, just by being human, are of equal dignity and worth, no matter where they are situated in society, and that the primary source of this worth is a power of moral choice within them, a power that consists in the ability to plan a life in accordance with one's own evaluations of ends. (p. 57)

According to Nussbaum (1999), modern thinkers also emphasize, 'that the moral equality of persons gives them a fair claim to certain types of treatment at the hands of society and politics' (p. 57). These principles are intended to apply, as well, to the 'lives that people are able to lead' (Sen, 2009, p. xi), which includes concerns with how people are able to reduce injustices and advance fairness. An emphasis on reasoning is not meant to minimize the role of emotions, which in Nussbaum's (2001) account are best construed as involving evaluative appraisals.

Development and domains of social judgments

In a general sense, these philosophical perspectives align with, and receive support from, research and theory in psychology – including research I have conducted over many years with a number of colleagues. We have found that at young ages children develop moral judgments first mainly about welfare and later in age better formed judgments about justice and rights. As already mentioned, children's moral judgments are constructed through their social interactions and relationships. Moral thinking is not solely a product of teachings from adults or exposure to societal standards, but emerge from everyday experiences in situations involving matters such as harm, sharing or failing to share, helping or failing to help, equalities and inequalities, and much more that occurs the world over in daily life (Nucci & Turiel, 1993; Turiel, 2015). Children also form judgments about other domains, including social conventions and areas of personal jurisdiction (Turiel, 1983, 2002). Distinguishing morality from other domains demonstrates that individuals think about social relationships, emotions, social practices, and social order, and that thinking about morality has features distinctive from thinking about other aspects of the social world. Individuals also form judgments about social systems, social organization, and the conventions that produce common expectations in social interactions within social systems. *Conventions* are a constitutive part of the social systems and these entail shared behaviours (uniformities, rules) whose meanings are defined by the system in which they are embedded. Making the distinction among domains also demonstrates that judgments about the social world include non-moral domains of importance. Individuals form judgments within the *personal domain* that pertain to actions considered outside the jurisdiction of moral concern or social regulation and legitimately within the jurisdiction of personal choice in arenas that do not involve impinging on the welfare of others.

We refer to these as domains because they differ from each other in systematic ways and do not solely involve simple discriminations. The domains constitute configurations of thought about dimensions related to rules, authority, and common practices. For example, moral issues are judged as non-contingent – as not necessarily tied to specific rules or authority dictates – and as applying across settings. By contrast, social conventions are judged to be contingent on rules and authority, and as specific to particular societies. With regard to the moral domain, children, adolescents, and adults judge that existing rules or the dictates of authority do not determine whether acts are right or wrong, but rather whether they meet standards of welfare and justice. As constitutive parts of the social system (such as specific rules regulating behaviour in an institution such as a school), conventions are seen as determined by existing rules and authority dictates (for extensive reviews, see Smetana, 2006; Turiel, 1983, 1998, 2002).

Processes of coordination in social decision-making

The domains do not only apply to children, but also to adolescents and adults since the distinctions are not age related. The domains are formed at early ages and each constitutes a separate developmental pathway. However, in addition to identifying individuals' moral judgments it is necessary to ascertain how and to whom they are applied. For example, concepts of equality and freedom as moral goals may be applied to some groups and not others. In his discussion of this issue, Sen (1997) points out that Aristotle wrote in support of freedoms and equality but did not apply it to women or slaves (as perhaps was the case for Jefferson). Similarly, it has often been the case that equality and freedom were strongly defended for upper classes or for Brahmins, but not for other groups (Sen, 1997).

Political thinking and decisions on the part of the public are complex topics to study from a psychological perspective. They are topics that should not be reduced to one domain of thought, such as morality, and require coordination of multiple features. One feature likely to be relevant to how judgments are made in the political realm is that of how moral judgments are applied in situational contexts, although our understanding of the failure to apply such concepts to all groups is currently quite limited. However, research has been conducted on another aspect of the application of moral judgments bearing on how decisions are made in situations entailing considerations from different domains or different considerations within the moral domain. Domains do intersect and are relevant to processes of social decision-making, which entail coordination between domains and between separable elements within domains. By coordination, I mean the process of weighing and balancing different considerations and goals and drawing priorities among them (a topic I do go into in more detail here than on the domains). Many social decisions – including political ones of the type considered above in the discussion of conservatives and liberals – involve such processes of coordination. Social situations often include varying components and require making choices by drawing priorities. The components and their potential conflicts can be between moral and non-moral goals, as well as between different moral goals.

An illustrative example of processes of coordination in social decision-making can be seen in the still well-known experiments conducted many years ago by Milgram (1963, 1974) – experiments supposedly on obedience to authority. I say *supposedly* because that way of interpreting the experiments shows how there is sometimes a tendency to focus only on one component of a situation and, thereby, obscure an understanding of multiple components in social situations and in people's decisions. In these experiments, participants were instructed by an experimenter to administer increasing levels of electric shocks (which were not real) to another person (a learner who was an accomplice of the researchers) in the guise of a study on the effects of punishment on learning and memory.

There are two problems and simplifications with the usual portrayal of findings by Milgram and others that they demonstrate that large numbers of people obey authority even when commanded to inflict severe pain on others (hence the title of Milgram's book *Obedience to authority*). One problem is that it does not account for the findings of most of the experimental conditions in Milgram's body of research, which showed that majorities defied the instructions of the experimenters. It was only in one experimental condition that most (about 65%) continued administering the shocks to the end of the scale. In that condition, the experimenter gave instructions directly to the participant who was in the same room while the person in the role of learner, who had been strapped to the electric shock apparatus, was not visible but within hearing range in an adjacent room. In other experimental conditions, producing little in the way of adherence to the experimenter's instructions, there were variations in the salience of the pain perceived by participants or of the role of the experimenter.

A second problem is that decisions in all these situations do not reflect straightforward obedience to authority. Instead, the decisions usually involved strong conflicts for participants between wishing to avoid inflicting physical pain on another and wishing to adhere to the procedures established by the experimenter in order to contribute to the goals of the scientific enterprise in which they had agreed to participate. In fact, Milgram (1974) noted that most participants, regardless of their ultimate decision, were experiencing conflict about the two considerations (e.g. even when continuing to administer the shocks, participants displayed a good deal of anxiety and would stop to tell the experimenter that the 'learner' was in pain and danger, that the experimenter should look to see if he was all right, that he did not want to harm the learner). Such conflicts, along with the findings from the other experimental conditions, strongly indicate that participants were attentive to both considerations and that they were weighing and balancing the two concerns. These considerations need to be taken into account if, for example, a goal is to promote greater scrutiny on the part of people of the commands of those in governmental leadership positions.

Coordination regarding rights, social inclusion, and honesty

I have described the Milgram experiments in a little detail to provide an illustration of how individuals attend to varying components in social situations and how they engage in a process of decision-making by weighing and balancing different and conflicting considerations (coordination). A related example is the research conducted by Asch (1952, 1956), often interpreted (inaccurately) to show people's propensities to conform to the group even with regard to erroneous responses to simple perceptual tasks such as estimating the comparative length of lines. The interpretation of the findings provided by Asch (1952) was, instead, that participants were not simply conforming, but attempting to make sense of a perplexing situation involving a discrepancy between their own perceptions and those of several others.

In the research on moral development, three topics of judgment have been studied – rights, social inclusion, and honesty – and shown to involve processes of coordination. A series of studies, conducted in several nations, looked at judgments about rights and freedoms of speech and religion in general and in contexts of conflicts between the freedoms and other social and moral considerations (Day, 2014; Helwig, 1995, 1997; Helwig & Turiel, in press; Helwig, Ruck, & Peterson-Badali, 2014; Turiel & Wainryb, 1998). In response to general questions bearing on decisions with political ramifications (e.g. should people be allowed to express their views or engage in their religious practices; would it be right or wrong for the government to institute laws restricting the freedoms), most endorsed the freedoms and judged them as moral rights independent of existing laws that are generalizable to other cultural contexts. These rights are also endorsed in certain situational contexts, but not in all situations. Often, rights are not endorsed when placed in situational contexts where an assertion of a right might conflict with, as examples, goals of preventing physical harm or equality of opportunity. The developmental findings, using interview methods, are consistent with the findings of several large-scale public opinion surveys at various times in the twentieth century (Hyman & Sheatsley, 1953; McClosky & Brill, 1983; Stouffer, 1955). Those surveys showed that large numbers of American adults endorse rights (e.g. to freedom of speech, religion, press, and assembly) in many situations, but in other situations subordinate rights to other social and moral goals.

Similar patterns have emerged in research with children and adolescents on their judgments about social inclusion and exclusion (Horn, 2003; Killen, Lee-Kim, McGlothlin, & Stagnor, 2002). In brief, exclusion based on gender and race is judged as wrong in many situations with reasons of fairness and equality. However, when judging situations that involve conflicting social goals, fairness can be subordinated to non-moral goals.

A third area is research with adolescents and adults on judgments about honesty, trust, and deception – research that also bears on judgments in the context of social hierarchies, power relations, and social inequalities. Honesty provides an example of a value that is not always straightforward from the moral point of view (Bok, 1978/1999). Philosophers have considered examples of situations in which honesty should be subordinated to other moral goals, such as when telling the truth might result in undue harm (think of deception to save lives in Nazi Germany).

A series of studies examined processes of coordination in decisions regarding honesty and deception. One example is a study with adolescents assessing their judgments about hypothetical situations bearing on deception of parents regarding activities in different domains (Perkins & Turiel, 2007). In this research, the large majority of adolescents (ages 12–13 and 16–17 years) judged it acceptable to deceive parents about demands made by parents considered morally wrong (regarding a parental directive to hit another; to engage in racial discrimination) on the grounds of preventing injustice or harm. The majority of adolescents also judged that deception was justified when parents directed personal choices (who to date; which club to join). By contrast, most judged deception as wrong when parents gave directives about prudential or pragmatic activities (not riding a motorcycle; completing homework). Such directives were seen as within parents' legitimate authority to place restrictions bearing on the welfare of their children. These and other findings indicate that adolescents value honesty and trust but coordinate that value with other considerations.

In the same study, it was found that fewer of the adolescents judged deception of peers acceptable than deception of parents for the morally relevant and personal issues. Although the adolescents thought that the restrictions directed by peers were not legitimate, they were less likely to accept deception of peers than of parents. The difference between how adolescents perceive the acceptability of deception of parents and friends points to another element of the coordination of different considerations in social and moral decision-making. The reason that deception of friends is considered less acceptable is that such relationships are seen as based on equality and mutuality, whereas relationships with parents involve greater inequality in power. Concerns with power differences, inequalities, and the acceptance of deception should not be seen as particular to the travails of adolescence. We have obtained comparable findings in adults' judgments about the acceptability of deception as a means of promoting welfare in marital relationships involving power differences (Turiel, Perkins, & Mensing, 2009).

Cultural practices, social opposition, and moral resistance

The studies on honesty and deception with adolescents and adults can be seen as contradictory with the interpretation of Milgram's (1963) findings as reflecting people's propensities to obey those in authority. Those findings show that in some realms of social activities individuals defy those in authority. In family relationships, individuals do not simply accept power differences or inequalities in all endeavours. It would be very informative for explanations of political discourse to conduct similar research on individuals' orientations to governmental authorities. However, research has been conducted on judgments and actions pertaining to cultural practices of inequality embedded in social hierarchies.

The research, psychological and anthropological, examined judgments and actions around inequalities between males and females in non-Western, patriarchal cultures. The research provides evidence that social inequalities in cultural practices produce social opposition and moral resistance. Studies conducted in patriarchal cultures in the Middle-East (Guvenc, 2011; Wainryb & Turiel, 1994), India (Neff, 2001), Colombia (Mensing, 2002), and Benin (Conry-Murray, 2009) assessed how adolescent and adult females and males think about inequalities between females and males that are institutionalized in cultural practices. These include inequalities regarding educational and work opportunities, recreational activities, and decision-making within the family. The research examined whether there are concerns with the individual, independence, and freedoms in the cultures, and whether individuals accept their roles and positions of inequality.

I summarize some of the findings with examples of representative responses from a few of the participants in studies conducted in a Druze Arab community in northern Israel. Perhaps not surprisingly, it was found that males assert their independence and autonomy, as well as their right to exert control over the activities of females in the family. An acceptance of personal choices, freedoms, and the idea of autonomy are very much a part of the cultures – as mainly granted to males. Females are also aware of the freedoms granted to males and in some respects females accept their roles as reflected in the responses of an adolescent (14 years old) female in the Druze community (Turiel, 2002, p. 247):

> Because in our culture a man is given complete freedom ... no one would oppose a man being free. ... That is the way it is among the Druze. [A male] has the right to choose his own way.

However, acceptance by females of their roles and control by males is often for pragmatic reasons; that is, they fear the consequences, which can be severe, of defiance. Nevertheless, females desire freedoms and equality, but think that these are difficult goals to achieve and that they must struggle to do so. As an example, an 18-year-old Druze female said (Turiel, 2002, p. 249):

> We live in a conservative culture. Maybe in the future I might want to treat my daughter in the same way I would treat my son, but the culture wouldn't let me do it. ... I believe in equality, but the culture would grant more to a male.

It was also found that the large majority of females judged the inequalities as unfair, as illustrated by the responses of an adult female (Turiel, 2002, p. 249):

> A man's life is simple. He works, he comes back home; he has no other responsibilities. I work too and I have kids and a home. He knows that when he comes back, everything will be ready

for him. That's such a pleasure. When I come home I have more work to do at home. So, who do you think deserves to get out a little and enjoy life?

In line with the findings of the psychological research are findings from anthropological studies using ethnographic methods involving observations of social interactions and interviews. The anthropological research shows that women act in covert (including the use of deception) and overt ways to assert freedoms, rights and avoid undue control by men. In one case, Wikan (1996) conducted fieldwork with people living in conditions of poverty in Cairo through visits to the same community over several years. She documented that there is a good deal of conflict in their relations with those in higher socio-economic classes and with governmental authorities. She also found that there are conflicts within the family around women's desire for greater equality.

Another anthropological study, conducted by Abu-Lughod (1993) in a rural Bedouin village in northwestern Egypt, found that women were often critical of the restrictions placed on them in their daily lives. Moreover, they sought ways to avoid the control that men exerted on them, using several means, sometimes involving deception, to evade restrictions placed on their personal choices, education, and work opportunities. They also used deceptive means to avoid general cultural practices such as arranged marriages and polygamy, practices they believed were unfair. As an example, Abu-Lughod reported that many of the women believed that the practice of polygamy was unfair and should be changed.

The findings from the psychological and anthropological studies are corroborated by journalistic reports from countries such as Iran and Afghanistan of underground activities aimed at circumventing governmental and religious restrictions on matters such as dress, listening to music, viewing videos, and consumption of alcohol (Turiel, 2003). Consistent with the research findings, people resist restrictions imposed by those in positions of authority but judged to be unfair. Such opposition and resistance indicate that the moral judgments of individuals are not derived from existing societal standards or practices. Opposition and resistance also indicate that social and moral reasoning involves scrutiny and reflection upon existing practices.

Conclusions

The research and theoretical approach I have discussed bear on how we think about different groups, including cultural groups and groups based on political affiliations. The research indicates that we cannot, as is often the case, view differences as due to cultural orientations entailing shared beliefs, values, and knowledge – such as the dichotomy between individualist and collectivist cultures (Markus & Kitayama, 1991; Shweder & Bourne, 1982; Triandis, 1990).

Research I have discussed yields different conclusions. First, the research on domains of moral, social, and personal judgments indicates that general cultural orientations such as individualism and collectivism fail to capture the heterogeneity evident in the social orientations of most individuals and peoples. Within cultures, we see varying perspectives on social relationships, including moral judgments bearing on concerns with welfare, justice, and rights and personal judgments with concerns with independence and autonomy.

These heterogeneous orientations are manifested in conflicts within cultures and decisions that involve coordination of considerations from the different domains and within domains.

A reason cultures are sometimes characterized as maintaining homogeneous, shared values may be that researchers often rely on those who are in positions of power and authority to inform them on the culture. By excluding those in positions of lesser power, researchers obtain a one-sided view, as has been noted by several commentators. As an example, Wikan (1991, p. 290) has stated: 'looking mainly at culture's spokesmen ... at the exclusion of the poor, the infirm, women, and youths' (has resulted in) 'the concept of culture as a seamless whole and of society as a bounded group manifesting inherently valued order ... that effectively masked human misery and quenched dissenting voices'. Making a similar point, the philosopher and political scientist, Okin (1989, p. 67) maintained that:

> Oppressors and oppressed – when the voice of the latter can be heard at all–often disagree fundamentally. Contemporary views about gender are a clear example of such disagreements; it is clear that there are no shared understandings on this subject, even among women.

The research in patriarchal cultures, which did include study of the perspectives of those in different positions on social hierarchies, shows both that there is a strong sense of independence and personal entitlements embedded in hierarchical arrangements as granted to those in dominant positions, and that those in subordinate positions are not entirely accepting of the morality of practices that unequally restrict their activities. There are commonalities between cultures in moral judgments, and there are differences in the ways they are applied and coordinated with other goals. Moreover, within cultures there are differences in perspectives between those in different positions on the social hierarchy. It may also be that in some respects there are more commonalities between those in similar positions on the hierarchies in different cultures than those in different positions in the same culture. With regard to the political sub-groups of conservatives and liberals, both make similar moral judgments and each group maintains positions that combine a reliance on institutions and authority and critical stances on some institutions and authorities – albeit with disagreements.

More generally, it seems to me that the study of the development of moral judgments has connections to political discourse. In drawing such connections, it is important to recognize that people reason about morality. It is also important to take into account the ways moral reasoning is applied in different situational contexts, with coordination of moral, social, and personal goals. The research on power relations, social hierarchies, and inequalities also bears on political thought. In weighing and balancing concerns with fairness and personal goals and commitments to cultural practices and systems of social organization, individuals engage in social opposition and moral resistance in their everyday lives. Critique of cultural practices and moral resistance indicate that in constructing moral judgments people do reflect on their social conditions.

The idea that moralities differ by culture (i.e. moral or cultural relativism) is inadequate, given the complexities of similarities and differences between cultures and within cultures. It fails to account for the commonalities across cultures in moral understandings of welfare, justice, and rights which develop through reciprocal interactions. However, the evidence also speaks against the idea of moral absolutism insofar as absolutism means that particular moral values or concepts must be categorically applied. People's understandings of social situations are too complex for such an inflexible morality. Social life is such that one moral good can conflict with another. In most cultures, choices must be made that can result in variations in the application of a moral good so as to maintain a moral good.

Disclosure statement

No potential conflict of interest was reported by the author.

References

Abu-Lughod, L. (1993). *Writing women's worlds: Bedouin stories*. Berkeley: University of California Press.

Asch, S. E. (1952). *Social psychology*. Englewood Cliffs, NJ: Prentice-Hall.

Asch, S. E. (1956). Studies of independence and conformity: A minority of one against a unanimous majority. *Psychological Monographs, 70*(9), 1–70.

Bellah, R. N., Madsen, R., Sullivan, W. M., Swidler, A., & Tipton, S. M. (1985). *Habits of the heart: Individualism and commitment in American life*. New York, NY: Harper & Row.

Bok, S. (1999). *Lying: Moral choice in public and private life*. New York, NY: Vintage Books. (Original work published 1979).

Bruner, J. (1960). *The process of education*. New York, NY: Vintage Books.

Conry-Murray, C. (2009). Adolescent and adult reasoning about gender roles and fairness in Benin, West Africa. *Cognitive Development, 24*, 207–219.

Day, K. (2014). The right to literacy and cultural change: Zulu adolescents in post-apartheid rural South Africa. *Cognitive Development, 29*, 81–94.

Dworkin, R. (1993). *Life's dominion: An argument about abortion, euthanasia, and individual freedom*. New York, NY: Alfred A. Knopf.

Dworkin, R. M. (1977). *Taking rights seriously*. Cambridge, MA: Harvard University Press.

Gewirth, A. (1982). *Human rights: Essays on justification and applications*. Chicago, IL: University of Chicago Press.

Graham, J., Haidt, J., & Nosek, B. A. (2009). Liberals and conservative rely on different sets of moral foundations. *Journal of Personality and Social Psychology, 96*, 1029–1046.

Guvenc, G. (2011). *Women's construction of familial-gender identities and embodied subjectivities in Saraycik, Turkey* (Unpublished manuscript). Isik University, Istanbul, Turkey.

Habermas, J. (1993). *Justification and application*. Cambridge, MA: MIT Press.

Haidt, J. (2001). The emotional dog and its rational tail: A social intuitionist approach to moral judgment. *Psychological Review, 108*, 814–834.

Haidt, J., & Graham, J. (2007). When morality opposes justice: Conservatives have moral intuitions that liberals may not recognize. *Social Justice Research, 20*, 98–116.

Helwig, C. C. (1995). Adolescents' and young adults' conceptions of civil liberties: Freedom of speech and religion. *Child Development, 66*, 152–166.

Helwig, C. C. (1997). The role of agent and social context in judgments of freedom of speech and religion. *Child Development, 68*, 484–495.

Helwig, C. C., Ruck, M., & Peterson-Badali, M. (2014). Rights, civil liberties, and democracy. In M. Killen & J. G. Smetana (Eds.), *Handbook of moral development* (2nd Ed., pp. 46–69). Mahwah, NJ: Taylor & Francis.

Helwig, C. C., & Turiel, E. (in press). The psychology of children's rights. In M. Ruck, M. Peterson-Badali, & M. Freeman (Eds.), *Handbook of children's rights: Global and multidisciplinary perspectives*. Taylor and Francis.

Horn, S. S. (2003). Adolescents reasoning about exclusion from social groups. *Developmental Psychology, 39*, 71–84.

Hyman, H. H., & Sheatsley, P. B. (1953). Trends in public opinion on civil liberties. *Journal of Social Issues, 9*, 6–16.

Jacobson, D. (2012). Moral dumbfounding and moral stupefaction. *Oxford studies in normative ethics* (pp. 289–316). New York, NY: Oxford University Press.

Kihlstrom, J. H. (2004). Is there a 'People are Stupid' school in social psychology? [Commentary on "Towards a balanced social psychology: Causes, consequences, and cures for the problem-seeking approach to social behavior and cognition" by J. I. Krueger and D. C. Funder.] *Behavioral & Brain Sciences, 27*, 348–349.

Kihlstrom, J. H. (2008). The automocity juggernaut – or, are we automatons after all? In J. Baer, J. C. Kaufman, & R. F. Baumeister (Eds.), *Are we free? Psychology and free will* (pp. 155–180). New York, NY: Oxford University Press.

Killen, M., Lee-Kim, J., McGlothlin, H., & Stagnor, C. (2002). How children and adolescents value gender and racial exclusion. *Monographs of the Society for Research in Child Development*. Serial No. 271, Vol. 67, No. 4. Oxford: Blackwell.

Markus, H. R., & Kitayama, S. (1991). Culture and the self: Implications for cognition, emotion, and motivation. *Psychological Review, 98*, 224–253.

McClosky, M., & Brill, A. (1983). *Dimensions of tolerance: What Americans believe about civil liberties*. New York: Sage.

Mensing, J. F. (2002). *Collectivism, individualism, and interpersonal responsibilities in families: Differences and similarities in social reasoning between individuals in poor, urban families in Colombia and the United States* (Unpublished doctoral dissertation). University of California, Berkeley.

Milgram, S. (1963). Behavioral study of obedience. *Journal of Abnormal and Social Psychology, 67*, 371–378.

Milgram, S. (1974). *Obedience to authority*. New York, NY: Harper & Row.

Neff, K. D. (2001). Judgments of personal autonomy and interpersonal responsibility in the context of Indian spousal relationships: An examination of young people's reasoning in Mysore, India. *British Journal of Developmental Psychology, 19*, 233–257.

Nucci, L. P., & Turiel, E. (1993). God's word, religious rules and their relation to Christian and Jewish children's concepts of morality. *Child Development, 64*, 1475–1491.

Nussbaum, M. C. (1999). *Sex and social justice*. New York, NY: Oxford University Press.

Nussbaum, M. C. (2000). *Women and human development: The capabilities approach*. Cambridge: Cambridge University Press.

Nussbaum, M. C. (2001). *Upheavels of thought: The intelligence of emotions*. Cambridge: Cambridge University Press.

Okin, S. M. (1989). *Justice, gender, and the family*. New York, NY: Basic Books.

Oxley, D. R., Smith, K. B., Alford, J. R., Hibing, M. V., Miller, J. L., Scalora, M., ... Hibbing, J. R. (2008). Political attitudes vary with physiological traits. *Science, 321*, 1667–1670.

Perkins, S. A., & Turiel, E. (2007). To lie or not to lie: To whom and under what circumstances. *Child Development, 78*, 609–621.

Putnam, R. D. (2000). *Bowling alone: The collapse and revival of American community*. New York, NY: Simon & Schuster.

Rawls, J. (1971). *A theory of justice*. Cambridge, MA: Harvard University Press.

Rawls, J. (1993). *Political liberalism*. New York, NY: Columbia University Press.

Sen, A. (1997, July 14 & 21). Human rights and Asian values. *The New Republic*, 33–39.

Sen, A. (1999). *Development as freedom*. New York, NY: Alfred A. Knopf.

Sen, A. (2006). *Identity and violence: The illusion of destiny.* New York, NY: Norton.

Sen, A. (2009). *The idea of justice.* Cambridge, MA: Harvard University Press.

Shweder, R. A., & Bourne, E. J. (1982). Does the concept of person vary cross-culturally? In A. J. Marsella & G. M. White (Eds.), *Cultural conceptions of mental health and therapy* (pp. 97–137). Boston, MA: Reidel.

Shweder, R. A., Turiel, E., & Much, N. C. (1981). The moral intuitions of the child. In J. H. Flavell & L. Ross (Eds.), *Social cognitive development: Frontiers and possible futures* (pp. 288–305). Cambridge: Cambridge University Press.

Smetana, J. G. (2006). Social domain theory: Consistencies and variations in children's moral and social judgments. In M. Killen & J. G. Smetana (Eds.), *Handbook of moral development* (pp. 119–153). Mahwah, NJ: Erlbaum.

Stouffer, S. (1955). *Communism, conformity and civil liberties.* New York, NY: Doubleday.

Triandis, H. C. (1990). Cross-cultural studies of individualism and collectivism. In J. J. Berman (Ed.), *Nebraska Symposium on motivation: 1989, Vol. 37. Cross-cultural perspectives* (pp. 41–133). Lincoln: University of Nebraska Press.

Turiel, E. (1983). *The development of social knowledge: Morality and convention.* Cambridge: Cambridge University Press.

Turiel, E. (1998). The development of morality. In N. Eisenberg (Ed.), *Social, emotional, and personality development. Volume 3 of the handbook of child psychology* (5th ed., pp. 863–932). Editor-in-chief: W. Damon. New York, NY: John Wiley & Sons.

Turiel, E. (2002). *The culture of morality: Social development, context, and conflict.* Cambridge: Cambridge University Press.

Turiel, E. (2003). Resistance and subversion in everyday life. *Journal of Moral Education, 32,* 115–130.

Turiel, E. (2010). The relevance of moral epistemology and psychology for neuroscience. In P. Zelazo, M. Chandler, & E. Crone (Eds.), *Developmental social cognitive neuroscience* (pp. 313–331). New York, NY: Taylor & Francis.

Turiel, E. (2015). Moral development. In W. F. Overton & P. C. Molenaar (Eds.), *Handbook of child psychology, Vol. 1: Theory & method, 7th edition* Editor-in-chief: R. M. Lerner (pp. 484–522). Hoboken, NJ: John Wiley & Sons.

Turiel, E., Hildebrandt, C., & Wainryb, C. (1991). Judging social issues: Difficulties, inconsistencies and consistencies. *Monographs of the Society for Research in Child Development, 56* (Serial No. 224).

Turiel, E., Perkins, S. A., & Mensing, J. F. (2009). *Judgments about deception in marital relationships* (Unpublished manuscript). University of California, Berkeley.

Turiel, E., & Wainryb, C. (1994). Social reasoning and the varieties of social experience in cultural contexts. In H. W. Reese (Ed.), *Advances in child development and behavior* (Vol. 25, pp. 289–326). New York, NY: Academic Press.

Turiel, E., & Wainryb, C. (1998). Concepts of freedoms and rights in a traditional hierarchically organized society. *British Journal of Developmental Psychology, 16,* 375–395.

Vlastos, G. (1962). Justice and equality. In R. B. Brandt (Ed.), *Social justice* (pp. 31–72). Englewood Cliffis, NJ: Prentice-Hall.

Wainryb, C., & Turiel, E. (1994). Dominance, subordination, and concepts of personal entitlements in cultural contexts. *Child Development, 65,* 1701–1722.

Wikan, U. (1991). Toward an experience-near anthropology. *Cultural Anthropology, 6,* 285–305.

Wikan, U. (1996). *Tomorrow, God willing: Self-made destinies in Cairo.* Chicago, IL: University of Chicago Press.

Conscientious politics and Israel's moral dilemmas

Uriel Abulof

ABSTRACT

This paper introduces 'conscientious politics', discusses their features and shows their resonance in the case of Israel. I define conscientious politics as politics informed by moral deliberations about legitimacy, and locate them in the larger matrix of conscience. In the balance between passion and persuasion, conscientious politics provide time and invite venues for deliberation on the social contract, challenging rulers' convenience and society's conventions. While the individual's freedom of conscience draws mainly on positive liberty (from within), conscientious politics also requires emancipation from without. However, conscientious politics are not necessarily harmonious or liberal, nor does liberalism necessarily entail free conscience. Conscientious politics are often 'hidden in plain sight', and the normative task of bringing them to light depends on revealing the moral dilemmas that underpin actual politics. I unearth such dilemmas with regard to Israel's 2011 social justice movement, the subsequent prisoner exchange and Israel's relations with the Palestinians.

> We are not looking for a leader to rule us, because everyone who went to Tahrir is a leader. We are looking for a conscience. – Ahmed Hassan, Egyptian activist, *The Square*. (Noujaim, 2013)

Public justification entails both practical reasoning and moral reasoning. Focusing only on the latter, this paper investigates whether and how conscience, which is usually seen as private (its reasoning internal to one's thoughts and emotions), can transcend the individual to inform and affect politics. I thus address one core question: Can conscience be public, and does it matter? I answer both questions in the affirmative. Conscience, as both idea and practice, may transcend the individual, and involve the public in ways that shape its politics. This is not merely about 'social conscience' – the individual's consideration of the common good, often drawing on shared principles and obligations (Walzer, 1970). Conscientious politics are about such individuals and groups engaging in moral conversations in order to influence their political life. By walking the line between the *is* and the *ought*, conscientious politics constitute the crux of *moral* public justification.

The study of conscientious politics is existentialist and phenomenological. Existentialism is a broad intellectual lodge and its denizens (not always subscribing to the term itself) are not of one voice (Crowell, 2012; Flynn, 2006; Jonas & Vogel, 1996; Luper, 2000;

Strenger, 2011; Tymieniecka, 2010). Still, while their normative conclusions often diverge, their empirical observations typically converge. From the biblical Ecclesiastes through Kierkegaard and Kafka to Dostoyevsky, Nietzsche and Sartre, thinkers have centred on humans as mortal agents, free to construct moral meaning in a meaningless universe. Conscientious politics foreground this individual moral freedom against the background of its modern predicament: a lingering crisis of political legitimation.

Ivan Karamazov may have been right, 'If there's no God and no life beyond the grave … everything is permitted.' With the 'murder of God', modern politics, especially in the west, lost an absolute anchor for values and virtues (Chadwick, 1990; Taylor, 2007). We cannot provide an external *post-hoc* justification, let alone a *raison d'être*, to socio-political order, for example, having non-liberal legitimation of liberalism. Rather than espying a towering lighthouse that embodies goodness and shows the right (and righteous) path, people are called upon to construct and construe their own individual moral compass, often seeing North in opposite directions. Creating moral havens in this modern wilderness is the task of contemporary conscientious politics: to effectively furnish public justification with moral coordinates to navigate through politics.

The socio-moral wandering and divergence underpin the emergence of 'multiple modernities' (Eisenstadt, 2003; Kupchan, 2012). Weber (1946, p. 147) recognized that in the moral vacuity of modern, bureaucratic legitimation 'the various value spheres of the world stand in irreconcilable conflict with each other'. By investigating moral divergence in a 'disenchanted world', political existentialism invites us to go beyond *political moralism*, 'the priority of the moral over the political', to *political realism*, revealing how we have tried to meet 'the basic legitimation demand' of political life (Williams, 2005, pp. 2, 3). It motivates us to embrace a phenomenological gaze at politics, to tap into the social actors' shared understanding of this world and of their political life in it without necessarily passing judgment on its merits and outcomes.[1] Conscientious politics are thus not predicated on their content, and need not be liberal or otherwise benign.

Though ethically agnostic, political existentialism is not amoral. Rather than favouring the ideal over the real or equating the former with the latter, political existentialism plumbs the gaping abyss between the *is* and the *ought*, and see this chasm as itself constituting the realm of humanity's most exciting, and daunting, features: death, freedom and the quest for meaning. Therefore, with political existentialism, the normative is empirical – the actors' divergent views of what *ought* to be, and *why*, is the object of inquiry – and the empirical is normative: investigating the social actors' legitimation efforts illuminates their socio-moral dilemmas, thus making us more aware of our freedom, more adept at discerning the right choice.

Below, I engage with this agenda in theory and practice, first outlining conscientious politics along the contentious contours of conscience, and then examine their resonance in contemporary Israel. For lack of space, my emphasis is theoretical. The empirical discussion is illustrative, not exhaustive. Extensive case studies are introduced elsewhere (e.g. Abulof, 2015b).

The contours of conscience

Insights from philosophy, sociology and psychology are invaluable for conceiving the moral motivations of public justification and for grasping how they underpin politics.

These insights may not provide us with an exact definition of conscience, but they can help us chart some of its defining features. Conscience, as both idea and practice, defies a simple either-or depiction. Lingering debates about the nature of conscience and its impact on politics have yielded substantial scholarship (Arendt, 1978; Braun & Vallance, 2011; Brownlee, 2012; Hitlin, 2008; Howard, 1978; Langston, 2001; Ojakangas, 2013; Schinkel, 2007; Strohm, 2011; Vischer, 2010). Below, I do not address the host of these debates, but identify and address four key questions, which should help us grasp the resonance of conscience in public justification, via conscientious politics. Is conscience character-based or circumstantial, intuitive or reflective, conformist or counter-conventional, certain or curious? Instead of resolving these conundrums and trying to pin down conscience, I explicate these contentious contours of conscience. Probing the resonance of each contour in the social realm, I crystalize the meaning and significance of conscientious politics.

Character and circumstances

What cause conscience – personal character or social circumstances? Weber (1922/1978, p. 25) acknowledged 'the great bulk of everyday action to which people have become habitually accustomed', but equally stressed the role of individual conscience as 'clearly self-conscious formulation, of the ultimate values governing the action', which 'always involves "commands" or "demands" which, in the actor's opinion, are binding on him'. What then invokes these moral 'commands' and activates our conscience?

Part of the answer may be found in biological traits (e.g. age and gender) and psychological dispositions. For example, Adorno (1950) suggests that certain childhood experiences, such as punitive parenting and suppressed homosexuality, engender the 'authoritarian personality', with specific right-wing, even fascist, inclinations, leaving little room to individual conscience. Rokeach (1960) likewise locates authoritarianism and diminished autonomy in different personalities, though without specific political correlation: both left and right have their share of 'open' and 'closed' minds. Notably, the latter's high score on 'dogmatism' often suggests a strong conviction, which many attribute to conscience.

Proceeding from open and closed minds to open and closed societies, conscience is arguably not merely the offshoot of a hardwired character; social circumstances and coincidence too play a role. Arendt (1978) grounds conscience in thinking, suggesting the latter is a natural, universal, human need, but equally pervasive is the inability to think. Does society push us one way or another? Studies in moral psychology indicate that time and social interaction are especially conducive to reasoned conscience. The more leisure we have to contemplate matters, and the more opportunities we have to discuss them with peers, the greater is our ability, and willingness, to activate our moral compass. Time and interaction are so crucial that given a while to think and deliberate, participants were persuaded by arguments defending incestuous behaviour, which commonly elicits instinctive emotional condemnation that defies reasoned persuasion (Paxton, Ungar, & Greene, 2012).

In the realm of conscientious politics, social conditions, rather than innate personal character, typically take front stage. Contemporary scholars submit that people are hardwired to hold different political views (e.g. Haidt, 2012; Hibbing, Smith, & Alford, 2014), but none suggest that a substantial group of people are physiologically incapable of having a conscience. The decline of virtue ethics in modern morality (MacIntyre, 2007) further undermines the role of character in fostering conscience.

The alternative is clear: conscience is lost due to a 'bad barrel', not 'bad apples' (Zimbardo, 2007). How then can we fix the barrels? One proposition is Bergson's 'open society', which is concerned less with social cohesion, more with inspirational conscience and creativity. Such open society fosters the 'duration' needed to cultivate the 'qualitative multiplicity' of human consciousness and conscience, a continuous heterogeneity of emotions and thoughts, which may ultimately breed moral progress, for example, in the 'transition from repugnance to fear, from fear to sympathy, and from sympathy itself to humility' (Bergson, 2001, p. 19). Cognitively, an open society further fosters a moral learning process on both the individual and social levels. Notably, Bergson's open society need not be liberal; enlightened absolutism can empower conscientious politics no less than a neo-liberal democracy (more on this below). Later, in the wake of the World War II, Popper (1945/2003) more strictly employed 'open society' to denounce teleological historicism in the name of liberal democracy. The latter, he argued, constitute a falsifiable social order, which is vital for fostering a free conscience.

Both Bergson and Popper largely dodged the 'material-moral paradox': does affluence encourage or curtail conscientious politics? Maslow (1971) famously suggested that striving for high goals, including morality and conscience, is predicated on satisfying lower, material needs. Yet, critics of capitalist consumerism suggest that wealth and overconsumption fosters 'affluenza', mind-numbing decadence on a mass scale (Hamilton & Denniss, 2005; Luthar, 2003; Wachtel, 1983). Furthermore, although affluence is typically contrasted with indigence (literally, being in need), abundance may foster new needs, which in turn encourage people to seek more material assets. A moral vacuity may ensue, undermining conscientious politics.

Conscientious politics and social transformations often intertwine. In and beyond the West, the secularization of conscience has affected its content and resonance (Moskos & Chambers, 1993). By suggesting 'good without God', secular conscience invites a moral 'peer review': accepting God's existence, or the right to believe in one, can no longer suffice; one is called upon to engage with the conscientious propositions of one's fellows, to ponder their moral dilemmas, and make a choice. Otherwise, there is no *moral* public justification. More recently, the post-industrial age has arguably undermined habits as reliable guides, and people, especially the young and educated, increasingly turn to reflective reasoning (Archer, 2012). We are also likely to resort to conscientious politics when facing acute dissonance between equally important, but non-sacred, values, especially when we sense that our decisions matter (Tetlock, Peterson, & Lerner, 1996). Importantly, conscientious politics are not only born out of circumstances but also can change them.

Intuition and reflection

Is conscience a moral sentiment, emotive and unreflective, or does it require contemplation and reason? Conscience involves both feeling and thinking, but their interplay varies. Conceptually, it might be useful to revive the scholastic distinction between *synderesis* and *conscientia*, an habituated moral intuition and a reasoned moral judgment, respectively (Langston, 2001, pp. 21–38). But distinction means neither divorce nor innate hierarchy.

Recent influential works downplay the role of reason. Haidt (2012) introduced 'social intuitionism' as the root of individual morality. Accordingly, unreflective sentiments motivate our moral judgment and actions to which reason provides only *post-hoc* justification. Intuitionism has gained much traction among sociobiologists. After all, if emotions, not reason, make morality, the moral gap between man and other animals, especially mammals, seems ever so slight. Haidt (2012, p. xxii) confidently proclaims, 'human beings are 90 percent chimp … selfish hypocrites … and 10 percent bee … cells in a larger body'.

Granted, we could not have a sense of right and wrong without either its emotional underpinning or our advanced prefrontal cortex; and certainly, humans share much of this mental 'software' and biological 'hardware' with apes (de Waal, 2006). Still, if we seek to learn not only what brings us together as animals but also what sets us apart as humans, we must probe also our distinctive traits, not least in the moral realm. Reason has become a paramount part of human morality, especially if we accept morality as interactionist and dynamic.

> Though a capacity to reason helps us to survive and reproduce, once we develop a capacity for reasoning, we may be led by it to places that are not of any direct advantage to us, in evolutionary terms. Reason is like an escalator – once we step on it, we cannot get off until we have gone where it takes us. (Singer, 2006, p. 146)

Endowed with freedom, we have much to say on 'where it takes us' – on what items to pick from the evolutionary menu, and how to expand it (Abulof, 2015a, pp. 43–61). Moral reasoning allows – though does not compel us – to transcend, even transform, seemingly hardwired instincts and intuitions, partly by broadening the bounds of empathy beyond kith and kin.[2]

Social intuitionism often alludes to Hume's dictum that 'reason is, and ought only to be the slave of the passions', and Haidt (2012, p. 29) purports to have 'found evidence for Hume's claim'. Hume's (1739/2007) claim, however, is that 'since a passion can never, in any sense, be called unreasonable … 'tis impossible, that reason and passion can ever oppose each other'. He proposed that in order to yield action, reason must resonate emotionally. Passions, broadly understood, empower reasons. Thus, Hume attested that his passions of 'curiosity' and 'ambition' drive his philosophical inquiries. Moreover, when passion is 'founded on a false supposition. Or when it chuses means insufficient for the design'd end', reason is there to correct it (see also Wright, 2009, pp. 166–168, 265–275).

Human exceptionalism and the existential search for meaning involve both 'moral emotions', like pride, shame and guilt, and the exercise of 'passions within reason' (Frank, 1988; Steinbock, 2014). Human morality ultimately fuses emotion and reason, and both are indispensable to mature conscience (Paxton & Greene, 2010). Toddlers may cry out 'This is not fair!' but mostly lack the capacity to fully feel and reason their moral defiance. Importantly, publicly articulating moral justification for our views and conduct is key to distinguishing conscientious objections from other forms of political resistance (Schinkel, 2007, pp. 516–520). Moral intuition without reflection lends itself to emotivism – justification based on emotional appeal (e.g. 'That's just the way I feel') and 'bad faith' ('That's just who I am'), thus extolling, for example, the 'wisdom of repugnance' (Kass, 2002). Conversely, the coalescence of emotion and reason, by encouraging articulated justification, advances the moral appeal of conscience beyond the individual in both interpersonal and social settings (Nussbaum, 2001, 2013).

Moral dilemmas and their emotive residue are the clearest manifestation of this emotional–rational interplay. Moral dilemma arises when there are moral reasons for each of two (or more) actions, but it is impossible to take no action or to act on all; a 'damned if you do, damned if you don't' situation. Moral residue relates to the emotional remnants of a dilemma – 'bad conscience' involving remorse, shame and regret (Gowans, 1987). Reason and emotion also meet in the *moral shock* at a transgression (Jasper, 1997). Such dynamics underpin conscience and render both *conversational* and *covenantal*.

Conscience is *conversational* since our moral 'self-knowledge' entails conversations we hold with the 'inner voice' of our 'better self', critically evaluating our conduct. By grounding conscience in thinking, Arendt (1971, p. 442) saw it as a Platonic 'silent dialogue between me and myself', constituting Socrates' 'two in one'. Some 'silent dialogues' are brisk – strict commands through moral intuition. Others are longer, allowing for inner-debate, and even deep 'meta-reflexivity' on past inner-dialogues (Archer, 2012). In between the intuitive dictate and the moral dialogue, conscientious politics push towards greater reflection by providing more time and venues for deliberation. The latter, however, need not amount to 'discourse ethics' (Habermas, 1999) and be open, inclusive, well-informed, equal or liberal; indeed, often it is not. In the realm of conscientious politics, deliberation is simply reasoned, public conversation. However, it requires individuals not just to be willing to communicate their conscientious beliefs, but to actually do so (Brownlee, 2012).

Conscience is *covenantal* since we regard our conversations with our 'better self' as quasi-sacrosanct obligations, whose breach engenders daunting emotions and thoughts, such as guilt and remorse. The covenant, however, is always a work in progress, a learning process, shifting with new life experiences. Conscientious politics effectively turns this individual covenant into a social contract, outlining virtues and values that legitimate politics. Public conscience involves the public's (moral) justification of identity, polity, authority and policy. This content of this social contract is not up to any particular individual, be she a philosopher or a politician, and need not be formal (indeed, typically, it is not). Rather, it is a dynamic, intersubjective and multifaceted construct, erected by individuals and groups to guide of their socio-political order (Abulof, 2016).

Convenience and conventions

Must conscience defy personal convenience and social conventions? Kohlberg (1981) disaggregated moral development into three progressive levels, two stages in each: from blind and instrumental egoism ('pre-conventional level'), through interpersonal accord and social conformism ('conventional level'), to prosocial and principled justification ('post-conventional level'). For example, in Kohlberg's famous dilemma, Heinz must decide whether to steal a drug to save his wife's life. Kohlberg was interested less in what we would like Heinz to do, more in how we morally reason our prescription. For example, in the pre-conventional level, we may argue that Heinz should steal the drug so as not to be blamed for her death (stage 1) or because he needs her alive (stage 2). If we are in the conventional level, we may argue that Heinz should not steal lest he be regarded as criminal (stage 3) or because he ought to obey extant laws (stage 4).

Finally, in the post-conventional level, we can reason that Heinz ought to steal the drug since human life precedes extant law (stage 5), or ought not to steal it, because others, whose lives are equally valuable, may need the medicine just as badly (stage 6).

Conscience cannot be pre-conventional, for it might, and often does, become personally inconvenient. Indeed, every active conscience involves *internal* conscientious objection: the better self's inner voice challenging our own thoughts and actions (not just the actions of others) through both shame and guilt. The existential dimension of this objection may even impel suicide. The Samurai's ritual suicide (*seppuku*) is a case in point. A vivid literary example is Kafka's *In the Penal Colony*: 'the officer' sentences himself to execution by his own 'remarkable apparatus' for violating the imperative to 'Be Just!' Mostly, however, our conscience does not take us that far.

Conscience need not be post-conventional even when it questions prevalent social norms. After all, defying a convention often means affirming or refining another, resonating in Durkheim's (1893/1997, p. 39) *conscience collective*. We should not, however, conflate the omnipresence of social conventions with inevitable social conformism. Consider Twain's (2010) *Huckleberry Finn*: Huck feels religiously compelled to write a letter revealing the whereabouts of the runaway slave, Jim, and then, reflecting upon their friendship, says to himself 'All right, then, I'll GO to hell' – and rips up the letter. Abolitionism predates Huck's awakened conscience, and the latter pledged not to principled, post-conventional, reasoning, but to 'lower', interpersonal sensibility – friendship; Huck ultimately takes a 'leap of love'. However, Huck's conscience rebelled against everything he was brought up to believe in, while embracing its cruel verdict. It comes as close as anything does to a nonconformist conscience.

Conscientious politics, like individual conscience, can include conventional moral reasoning, but must also involve post-conventional arguments. After developing his six-stage scale, Kohlberg added another: 'stage 4.5'. He noticed that many teenagers and college students embrace moral scepticism and relativism, coming to believe in the arbitrary, often personal and emotional, basis of moral judgments. This stage readily fosters pre-conventional 'might makes right' reasoning. If 'everything is permitted', the moral absolutism of the other should likewise be accepted, for, if rejected, moral relativism (read pluralism) itself becomes absolute. While such postmodern social climate allows individual conscience to flourish, it does not help conscientious politics. There is simply no common ground on which to converse and contest, only separate grounds of isolated individuals, bubbles of like-minded.

Conscientious politics cannot wallow in the mire of moral relativism. To thrive, conscientious politics must also offer universalizable principles and through them challenge the rulers' convenience and the society's conventions. They must go against the grain of established ideologies and system justification (Jost, Kay, & Thorisdottir, 2009). Modernity transformed the socio-moral imagery of 'public opinion'; by the end of the eighteenth century it had come to signify 'the authoritative judgment of a collective conscience, the ruling of a tribunal to which even the state was subject' (Vopa, 1992, p. 79). Conscientious politics draws on this modern ethos to win, through moral passion and persuasion, the 'hearts and minds' of people. It does so, however, by invoking sense of freedom and responsibility among the people for their moral choices. The 'common good' here is not an all-beneficial commodity but a common moral ground – an elusive, if not illusive, horizon, but a coveted one nonetheless. Thus, conscientious politics entwine the moral reasoning of agents with its resonance in the wider public sphere to chart, and re-chart, modes of socio-political legitimation. Such politics may, but need not, involve social movements, although the latter are often underpinned by emergent public conscience. Some instances of counter-conventional moral reasoning are abrupt, like Occupy Wall Street. Other moral transitions are slower in the making, like the growing western tolerance, even celebration, of gay marriage (Baunach, 2011).

Conviction and curiosity

Does conscience require self-confidence or uncertainty? Again, the *synderesis/conscientia* distinction is illuminating, especially as used by casuists to distinguish between divine, immutable truths and their contingent application, the former fostering stability, the latter connoting subversion (Gallagher, 1991). From Catholic to Protestant casuistry, the conscience's subversive potential became apparent (Slights, 1981). Still, retaining the aura of *synderesis* as 'the voice of God in man' may give rise to a sense of infallibility, allowing one to doubt others, but not the self. In the popular conception of conscience, such conviction has remained its hallmark.

It is, however, in recognizing its contingency that conscience finds its own freedom, and warrants other liberties, which in turns allow free conscience to flourish. It is useful to draw here on Berlin's (2002, p. 36) distinction between positive and negative liberty, the former being about 'who is master', the latter 'over what area am I master'. The relation of conscience to these two liberties is intriguing. John Milton famously entreated, 'Give me the liberty to know, to utter, and to argue freely according to conscience, above all liberties' (Milton, 1753, p. 169). The liberties to utter and argue are negative, bestowed or granted by others; the liberty, even courage, to know (*sapere audeis!*) is positive. It is the latter that gives conscience its creative content. This freedom of conscience lies in one's self-liberation from social conventions and individual convictions, questioning right and wrong, both factually and morally. Both excessive doubt and confidence can lead our conscience astray. The former produces confusion by fostering 'postmodern conscience' that subscribes to relative truth and morality (Kohlberg's 'stage 4.5' above). Overconfident conscience breeds confusion when encountering life's complexity and coincidence.

While the individual's free conscience draws mainly on developing positive liberty (from within), conscientious politics require also emancipation from without. This, as well as the realization that truth and ethics interlace, and freedom of conscience is gained by seeking both, are at the heart of Orwell's (1983, p. 81) suggestion, through *1984*s protagonist Winston, that 'Freedom is the freedom to say that two plus two makes four. If that is granted, all else follows'. Winston holds on to such 'truisms' in his secret diary, well aware that going public would be his ruin. Still, while his private musings maintains his individual conscience, in *1984* conscientious politics are impossible. There is virtually no room for public deliberation, however circumscribed.

Yet more horridly, Winston learns that even private conscience can be undone. Here, we may distinguish between liberty as mastery (à la Berlin) and freedom as choice, further distinguishing between closed freedom (where one selects from a given, limited menu of choice) and open freedom (where one prepare one's own menu). In Room 101, Winston betrays his love, and willingly submits to 'doublethink': to choose not to choose, to 'repudiate morality while laying claim to it', and 'the ultimate subtlety:

consciously to induce unconsciousness, and then, once again, to become unconscious of the act of hypnosis you had just performed'. Winston at last accepts that 'Freedom is Slavery', and indulges in the one-item menu Big Brother concocts.

Even beyond Orwell's dystopia, choice is daunting, and the flight from freedom always lurks, making moral inquiry a potential prelude to submission (Fromm, 1941). We may not always recognize our submission as such, and seamlessly succumb to 'bad faith' (Sartre, 1965, pp. 147–186): embracing essentialism and determinism; thinking 'I must', instead of 'I choose', saying 'I cannot' instead of 'I refuse'. Rorty (1989, p. 73) anchored this practice in 'final vocabulary':

> All human beings carry about a set of words which they employ to justify their actions, their beliefs, and their lives … [This vocabulary] is 'final' in the sense that if doubt is cast on the worth of these words, their user has no noncircular argumentative recourse. Those words are as far as he can go with language; beyond them there is only helpless passivity or a resort to force.

This again is at the heart of the modern impasse of secular public justification. Human rights often serve as the liberal 'final vocabulary', but without God in whose image humans are created, this is where justification often ends. Rorty offers no panacea, but the limited remedy of playful humility. Unlike those who subscribe, often unwittingly, to the 'common sense' of a particular 'language game', Rorty (1989, p. 75) applauds 'the ironist [who] spends her time worrying about the possibility that she has been initiated into the wrong tribe, taught to play the wrong language game'.

Curious conscience is the cradle of true autonomy, for moral self-determination can only flourish through doubt that opens up free choice. Sans free choice we live according to the predicates of the other, whether divine or human – or of our own 'past self'. Still, the opposite is false: predicating conscience on autonomy is a step too far. Conscience ultimately evolves in-between being automatous and autonomous, seeking the latter. The challenge lies in fostering a curious conscience while acknowledging our 'bounded freedom': to be able to laugh at ourselves, occasionally criticize our own conscience, and willingly 'go to hell'.

Conscientious politics are not harmonious. Thus, both Royalists and Parliamentarians could fight the English Civil War as a cause of conscience. Conscientious politics are also not necessarily liberal, nor does liberalism necessarily entail a curious (public) conscience. We may allow the 'voice of God in man' as well as the 'Führer within' to police our thoughts and actions. Personal convenience notwithstanding, both Antigone and Eichmann sanctified their moral reasoning, subduing future doubt. Arendt's (1964) famous thesis about the latter was less about the 'banality of evil', more about the 'evil of banality', the terrible offshoots of stop thinking critically. Critical thinking, however, can also lead one – indeed have led many – to embrace 'Nazi conscience', finding inherent righteousness in the volk and its leader (Koonz, 2003), evincing that moral reasoning itself is morally agnostic. The continuous effort to retain moral curiosity, to embrace irony (indeed, the Absurd), can keep conscience brave, and, with empathy and guilt, benign as well.

Václav Havel found hope in the regime's fear: curious conscience, both private and public, is totalitarianism's weak spot, rendering the morality of 'living in truth' the ultimate subversion against it (Havel, 1978/1985). However, Havel was careful not to anoint liberalism. Indeed, liberalism allows, but does not prescribe, self-doubts, and may ossify. Neo-liberalism, as much as Marxism, can hallow its doctrines – veil decisions behind 'no-choice' – and vilify curious minds who question its 'givens'. For Durkheim (1958, p. 12), the 'amoral character of economic life amounts to a public danger ... If we live amo-rally for a good part of the day, how can we keep the springs of morality from going slack in us?' More recently, postmodernism and 'lifestyle psychology' may engender moral vacuity and atomization that can undermine conscientious politics and invite anti-liberal reactions.

The above contours of conscience paint the background for contemporary treatises' lament on the withdrawal of conscience from modern moral theory (e.g. Langston, 2001). The decline may go further. Corpus linguistics of western public discourse – in books, broadcasts, magazines and newspapers – suggest the concept's demise over the last two centuries (Figure 1).[3]

Can, and should, scholars of conscience aid its revival? We may criticize people for their lack of conscience (Arendt), or advise them what to think and do (Rawls). We may also go about the existentialist path and encourage people to flex their moral muscles by acknowl-edging their freedom and its call for personal responsibility (Sartre) and social solidarity (Camus), with imaginative, meaningful, art encouraging both (the later Rorty). Meta-moral agents turn one-way roads into crossroads, engendering a 'moral exception' that invites their peers to reaffirm, or renounce, the socio-political order. Optimally, rather than submitting to state decisionism (Schmitt, 2005), these agents of conscientious politics foster moral dilemmas to be ethically, dialogically, resolved. In political existentialism, private and public acts of conscience are often 'hidden in plain sight', and it is by illumi-nating the moral dilemmas underpinning our political life that we seek to uncover and awaken conscientious politics. In what follows, I undertake this task.

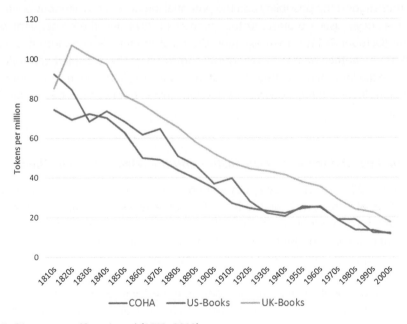

Figure 1. Discourse on 'Conscience' (1810–2010).

Israel

The politics of conscience in Israel are typically discussed through the lens of conscientious refusal. Conscientious refusal to serve in the Israel Defense Force (IDF) or to obey certain commands (*sarvanut* in Hebrew) goes back to Israel's establishment (1948), its scope and publicity mounting after the 1967 War (Linn, 1996). Both political camps, but mainly the left, have signed petitions and collective letters of refusal, occasionally endorsed by IDF elite units. Israeli politicians have usually shied away from endorsing *sarvanut*. Legally, Israel's Supreme Court (7622; 23 October 2002) reaffirmed that 'in Israel, everyone enjoys freedom of conscience', but warned, 'Recognizing selective conscientious objection [unlike universal pacifism] may lessen the ties that hold us as a people … The people's army might become an army of peoples with different units, each operative or non-operative according to its unique conscience.' To-date, only religious or pacifist claims for refusing military service were accepted (Friedman, 2006). Notably, while most Israeli Jews reject *sarvanut* on principle, they are more tolerant towards its right-wing religious incarnation (18%) (Yaar & Hermann, 2014; public opinion poll from November 2009). *Sarvanut* underscores the importance of both character and circumstance in engendering a conscience that defies, often against personal convenience, social conventions in an authoritarian sphere within a democratic state. *Sarvanut* has further intertwined with the wider public justification for, or against, Israeli policies.

Sarvanut, however, remains a marginal phenomenon and has yet to shape Israeli policies. Israeli conscientious politics have gone far beyond it, and have permeated some of Israel's key initiatives in the 2000s. Granted, Israeli policies have often favoured might over right, underpinned by *pragmatic* public justification. Indeed most scholarship on Zionism and Israel downplays the role of morality in their emergence and conduct. This, I submit, is a very partial picture (Abulof, 2014a, 2014b). To wit, my aim here is not to substitute moral for practical accounts, but to add the former to the mix. The illustrative case studies thus suggest the possibility and the potential impact of conscientious politics. I first discuss the social justice protests in the summer of 2011 and the subsequent prisoner exchange (October 2011). I then examine the most intractable conundrum Israel faces since 1967 – whether or not to relinquish control over the occupied territories. Both cases evince the importance of freedom, not merely liberty, in fostering conscientious politics. Decisions involving high 'degrees of freedom' invite, but need not exact, *moral* public justification.

Behind and beyond the veil: social justice and the release of Gilad Shalit

Beginning July 2011, Israel was swept by an unprecedented wave of mass demonstrations calling for 'social justice', with multitude 'tent towns' established in various cities, ongoing protests and stormy discourse in both traditional and new media. Demands for easing the cost of living (mainly housing) expanded to challenging the socio-economic order, especially inequality, the rise of tycoons, crony capitalism and the dwindling middle class. The government, headed by Benjamin Netanyahu, outlined reform plans, and then appointed a public committee to address the grievances, but the demonstrations mounted, reaching an apex on 3 September with nearly half a million protesters countrywide. Thereafter, however, the demonstrations subsided.

The rise and demise of the protest have many causes, some material, others moral. Here, I focus on the latter, especially the resonance of the idea and ideal of 'social justice'. Whether Arab or Jewish, secular or religious, poor or middle class, seeking to lower the cost of housing or childcare, protesters united behind a key slogan, chanted incessantly in the streets: 'the people demand(s) social justice'.

In *A theory of justice*, Rawls famously suggested that in order to imagine a just society, 'we must nullify the effects of specific contingencies which put men at odds and tempt them to exploit social and natural circumstances to their own advantage' by going behind 'the veil of ignorance' into the 'original position' (Rawls, 2003, pp. 118, 464). The social justice protesters followed, in their discourse, a similar moral path. Responding to deteriorating socio-economic circumstances, and emboldened by the activism of their peers, they took to the streets. Employing both intuition and reflection, they challenged conventional ideas and practices, albeit typically without substantially compromising their personal convenience.

The demonstrations awakened Israelis' socio-economic conscience. Whether or not they read Rawls, the protestors have denounced Israel's market economy as unfair, thus unjust. Protesters claimed that instead of employing unbiased rules for the benefit of all, Israel's neo-liberal policies have privileged the privileged. If the overall economy prospers, they asked, why have most people been losing their economic security, why has poverty grown, and why were occupations that are for the benefit of all (health, arts, academia and social work) undercut? The protesters thus demanded 'Justice, not Charity' (*tzedek, lo tzedaka*), realigning Israel's social contract with its founding Zionist ethos of socio-economic solidarity (Grinberg, 2013).

While going behind the veil to chart the right economic path, the protesters also sought to tear down the veil of ignorance: to reveal what they regarded as the inconvenient truth about 'the power matrix of Israel's economy'. Their core proposition was that the 'system is rigged', that the politicians, banks and media connive with the wealthy, rendering Israel an oligarchy, not a democracy. Privatization, for example, is abused by Israel's crony capitalism to enrich the rich and impoverish the rest. The protesters thus demanded transparency about decision-making so as to foster equal distribution of wealth (Oren, 2012; see also the Hebrew journal *Theory and Criticism*, issue 41, 2013). It is easy to dismiss these calls as naïve, their political outcome as marginal, but they have struck roots in Israeli discourse. For example, the willingness of Israel's antitrust chief to challenge the natural gas monopoly (*Haaretz*, 23 December 2014), threatening its break up, was hardly conceivable before the summer of 2011.

Still, that summer ended as abruptly as it started, and here too, conscientious politics played a role. Even if we manage to go behind the veil, beyond it we are not detached spirits, devoid of social positions or identities. We connect to family, friends and foes, and develop a sense of communal belonging. This familiar criticism of Rawls' theory revealed its practical potency in the twilight of the demonstrations. PM Netanyahu made a deal with the Hamas, releasing Gilas Shalit in exchange for 1027 prisoners, collectively responsible for the killing of hundreds of Israelis. Netanyahu, who had always spoken strongly against such deals (e.g. Netanyahu, 1995, pp. 208–209), claimed to have been swayed by his wife's plea to 'think of him [Shalit] as our son' (*Bild*, 10 June 2012), but his emissary to the negotiations disclosed that the summer demonstrations underlay the decision (*Haaretz*, 24 July 2012).

If that was the case, it worked. The news about the upcoming release of Shalit, and the release itself, eclipsed the demands for 'social justice'. The role of morality in the deal is elusive, but significant. The notorious 'trolley problem' provides a lens onto the conscientious politics surrounding the deal and its link to the 'social justice' protests. Briefly, in the original problem, a trolley would kill five people tied to its current track, but we can save their lives by pushing a button, diverting the trolley's course to a track where one person is tied. In a variation, we stand on a footbridge above the track and can stop the advancing trolley from killing the five people by pushing, thus killing, a fat man standing next to us. Numerous experiments to date have shown people overwhelmingly willing to push to button, but not the fat man (Edmonds, 2014).

Such artificial dilemmas may seem even more aloof than Rawls' 'original position', yet here too, their illuminating power is revealed through the lens of actual socio-political dynamics. The mounting public plea for Shalit's release started soon after his capture, June 2006, and quickly gathered momentum, making Gilad Shalit a household name, 'the son of us all'. Ultimately, the mass movement for Shalit's release transformed the dilemma about striking a deal with the Hamas from 'pushing the button' to 'pushing the fat man'. This movement challenged personal convenience to foster 'bad conscience' on the part of many Israelis who felt guilt and shame in the face of the imprisoned son. Instead of risking the life of a single soldier so as not to further risk the lives of many other civilians, a clear majority in Israeli public held Shalit to be so close and familiar as to render such cold calculation morally unacceptable. Many 'social justice' activists willingly incorporated this massage in their list of demands, as it underscored their call for renewed solidarity with strong emotional and ethnonational appeal. In retrospect, however, it was their undoing. Shalit's release forcefully brought the Israeli public from behind the veil, to hail the son's return to the ethnonational family, and ultimately grant Netanyahu another term.

The resolution of this 'prisoner's dilemma' is a landmark in the ongoing learning process of Israeli public conscience. It had already revived the secret IDF 'Hannibal Directive', aimed at preventing the capture of Israeli soldiers at virtually any cost. The lesson was soon employed. During Operation Protective Edge in the Gaza strip (summer 2014), the Hamas kidnapped IDF soldier Hadar Goldin, and the IDF forcefully retaliated. The officer leading the chase later reasoned, 'I knew that even if we kill Hadar, then as much as it hurts – it's better that way.' (Channel 2 News and *Haaretz*, 9 August 2014)

Samson's option and Solomon's judgment: the Israeli–Palestinian conflict

Attempts at capturing the 'Zionist psyche' have often invoked the myth of Masada, the defiant stand of a handful of zealous Jews against the Roman Empire in the twilight of the Second Temple period (Zerubavel, 1995). This analogy has merits, not least since Zionists themselves have occasionally invoked the myth, but it misses the transformation of the Jewish self-imagery since 1948, especially after 1967. To better grasp it, we may turn to the biblical story of Judge Samson. Divinely endowed with immense strength, Samson was betrayed by Delilah, and delivered to his sworn enemies, the Philistines of Gaza, to be put on humiliating display, his eyes torn out. In the temple of Gaza, Samson asked God to give him back his strength for the last time, cried out, 'Let my soul die with the Philistines', and brought the temple down.

Like the Masada myth, the story of Samson too resonates in Zionist chronicles. PM Levi Eshkol in 1963 suggested portraying Israel as 'poor little Samson' (*Shimshon der nebechdikker*) to impress upon others the need to aid it. Since then, Israel's real power has only mounted. *Samson's option*, a title of a study on Israel's nuclear project encapsulates the strategy: if Israel seeks survival, it must be willing to play the card of mutual destruction (Hersh, 1991). Military Historian Martin van Creveld thus responded to the potential Iranian nuclear threat: 'We have the capability to take the world down with us. And I can assure you that that will happen before Israel goes under' (Hirst, 2003).

Samson's option is about the frustrating, humiliating, gap between the immense potential and the distressed present. This gap resonates with the plight of the Palestinians, ostensibly enjoying the support of the entire Arab and Muslim world, but mostly facing Israel alone. Israeli Jews too live with this humiliating gap, between their state's military might (alongside its special relations with the U.S.) and its inability to protect its own citizens, mainly in the south, who, since 2001 have been subjected to rockets and mortar fire, while the state's international standing, perhaps even its core legitimacy, is increasingly contested.

Embracing Samson's option has had a profound impact. Many right-wingers have turned to name and shame the metaphorical *Delilah* within (mostly left wing) and without (mostly in the west) for Israel's troubles. Moreover, like Samson in his final moments, Israel's public conscience has increasingly turned to God, to a conversation that predicates the collective's political fate on its religious faith – a patent deviation from the founding, secular Zionism (Abulof, 2014b). Thus, for example, in a 2013 survey, 64% of all Israeli Jewish respondents stated that the Jews are 'the chosen people' (Hermann, 2013, pp. 62–73). That such transformation may inspire calls of 'holy war' became apparent at the onset of Protective Edge, when IDF Colonel Ofer Winter's 'battle call' asked for God's help in 'fighting (against) the terrorist "Gazan" enemy which abuses, blasphemes and curses the God of Israel's battles' (*Haaretz*, 12 July 2014).

Another biblical story sheds a complementary light on Israel's conscientious politics regarding the Palestinians and territorial compromise. King Solomon was approached by two women, who gave birth on the same day. Only one son survived, and each mother claimed it as hers. Solomon ordered the living son split in two, each mother receiving half. One woman pleaded with the King to keep the baby alive and give it to the other woman, but the latter accepted the verdict. Solomon judged the former to be the true mother, and gave her the son.

Solomon's judgment captures how many Israeli Jews (and Palestinians too) frame the moral dilemma involved in the two-state solution. Refusal to divide the land is seen as evincing true love for it, which should thus be rewarded by having it all. By framing their conscientious cause as full of conviction, earthily and divine, while compromising their material comfort (e.g. by living in illegal settlements or committing suicidal Jihad), these agents strike moral and emotional cords with many Israeli Jews. Consequently, among both peoples, opposition seems to hold a moral veto right over compromise, leaving the moderates to defend their views by resorting to the practicalities of realpolitik.

This moral framing obviously misses much. The true mother (if we accept Solomon's judgment) was granted the son only after willingness to give it to the other mother, the land is not human, and saving people might actually require a division. Ultimately, a key to Solomon's judgment was his ability to convince the mothers of his plan, thereby prompting them to realize their freedom to make a moral choice, and take responsibility for it. By turning a dispute into a moral dilemma, Solomon's judgment awakened their conscience. It remains to be seen if the Israel–Palestinian conflict might undergo, and benefit from, such a moral awakening.

Conclusion

This paper delved into the moral aspect of public justification through conscientious politics and its resonance in contemporary Israel. My claim is not that conscientious politics is omnipresent or all-important, but that it is part of our political life, that recognizing, and studying, it, is valuable – for better understanding this world, and making it better. To conclude, I would like to underscore this promise from a broader scholarly perspective.

In political science, we often defer questions of morality to political theorists and philosophers. Empirical research has supposedly little to say about humans' unique capacity, and inclination, to construct, construe and apply categories of good and evil. This 'scholarly imaginary', however, is wrong, both descriptively and prescriptively. Whenever we study agents, we engage with human morality. By ascribing motivations to actors, we subscribe – both empirically and normatively – to a certain moral view.

Critics of social contract theory, and state-of-nature theory in particular, are quick to denounce its rationale as fictitious, thus false: The state-of-nature narratives suggest a mere myth of man, providing a poor moral and empirical guidance to socio-political arrangements. However, in running away from one fiction, we have embraced another: side-stepping agents for structures, or else framing the former as either purely rational or emotional. In principle, we are well aware that humans are complex beings, driven by multiple motivations, and thus shy away from reductionism. Still, in practice, to simplify matters, we often reduce human motivations to their single, arguably most important, core.

In the social sciences, three ideal-type models of human motivations have been particularly prominent: *homo economicus*, driven by material cost-benefit calculation; *homo sociologicus*, driven by social identities; and *homo psychologicus*, driven by emotional processes. Less popular, but coming to the fore, are images of humans as driven by evolutionary imperatives (*homo biologicus*) or by seeking the common good (*homo civicus*). This paper ultimately uncovers one missing motivational model: *Homo conscientious*, the image of man as searching for moral meaning. It provides an agential base for conscientious politics: the moral dimension of public justification amidst the ontological gap between *is* and *ought*. To reveal this image's merits and remit require that we further probe both its theoretical foundations and actual place in our societies. I hope this paper showed this nascent endeavour to be a worthwhile, and a worthy, pursuit.

Notes

1. I share much of Taylor's (1985, p. 1) critique of 'naturalism', namely 'the ambition to model the study of man on the natural sciences' (see also Tully & Weinstock, 1994). Naturalism is prone to 'reification': turning human qualities into 'things', stripping individuals of their autonomy and reducing them to cogs of an abstract social machinery (Vandenberghe, 2001). I, thus, prefer hermeneutic understanding of the agents' intersubjective (shared and socially embedded) reasoning.

2. Pinker (2011, p. 182) regards the 'interchangeability of perspectives' at the heart of the Golden Rule as the 'foundation of morality' across time and cultures. There is much to support here (Gibbs, 2014; Turiel, 2002), but it requires consideration beyond the scope of this paper.
3. My findings draw on the three largest modern diachronic datasets (Davies, 2015): Corpus of Historical American English (COHA, 1810–2009); Google Books: American English (1500s–2000s); and Google Books: British English (1500s–2000s). 'Tokens' refer to the number of appearances of the specified word/s in the corpus.

Disclosure statement

No potential conflict of interest was reported by the author.

References

Abulof, U. (2014a). National ethics in ethnic conflicts: The Zionist 'iron wall' and the 'Arab question'. *Ethnic and Racial Studies, 37*(14), 2653–2669. doi:10.1080/01419870.2013.854921
Abulof, U. (2014b). The roles of religion in national legitimation: Judaism and Zionism's elusive quest for legitimacy. *Journal for the Scientific Study of Religion, 53*(3), 515–533. doi:10.1111/jssr.12132
Abulof, U. (2015a). *The mortality and morality of nations.* New York: Cambridge University Press.
Abulof, U. (2015b). "The people want(s) to bring down the regime": (Positive) nationalism as the Arab spring's revolution. *Nations and Nationalism, 21*(4), 658–680. doi:10.1111/nana.12137
Abulof, U. (2016). Public political thought: Bridging the sociological-philosophical divide in the study of legitimacy. *British Journal of Sociology, 67*(2), 371–391. doi:10.1111/1468-4446.12192
Adorno, T. W. (1950). *The authoritarian personality* (1st ed.). New York: Harper.
Archer, M. S. (2012). *The reflexive imperative in late modernity.* New York: Cambridge University Press.
Arendt, H. (1964). *Eichmann in Jerusalem; a report on the banality of evil* (Rev. and enl. ed.). New York: Viking Press.
Arendt, H. (1971). Thinking and moral considerations: A lecture. *Social Research, 38*(3), 417–446. doi:10.2307/40970069
Arendt, H. (1978). *The life of the mind* (1st ed.). New York: Harcourt Brace Jovanovich.
Baunach, D. M. (2011). Decomposing trends in attitudes toward gay marriage, 1988–2006. *Social Science Quarterly, 92*(2), 346–363. doi:10.1111/j.1540-6237.2011.00772.x
Bergson, H. (2001). *Time and free will: An essay on the immediate data of consciousness.* Mineola, NY: Dover Publications.
Berlin, I. (2002). *Liberty: Incorporating four essays on liberty.* Oxford: Oxford University Press.
Braun, H., & Vallance, E. (2011). *The renaissance conscience.* Malden, MA: Wiley-Blackwell.
Brownlee, K. (2012). *Conscience and conviction: The case for civil disobedience.* Oxford: Oxford University Press.
Chadwick, O. (1990). *The secularization of the European mind in the nineteenth century* (Canto ed.). New York: Cambridge University Press.

Crowell, S. G. (Ed.). (2012). *The Cambridge companion to existentialism*. New York: Cambridge University Press.

Davies, M. (2015). *The Corpus of Historical American English: 400 million words, 1810–2009; Google Books (US and UK)*. Retrieved January 20, 2015, from Brigham Young University http://corpus.byu.edu/

Durkheim, E. (1958). *Professional ethics and civic morals*. Glencoe, IL: Free Press.

Durkheim, E. (1893/1997). *The division of labor in society*. New York: Simon and Schuster.

Edmonds, D. (2014). *Would you kill the fat man?: The trolley problem and what your answer tells us about right and wrong*. Princeton, NJ: Princeton University Press.

Eisenstadt, S. N. (2003). *Comparative civilizations and multiple modernities*. Boston, MA: Brill.

Flynn, T. R. (2006). *Existentialism: A very short introduction*. New York: Oxford University Press.

Frank, R. H. (1988). *Passions within reason: The strategic role of the emotions* (1st ed.). New York: Norton.

Friedman, R. (2006). The challenge of selective conscientious objection in Israel. *Theoria: A Journal of Social and Political Theory*, (109), 79–99.

Fromm, E. (1941). *Escape from freedom*. New York: Farrar & Rinehart.

Gallagher, L. (1991). *Medusa's gaze: Casuistry and conscience in the renaissance*. Stanford, CA: Stanford University Press.

Gibbs, J. C. (2014). *Moral development and reality: Beyond the theories of Kohlberg and Hoffman*. New York: Oxford University Press.

Gowans, C. W. (Ed.). (1987). *Moral dilemmas*. New York: Oxford Uiversity Press.

Grinberg, L. L. (2013). The J14 resistance mo(ve)ment: The Israeli mix of Tahrir Square and Puerta del Sol. *Current Sociology, 61*(4), 491–509. doi:10.1177/0011392113479748

Habermas, J. (1999). *Moral consciousness and communicative action*. Cambridge: MIT Press.

Haidt, J. (2012). *The righteous mind: Why good people are divided by politics and religion*. New York: Pantheon Books.

Hamilton, C., & Denniss, R. (2005). *Affluenza: When too much is never enough*. Crows Nest: Allen & Unwin.

Havel, V., & Keane, J. (Eds.). (1978/1985). *The power of the powerless: Citizens against the state in central-Eastern Europe*. Armonk, NY: M.E. Sharpe.

Hermann, T. (2013). *Israeli Democracy Index 2013*. Jerusalem: Israeli Democracy Institute.

Hersh, S. M. (1991). *The Samson option: Israel's nuclear arsenal and American foreign policy* (1st ed.). New York: Random House.

Hibbing, J. R., Smith, K. B., & Alford, J. R. (2014). Differences in negativity bias underlie variations in political ideology. *Behavioral and Brain Sciences, 37*(3), 297–307.

Hirst, D. (2003). *The gun and the olive branch: The roots of violence in the Middle East*. New York: Thunder's Mouth Press/Nation Books.

Hitlin, S. (2008). *Moral selves, evil selves: The social psychology of conscience* (1st ed.). New York: Palgrave Macmillan.

Howard, M. (1978). *War and the liberal conscience*. London: Temple Smith.

Hume, D. (1739/2007). *A treatise of human nature: A critical edition*. New York: Oxford University Press.

Jasper, J. M. (1997). *The art of moral protest: Culture, biography, and creativity in social movements*. Chicago, IL: University of Chicago Press.

Jonas, H., & Vogel, L. (1996). *Mortality and morality: A search for the good after Auschwitz*. Evanston, IL: Northwestern University Press.

Jost, J. T., Kay, A. C., & Thorisdottir, H. (Eds.). (2009). *Social and psychological bases of ideology and system justification*. New York: Oxford University Press.

Kass, L. (2002). *Life, liberty, and the defense of dignity: The challenge for bioethics* (1st ed.). San Francisco, CA: Encounter Books.

Kohlberg, L. (1981). *The philosophy of moral development: Moral stages and the idea of justice*. San Francisco, CA: Harper & Row.

Koonz, C. (2003). *The Nazi conscience*. Cambridge, MA: Belknap Press.

Kupchan, C. (2012). *No one's world: The west, the rising rest, and the coming global turn*. New York: Oxford University Press.

Langston, D. C. (2001). *Conscience and other virtues: From Bonaventure to Macintyre.* University Park: Pennsylvania State University Press.

Linn, R. (1996). *Conscience at war: The Israeli soldier as a moral critic.* Albany: State University of New York Press.

Luper, S. (2000). *Existing: An introduction to existential thought.* Mountain View, CA: Mayfield Pub.

Luthar, S. S. (2003). The culture of affluence: Psychological costs of material wealth. *Child Development, 74*(6), 1581–1593. doi:10.1046/j.1467-8624.2003.00625.x

MacIntyre, A. C. (2007). *After virtue: A study in moral theory* (3rd ed.). Notre Dame, IN: University of Notre Dame Press.

Maslow, A. H. (1971). *The farther reaches of human nature.* New York: Viking Press.

Milton, J. (1753). *The works of John Milton, historical, political and miscellaneous.* London: A. Millar.

Moskos, C. C., & Chambers, J. W. (Eds.). (1993). *The New conscientious objection: From sacred to secular resistance.* New York: Oxford University Press.

Netanyahu, B. (1995). *Place among the nations [Hebrew: Makom taḥat ha-shemesh].* Tel Aviv: Yedi'ot Aḥaronot.

Noujaim, J. (Director), & Amer, K. (Producer). (2013). *The square.* Egypt, United States: GathrFilms, Participant Media.

Nussbaum, M. C. (2001). *Upheavals of thought: The intelligence of emotions.* New York: Cambridge University Press.

Nussbaum, M. C. (2013). *Political emotions: Why love matters for justice.* Cambridge, MA: Harvard University Press.

Ojakangas, M. (2013). *The voice of conscience: A political genealogy of western ethical experience.* New York: Bloomsbury.

Oren, B. (2012). *Field of tents: Conclusions from the social justice protest [Hebrew: Sde haOhalim].* Givat Ada.

Orwell, G. (1983). *1984: A novel* (1984 commemorative ed.). New York: New American Library.

Paxton, J. M., & Greene, J. D. (2010). Moral reasoning: Hints and allegations. *Topics in Cognitive Science, 2*(3), 511–527. doi:10.1111/j.1756-8765.2010.01096.x

Paxton, J. M., Ungar, L., & Greene, J. D. (2012). Reflection and reasoning in moral judgment. *Cognitive Science, 36*(1), 163–177. doi:10.1111/j.1551-6709.2011.01210.x

Pinker, S. (2011). *The better angels of our nature: Why violence has declined.* New York: Viking.

Popper, K. R. (1945/2003). *The open society and its enemies* (5th ed.) (Vol. 1) (The spell of Plato). New York: Routledge.

Rawls, J. (2003). *A theory of justice* (Original ed.). Cambridge, MA: Harvard University Press.

Rokeach, M. (1960). *The open and closed mind; investigations into the nature of belief systems and personality systems.* New York: Basic Books.

Rorty, R. (1989). *Contingency, irony, and solidarity.* New York: Cambridge University Press.

Sartre, J.-P. (1965). *Essays in existentialism.* Secaucus, NJ: Citadel.

Schinkel, A. (2007). *Conscience and conscientious objections.* Amsterdam: Pallas Publications.

Schmitt, C. (2005). *Political theology: Four chapters on the concept of sovereignty* (University of Chicago Press ed.). Chicago, IL: University of Chicago Press.

Singer, P. (2006). Morality, reason, and the rights of animals. In F. de Waal (Ed.), *Primates and philosophers: How morality evolved* (pp. 140–158). Princeton, NJ: Princeton University Press.

Slights, C. W. (1981). *The casuistical tradition in Shakespeare, Donne, Herbert, and Milton.* Princeton, NJ: Princeton University Press.

Steinbock, A. J. (2014). *Moral emotions: Reclaiming the evidence of the heart.* Evanston, IL: Northwestern University Press.

Strenger, C. (2011). *The fear of insignificance: Searching for meaning in the twenty-first century.* New York: Palgrave Macmillan.

Strohm, P. (2011). *Conscience: A very short introduction.* New York: Oxford University Press.

Taylor, C. (1985). *Philosophy and the human sciences.* New York: Cambridge University Press.

Taylor, C. (2007). *A secular age.* Cambridge, MA: Belknap Press of Harvard University Press.

Tetlock, P. E., Peterson, R. S., & Lerner, J. S. (1996). Revising the value pluralism model: Incorporating social content and context postulates. In C. Seligman, J. M. Olson, & M. P. Zanna (Eds.), *The psychology of values: The Ontario symposium* (Vol. 8) (pp. 25–51). Hillsdale, NJ: Lawrence Erlbaum Associates.

Tully, J., & Weinstock, D. M. (Eds.). (1994). *Philosophy in an age of pluralism: The philosophy of Charles Taylor in question*. New York: Cambridge University Press.

Turiel, E. (2002). *The culture of morality: Social development, context, and conflict*. New York: Cambridge University Press.

Twain, M. (2010). *Adventures of Huckleberry Finn*. New York: Oxford University Press.

Tymieniecka, A.-T. (Ed.). (2010). *Phenomenology and existentialism in the twentieth century (book I, II, III)*. New York: Springer.

Vandenberghe, F. (2001). Reification: History of the concept. In N. J. S. B. Baltes (Ed.), *International encyclopedia of the social & behavioral sciences* (pp. 12993–12996). Oxford: Pergamon.

Vischer, R. K. (2010). *Conscience and the common good: Reclaiming the space between person and state*. New York: Cambridge University Press.

Vopa, A. J. L. (1992). Conceiving a public: Ideas and society in eighteenth-century Europe. *The Journal of Modern History, 64*(1), 79–116. doi:10.2307/2124716

de Waal, F. (Ed.). (2006). *Primates and philosophers: How morality evolved*. Princeton, NJ: Princeton University Press.

Wachtel, P. L. (1983). *The poverty of affluence: A psychological portrait of the American way of life*. New York: Free Press.

Walzer, M. (1970). *Obligations; essays on disobedience, war, and citizenship*. Cambridge: Harvard University Press.

Weber, M. (1946). *From Max weber: Essays in sociology*. New York: Oxford university press.

Weber, M. (1922/1978). *Economy and society: An outline of interpretive sociology*, In G. Roth & C. Wittich (Eds.). Berkeley: University of California Press.

Williams, B. (2005). *In the beginning was the deed: Realism and moralism in political argument*. Princeton, NJ: Princeton University Press.

Wright, J. P. (2009). *Hume's 'A treatise of human nature': An introduction*. New York: Cambridge University Press.

Yaar, E., & Hermann, T. (2014). *War and Peace index, June 1994–October 2014*. Tel-Aviv: Tel-Aviv University.

Zerubavel, Y. (1995). *Recovered roots: Collective memory and the making of Israeli national tradition*. Chicago, IL: University of Chicago Press.

Zimbardo, P. G. (2007). *The Lucifer effect: Understanding how good people turn evil* (1st ed.). New York: Random House.

The fusion of the private and public sectors*

Amitai Etzioni

ABSTRACT
Much of contemporary analysis treats the public and private sectors as two rather separate and fundamentally different realms. Many see one of the two sectors as inherently virtuous and the other as corrupt. The paper shows, in considerable detail, that the two sectors are deeply intertwined. It follows that we need a rather different framework to study state and society.

Introduction

The distinction between the public and private sectors has been called one of the 'grand dichotomies' of Western thought (Bobbio, 1989, pp. 1–2), informing 'key issues of social and political analysis, of moral and political debate, and of the ordering of everyday life' (Weintraub, 1997, p. 1). In particular, it is used to limit 'legitimate government interference with individuals' in liberal political theory, to differentiate public and private organizations in public administration theory,[1] and to differentiate public and private goods and services in economic theory (Pattison, 2014, pp. 63–74). In this view, the two sectors are character-ized by conflicting values, such as the community versus the individual, or solidarity versus self-interest (Gal, 2002, pp. 77–78). This view is particularly present in the U.S.: according to Alan Freeman and Elizabeth Mensch, the public-private divide is

> the premise which lies at the foundation of American legal thought, and it shapes the way in which we relate to each other in our daily lives. We consistently take for granted that there is both a public realm and a private realm. (Freeman & Mensch, 1987, p. 237)

This dichotomy has come under criticism from a variety of perspectives. Social science has long established that the public-private distinction is more blurred than is often assumed in public discourse. Feminist scholarship has argued that 'most social practices, relations, and transactions' are neither purely public nor private, and that the 'personal is political' due to the way 'private institutions such as families often operate, like the polity, through conflict, power hierarchies, and violence' (Gal, 2002, p. 78). And some public administration and management scholars have long criticized the distinction between public and private organizations as an oversimplification, or portrayed it in terms of a con-tinuum rather than a dichotomy.[2]

---

*I am indebted to Rory Donnelly for research and editorial assistance on this paper.

This article argues that the distinction between the public and private realms is both overstated and is becoming increasingly obsolete. The two sectors are increasingly intertwined. Moreover, it appears that that the two realms are affected by the same historical forces, not only blurring their boundaries but also moving them in unison. If this is the case, we cannot assume that one realm is either the main benefactor or the main cause of harm inflicted on the other.

This is not, per se, a wholly new idea. However, a targeted reexamination and expansion of the idea is particularly important at this juncture because major fields of social science (and policy) still rely heavily on the public/private distinction. Major segments of neoclassical economics, the dominant school of economics in the U.S., sharply distinguish the market forces of supply and demand from government interventions such as regulations. Likewise, American jurisprudence typically views the Bill of Rights as protecting citizens from the government, but not from private actors such as corporations. And quite a few political scientists and sociologists do not fully take into account the significance of the high interpenetration of the two realms. In short, this article offers a concrete illustration of the phenomenon and its consequences.

This article will proceed by defining the key terms and introducing essential qualifications of the main thesis. It will next illustrate the merging of the public and private sectors through the case study of national security. Finally, the article briefly mentions other examples of the merging of the public and private sectors.

Public versus private

The terms 'private' and 'public' have many definitions and uses. For example, nonprofit organizations are seen as private in the sense that they are not part of the government public sector, but public in the sense that they serve the public interest and provide a 'public benefit' (Salamon, 1999, p. 10); on the other hand, the IRS divides nonprofits into 'private foundations' and 'public charities' depending on their activities and sources of funding (Internal Revenue Service, 2015). For the purposes at hand, the article follows a common practice in public discourse that uses 'public' more or less synonymously with governmental organizations and activities and 'private' to refer to nongovernmental ones.

The fact that developments in one realm are often and increasingly paralleled or closely followed by changes in the other, does not mean that the two realms are becoming indistinguishable, but rather that the walls presumed to separate them, which were never nearly as tall as the dominant public philosophies assumed, have already been significantly breached and have been further eroded since the advent of the cyber age. There remains considerable 'slack' in their integration, in the sense that developments in one realm can take place to a considerable extent without parallel developments in the other. However, such developments are limited compared to those that are co-joined and co-vary and the extent of such 'slack' is declining.

Of the many scholarly positions on the relationship between the public and private sector, several stand out. Historian William J. Novak argues that baseline integration between the two sectors is greater than often assumed:

most compelling analyses of American power have always refused to split the problem along a single either–or, public–private binary (for example, the people vs. the interests; public good vs. private right; the state vs. the individual; regulation vs. the market). Instead, realistic and pragmatic approaches to American state development emphasize the interpenetration of public and private spheres – the convergence of public and private authority in everyday policymaking. (Novak, 2008, pp. 769–770)[3]

Rather than view them as moving in tandem, Grant McConnell takes a zero-sum approach to the two sectors, holding that the weaker and more dispersed public power becomes, the stronger and more centralized private power becomes (McConnell, 1966). E.E. Schattschneider did see a parallel between private and public conflicts, holding that these conflicts originate in the private realm and studied the conditions under which they become public (Schattschneider, 1960). For his part, C. Wright Mills saw a convergence of political (public) and economic (private) power, which could lead the two power elites to function as one (Mills, 2000), a thesis also reflected in the term 'military–industrial complex'. Finally, Theodore Lowi and Mancur Olson saw interest groups as a force that bridges the two sectors and moves them in tandem (Lowi, 1979; Olson, 1982). Though some of these writings, in particular those by C. Wright Mills, gained currency outside academic circles, public discourse is often still conducted as if the two realms are distinct and one largely drives the other.

Several scholars have examined the issue from a specifically security-oriented standpoint. As contributors to Rodney Bruce Hall and Thomas J. Biersteker's *The emergence of private authority in global governance* point out, private actors such as organized criminals and mercenaries alternately provide and threaten security in ways only the public sector was equipped to do in the past (Hall & Biersteker, 2002). For example, in certain weak states in sub-Saharan Africa, non-state actors have 'transformed' security into 'a market good for those who can afford it' (Hall & Biersteker, 2002). Cutler, Haufler, and Porter's (1999) book *Private authority and international affairs* (pp. 4–5), meanwhile, points out that in many industries, non-state for-profit entities, rather than the state, voluntarily established the norms and institutions that guarantee international cooperation across those industries. Nathan E. Busch and Austen D. Givens describe the proliferation of public–private partnerships in national security, arguing that the private sector began to take 'a more expansive role' in the field during the late twentieth century; they identify critical infrastructure protection, cybersecurity, port security, and energy management as key sub-sectors of national security in which private actors play a substantial role (Busch & Givens, 2012). These public–private partnerships involve 'collaboration' between both sectors.

Case study: national security

Although each of these conceptual lenses enriches the dialogue about the public–private distinction in contemporary times, none of them describes the relationship between the public and private sectors in the realm of U.S. national security in the terms here used. Here and elsewhere, the public sector may be seen as 'annexing' portions of the private sector to accomplish its objectives, such that the distinction between the two sectors functionally disappears. By instrumentalizing private sector companies to accomplish its ends, and setting the terms by which the partnership exists, the public sector in effect absorbs the private companies for the duration of the partnership.

The modern state is often seen both as being the most important provider of security, and as having security as its most important responsibility. Thus, Max Weber defined the state as 'a human community that (successfully) claims the monopoly of the legitimate use of physical force within a given territory' (Weber, 1946). Modern development theory holds security to be an essential 'survival'[4] or 'constitutive' (Fritz & Menocal, 2007) function of the state. According to Deborah Avant, Weber's definition of the state is typically seen as 'common sense' and the 'obvious starting point in most investigations' of security and violence, as even scholars of globalization and non-state actors 'generally assume that coercive power still resides with the state' (Avant, 2005, p. 1). As a result, few see national security as a matter for the private sector.

Actually, a very large amount of the work required to ensure national security, including building the tools and providing the needed personnel and services, is carried out in the modern state, especially in the U.S., by and in the private sector. In fiscal year 2013, the federal government awarded a total of $460 billion in contracts to the private sector, much of which went to defence contractors (Ivory, 2014). Of the top 10 contracts working for the government in FY 2014, all were defence contractors or significantly involved in defence, with contractors Lockheed Martin, General Dynamics, and Boeing at the top of the list (Federal Procurement Data System – Next Generation, 2015). For its part, the Department of Defense accounted for 70% of federal spending on contracts in 2012, allocating 56% of its own budget on contracts, both of which percentages rose significantly over the last decade (Van Hollen, 2015). Private contractors provide vehicles, armour, weapons, transportation, logistical support, and many other goods and services, which range from aircraft carriers and nuclear submarines to hand grenades and MREs. The government also outsources much intelligence collection and analysis to private sector contractors, who make up about a quarter of intelligence workers, and absorb '70% or more of the intelligence community's secret budget' (O'Harrow, Priest, & Censer, 2013). Such private security firms often play a complementary rather than replacement role, with companies such Academi (formerly Blackwater) contracted to protect diplomats (The Associated Press, 2013), provide counterterrorism training, and supplement U.S. military forces abroad (Scahill, 2010).

The growing reliance on computer and internet technology further undermine the status of the public sector as the provider of security (Avant, 2005, p. 33). U.S. intelligence agencies placed cyberattacks by foreign governments and criminals on both public and private targets at the top of their list of security threats in 2015 (Clapper, 2015). Commentators and analysts typically view public–private collaboration as essential to cyber security.[5]

Inadequate cybersecurity at private firms has become a major concern due to the risk that adversarial governments or non-state actors could compromise U.S. national security through espionage or cyberattacks. The most obvious example of this was the 2013 Snowden leaks, in which a former private contractor leaked extensive information on U.S. intelligence activities. Senate investigators held in 2014 that the Chinese military 'hacked into computer networks of civilian transportation companies hired by the Pentagon at least nine times', and moreover stated that 'defense contractors have generally failed to report to the Pentagon hacker break-ins of their systems as required under their business agreements' (The Associated Press, 2014). Major defence contractors that have suffered cyberattacks include General Dynamics, Boeing, Lockheed Martin, Raytheon, and Northrop Grumman (Greenberg, 2010). One such attack on Lockheed Martin in 2007 secured for China the design details of the F-35 fighter aircraft, which facilitated China's development of its own J-20 stealth fighter (Gertz, 2014). The reverse is also true: inadequate government computer security creates risks for private individuals, as shown by the 2015 hacking of the Office of Personnel Management, which likely acquired personal information on 'every person given a government background check for the last 15 years', as well as their families, some 21.5 million people (Davis, 2015).

At the same time, the private sector supplies and maintains much of the information technology used by the government. Prior to the 1990s, the Pentagon used in-house pro-grammers to design secure software tailored to the military's needs. However, the military has since increasingly shifted to off-the-shelf commercial software as a means of cutting costs and satisfying Congress, which is influenced by private sector lobbying (Clarke, 2010). More broadly, the federal government as a whole now uses computers and software designed, manufactured, and often serviced by the private sector. This makes the military vulnerable to decisions made by the private sector. For example, Microsoft's decision to end support for its Microsoft XP operating system left the Navy, which still relies on that aging software, 'susceptible to intrusion' and faced with the prospect of 'loss of data integrity, network performance and the inability to meet mission readiness of critical networks'. This forced the Defence Department to negotiate a $31 million contract with Microsoft to continue updating the software (McGarry, 2015). An additional vulnerability stems from the private sector's own reliance on equipment and components imported from overseas. In March 2013, for example, Congress passed a law requiring 'NASA, and the Justice and Commerce Departments' to secure the approval of federal law enforce-ment officials before purchasing information technology systems, based on an assessment of 'cyber-espionage or sabotage' risks including those associated with 'being produced, manufactured or assembled by one or more entities that are owned, directed or subsi-dized' by China (Selyukh & Palmer, 2013).

The private sector is also responsible for maintaining much of the U.S.' critical infrastruc-ture in sectors including energy, telecommunications, transportation, health services, and finance. Without improved cyber security measures, this infrastructure remains vulnerable to 'kinetic' cyberattacks, or those that 'cause direct or indirect physical damage, injury or death solely though the exploitation of vulnerable information systems and processes' (Applegate, 2013). In June 2014, for example, a report by the Financial Stability Oversight Council asserted that cyberattacks to 'disrupt, degrade, or impact the integrity and avail-ability of critical financial infrastructure' could 'threaten the stability of the financial system' (Financial Stability Oversight Council, 2014). The Government Accountability Office like-wise warned that 'maritime security plans required by law and regulation' do not address the threats posed by cyberattacks, to U.S. ports, which handle more than $1.3 tril-lion in goods per year (United States Government Accountability Office, 2014). In short the government cannot secure the nation's infrastructure without extended collaboration with the private sector.

Finally, the provision by private companies of various strong encryption measures, while of significant benefit to cyber security in some aspects, also hampers the public sector in its law enforcement and counterterrorism efforts. While encryption debates date back decades, the issue returned to prominence in 2014 when Apple added default encryption to its latest smartphones without retaining the capacity to comply with government search warrants. Apple previously bypassed the password on its phones upon receipt of a search warrant, but now by its own admission 'wouldn't be able to comply with a wiretap order even if we wanted to' (Apple, 2015a). The trend towards private sector encryption is on the rise more broadly, in part due to a consumer backlash against the cooperation of private sector tech companies with government surveillance as revealed by the Snowden leaks.[6] While some tech executives and journalists argue that forcing tech companies to comply with search warrants would weaken protections against cyberattacks,[7] law enforcement officials warn that stronger and more prevalent encryption 'will have very serious consequences for law enforcement and national security agencies at all levels' (Comey, 2014) given that it undermines the government's ability to counter crime and terrorism (Peterson, 2015). While in some ways an example of an antagonistic relationship between elements of the public and private sector, encryption also illustrates the growing linkage between the two sectors.

The brief study of national security illustrates that the difference between the public and private sectors is much smaller than is often assumed in public discourse.

The disappearing public–private divide

While this essay used for illustrative purposes one single case, several others are next briefly cited. The Obama administration, in policy discussions and public debate on the war in Iraq and Afghanistan, focused largely on U.S. military troop levels; the Afghanistan surge, for example, followed a debate within the administration on whether to send 80,000, 40,000, or as few as 10,000 additional U.S. troops (Baker, 2009). Rarely has it been noted that in both arenas the US military hired a similar number of private contractors that carried out military missions (Dunigan, 2013)![8] Moreover, because the two numbers were not combined, it was possible to add x thousands in one sector and y thousands to another – or otherwise affect the final outcome without proper public and congressional scrutiny. Indeed, the Obama administration has rarely mentioned the role the private sector plays in supporting the military; the White House's calls to improve defence technology, 'maintain dominance', and otherwise guarantee a strong military tend to gloss over the substantial role that the private sector defence industry plays in outfitting and supporting the military.

The private sector also plays a major role in policing and the criminal justice system. For every public sector police officer in the U.S., there are three private police, a category including security guards, bodyguards, private detectives, and contractors working as police (Joh, 2005; Pastor, 2003). It is not possible to gain an even roughly correct picture of the measures the US takes to curb crime without taking both private and public cops into account.

Most of the debate about privacy concerns government surveillance. However, private corporations keep very detailed dossiers on most Americans. And they sell that information – to the government.[9] It follows that if one feels that privacy is well-protected just because the government is banned from directly collecting certain categories of information, one had better look also at the private sector privacy merchants.[10] (In this sector, the Obama administration has acknowledged the private sector's capabilities, but in a

White House speech in response to Edward Snowden's revelations about the NSA, President Obama drew a distinction between corporate dossiers of information and the surveillance conducted by the federal government. In reality, the relationship between the public and private sectors in surveillance is more symbiotic [Obama, 2014].)

In conclusion

The fusion of the private and the public realms directly challenges the key assumptions that underlie democratic liberalism; the foundations of the central contested ideological issues of the era; and demand a foundation of the inclusive social order. Rather than seeking for part of the societal realm to be accountable to the other – the whole society formation must be justified in terms of shared values. Thus it is no longer possible to hold that if the public officials are accountable to the citizens (presumably in the private realms) – the public realm actions are legitimate. This is the case, for instance, becuse the elected officials affect what the public expect of them and value about them, and because private citizens garner public influence in illegitimate means and so on. The whole design must be normally reassessed.

Furthermore, the thesis that one sector is vastly normatively superior to other or that it may bring the good life to the other, is rejected by the preceding observations. The left liberal thesis that the state will protect citizens from excessive accumulation of private power is challenged by the finding that the state is often captured by private interest. And the thesis that the private sector is the foundation of liberty and the state – of coercion is challenged by the same finding: if the private sector can use the state to abuse people, it cannot be treated as, in principle, normatively superior.

As is often the case, one can quite readily point to a challenge but not necessarily to ways to cope with it. This is especially true about a challenge of the order of the one posed to both key democratic liberalism and to key ideologies by the fusion of the private and public sectors.

Notes

1. See, for example, Malatesta and Carboni (2014, pp. 63–74).
2. See, for example, Radford (1965, pp. 63–85), Lorch (1978), Sapru (2013), and Cassel (1988).
3. See also Polanyi (2001).
4. See, for example, Whaites (2008).
5. See, for example, Germano (2014).
6. See, for example, Hern (2014), Arce (2014), Apple (2015b), and Lowenthal (2015).
7. See, for example, Timm (2015).
8. See also 'Contractors who worked in conflict zones suffer high rates of PTSD, depression and get little help' Rand Corporation, 10 December 2013
9. See, for example, Senate Committee on Commerce, Science, and Transportation (2013).
10. See, for example, Etzioni (2012).

Disclosure statement

No potential conflict of interest was reported by the author.

References

Apple. (2015a). *We've built privacy into the things you use every day*. Retrieved from http://www.apple.com/privacy/approach-to-privacy/

Apple. (2015b). *Legal process guidelines*, April 10. Retrieved from https://www.apple.com

Applegate, S. D. (2013). The dawn of kinetic cyber. In K. Podins, J. Stinissen, & M. Maybaum (Eds.), *5th international conference on cyber conflict*. Tallinn: NATO CCD COE Publications.

Arce, N. (2014, November 19). WhatsApp encryption has just made it more difficult for gov't to spy on you. *Tech Times*. Retrieved from http://www.techtimes.com

The Associated Press. (2013). Case against contractors resurfaces. *New York Times*. Retrieved from http://www.nytimes.com/2013/10/18/us/case-against-contractors-resurfaces.html?_r=0

The Associated Press. (2014). China's military cyberattacked defense contractors several times, report claims. *CBS News*. Retrieved from http://www.cbsnews.com/news/china-military-cyberattacked-defense-contractors-several-times-report-claims/

Avant, D. (2005). *The market for force*. Cambridge: Cambridge University Press.

Baker, P. (2009, December 5). How Obama came to plan for 'surge' in Afghanistan. *New York Times*.

Bobbio, N. (1989). The great dichotomy: Public/private. In N. Bobbio (Ed.), *Democracy and dictatorship: The nature and limits of State Power* (pp. 1–21). Minneapolis: University of Minnesota Press.

Busch, N. E., & Givens, A. D. (2012). Public–private partnerships in homeland security: Opportunities and challenges. *Homeland Security Affairs, 8*, 18.

Cassel, F. H. (1988). The public–private distinction in organizational theory. *Academic Management Review, 13*, 182–201.

Clapper, J. R. (2015). *Statement for the record worldwide threat assessment of the US intelligence community*. Retrieved from http://www.dni.gov/files/documents/Unclassified_2015_ATA_SFR_-_SASC_FINAL.pdf

Clarke, R. A. (2010). *Cyber war: The next threat to national security and what to do about it*. New York, NY: Harper Collins.

Comey, J. (2014, October 16). *Going dark: Are technology, privacy, and public safety on a collision course?* (Speech). Washington, DC: Brookings Institution. Retrieved from http://www.fbi.gov

Cutler, A. C., Haufler, V., & Porter, T. (Eds.). (1999). *Private authority and international affairs*. New York, NY: State University of New York Press.

Davis, J. H. (2015, July 9). Hacking of government computers exposed 21.5 million people. *The New York Times*.

Dunigan, M. (2013, March 19). A lesson from Iraq war: How to outsource war to private contractors. *Christian Science Monitor*.

Etzioni, A. (2012). The privacy merchants: What is to be done? *University of Pennsylvania Journal of Constitutional Law, 14*(4), 929–951.

Federal Procurement Data System – Next Generation. (2015). *Top 100 contractors report*. Retrieved from https://www.fpds.gov

Financial Stability Oversight Council. (2014). *2014 annual report*. Retrieved from http://www.treasury.gov/

Freeman, A., & Mensch, E. (1987). The public–private distinction in American law and life. *Buffalo Law Review, 36*, 237–258.

Fritz, V., & Menocal, A. (2007). *Understanding state-building from a political economy perspective.* London: Overseas Development Institute (ODI). Retrieved from http://www.gsdrc.org/go/display&type=Document&id=3178

Gal, S. (2002). A semiotics of the public/private distinction. *Differences: A Journal of Feminist Cultural Studies, 13*(1), 77–95.

Germano, J. H. (2014). *Cybersecurity partnerships: A new era of public–private collaboration.* NYU Center on Law and Security. Retrieved from http://www.lawandsecurity.org/Portals/0/Documents/Cybersecurity.Partnerships.pdf

Gertz, B. (2014, March 13). *Top gun takeover: Stolen F-35 secrets showing up in China's stealth fighter. Washington Times.* Retrieved from http://www.washingtontimes.com

Greenberg, A. (2010, February 17). For pentagon contractors, cyberspying escalates. *Forbes.* Retrieved from http://www.forbes.com/2010/02/17/pentagon-northrop-raytheon-technology-security-cyberspying.html

Hall, R. B., & Biersteker, T. J. (Eds.). (2002). *The emergence of private authority in global governance.* Cambridge: Cambridge University Press.

Hern, A. (2014, October 17). Apple defies FBI and offers encryption by default on new operating system. *The Guardian.* Retrieved from http://www.theguardian.com

Internal Revenue Service. (2015, April 24). *EO operational requirements: Private foundations and public charities.* Retrieved from http://www.irs.gov/

Ivory, D. (2014). Federal contracts plunge, squeezing private companies. *New York Times.* Retrieved from http://www.nytimes.com/2014/01/16/business/federal-contracts-plunge-squeezing-private-companies.html

Joh, E. (2005). *Conceptualizing the private police.* UTAH L. REV. 573.

Lorch, R. S. (1978). *Public administration.* St. Paul, MN: West Publishing.

Lowenthal, T. (2015, April 9). Yahoo's end-to-end email promises greater protection for journalists. *PBS.* Retrieved from pbs.com.

Lowi, T. (1979). *The end of liberalism* (2nd ed.). New York, NY: Norton.

Malatesta, D., & Carboni, J. (2014). The Public–private distinction: Insights for public administration from the State action doctrine. *Public Administration Review, 75*(1), 63–74.

McConnell, G. (1966). *Private power and American democracy.* New York, NY: Knopf.

McGarry, B. (2015, June 24). Fixing the Pentagon's windows XP problem. *Defense Tech.*

Mills, C. W. (2000). *The power elite* (New ed.). Oxford: Oxford University Press.

Novak, W. J. (2008). The myth of the 'weak' American State. *American Historical Review, 113,* 752–772.

Obama, B. (2014, January 17). *Remarks by the president on review of signals intelligence* (Speech). Washington, DC. Retrieved from https://www.whitehouse.gov/the-press-office/2014/01/17/remarks-president-review-signals-intelligence

O'Harrow, Jr, R., Priest, D., & Censer, M. (2013). NSA leaks put focus on intelligence apparatus's reliance on outside contractors. *Washington Post.* Retrieved from http://www.washingtonpost.com/business/nsa-leaks-put-focus-on-intelligence-apparatuss-reliance-on-outside-contractors/2013/06/10/e940c4ba-d20e-11e2-9f1a-1a7cdee20287_story.html

Olson, M. (1982). *The rise and decline of nations.* New Haven, CT: Yale University Press.

Pastor, J. F. (2003). *The privatization of police in America: An analysis and case study.* Jefferson, NC: McFarland.

Pattison, J. (2014). *The morality of private war: The challenge of private military and security companies.* Oxford: Oxford University Press.

Peterson, A. (2015). FBI official: Companies should help us 'prevent encryption above all else'. *The Washington Post.* Retrieved from http://www.washingtonpost.com/

Polanyi, K. (2001). *The great transformation: The political and economic origins of our time.* Boston, MA: Beacon Press.

Radford, E. (1965). Business as government. In R. C. Martin (Ed.), *Public administration and democracy* (pp. 63–82). Syracuse: Syracuse University Press.

Salamon, L. M. (1999). *America's nonprofit sector: A primer.* New York, NY: The Foundation Center.

Sapru, R. K. (2013). *Administrative theories and management thought.* Delhi: PHI Learning.

Scahill, J. (2010). Blackwater's secret ops. *The Nation*. Retrieved from http://www.thenation.com/article/154739/blackwaters-black-ops#

Schattschneider, E. E. (1960). *The Semi-sovereign people: A realist's view of America*. Chicago, IL: Holt, Rinehart, and Winston.

Selyukh, A., & Palmer, D. (2013, March 28). U.S. law to restrict government purchases of Chinese IT equipment. *Reuters*. Retrieved from http://www.reuters.com/article/us-usa-cybersecurity-espionage-idUSBRE92Q18O20130328

Senate Committee on Commerce, Science, and Transportation. (2013, December 18). A review of the data broker industry: Collection, use, and sale of consumer data for marketing purposes. Staff report for Chairman Rockefeller. Retrieved from http://www.commerce.senate.gov/

Timm, T. (2015, June 9). If the FBI has a backdoor to Facebook or Apple encryption, we are less safe. *The Guardian*.

United States Government Accountability Office. (2014). *Maritime critical infrastructure protection: DHS needs to better address port security*. Retrieved from http://www.gao.gov/assets/670/663828.pdf

Van Hollen, C. (2015). Re: federal contracts and the contracted workforce. *Congressional Budget Office*. Retrieved from https://www.cbo.gov

Weber, M. (1946). *Essays in sociology* (pp. 77–128). New York, NY: Oxford University Press. Retrieved from http://www.sscnet.ucla.edu/polisci/ethos/Weber-vocation.pdf

Weintraub, J. (1997). *The theory and politics of the public–private distinction: Public and private in thought and practice*. Chicago, IL: University of Chicago Press.

Whaites, A. (2008). *States in development: Understanding state-building*. UK Department for International Development. Retrieved from http://tna.europarchive.org/20081212094836/http://dfid.gov.uk/pubs/files/State-in-Development-Wkg-Paper.pdf

Empirical legitimation analysis in International Relations: how to learn from the insights – and avoid the mistakes – of research in EU studies

Achim Hurrelmann

ABSTRACT
The political legitimation (or de-legitimation) of the European Union (EU) has been the object of much empirical research. This paper argues that this research holds lessons that can inform debates about the legitimation of global governance more generally. After some conceptual clarifications, the paper presents a critical review of the literature on the EU's legitimation, focusing on six crucial aspects – (1) the emergence and change of legitimation debates; (2) the arenas where legitimation occurs; (3) the role of the state as a reference point in legitimacy assessments; (4) the difference between various objects of legitimation; (5) the actors that trigger legitimation change; as well as (6) the relationship between legitimation and polity development. In each of these respects, the paper identifies important insights that can be gained from EU Studies, but also conceptual and methodological weaknesses in the EU-related literature that researchers working on other aspects of global governance should avoid. The paper closes by formulating a set of general desiderata for empirical legitimation research in International Relations.

Introduction

In the past two decades, scholarly interest in the analysis of legitimacy has grown markedly in International Relations (IR). This development is usually attributed to the growing authority of global governance institutions, which implies that the state – the traditional focal point for assessments of legitimacy – is no longer the only political unit perceived as being in need of explicit legitimation (Bernstein & Coleman, 2009; Hurrelmann, Schneider, & Steffek, 2007; Nullmeier et al., 2010). While some of the resulting scholarly work has concentrated on the normative evaluation of global governance (Buchanan & Keohane, 2006; Coicaud & Heiskanen, 2001), the increased interest in legitimacy among IR scholars has also resulted in a number of studies that approach legitimation processes from an empirical perspective, examining for instance explicit challenges to the legitimacy of global political actors (Clark & Reus-Smit, 2007), their self-legitimation strategies (Dingwerth, Lehmann, Reichel, Weise, & Witt, 2015; Steffek, 2003; Zaum, 2013), the emergence of new legitimation principles (Clark, 2007), the ways in which citizens perceive the legitimacy of international organizations (Dellmuth & Tallberg, 2015), or the politicization of world politics in the population, including the resulting legitimation debates (Ecker-Ehrhardt, 2015; Zürn, 2014; Zürn, Binder, & Ecker-Ehrhardt, 2013; Zürn & Ecker-Ehrhardt, 2013).

This article seeks to make a contribution to this latter, empirical strand of the debate by reviewing the relevant literature that has been published about the legitimacy of the European Union (EU). Its starting point is the observation that, in the IR discourse on legitimacy, frequent reference is made to the EU example. This is unsurprising given the EU's comprehensive scope of policy competencies and extraordinarily high level of supranational institutionalization, which make it a poster-child for academic discussions about the internationalization of political power. In other words, the increase in international authority that is usually credited with triggering the 'legitimacy turn' in IR has proceeded unusually far in the EU context, which means that the EU can be interpreted as something like a forerunner for developments that might occur, over time, on other contexts of global governance as well. This makes it interesting for IR scholars to take a close look at the extensive empirical work on legitimation that has been done in EU Studies.

In this paper, I want to give a critical overview of this work, pointing to some of the insights that have been gained for the empirical analysis of legitimacy more broadly, but also to some of the problems that have hampered the scholarly quality of EU-related legitimation research, and that researchers working on other aspects of global governance might wish to avoid. After some conceptual clarifications, the article will highlight six important aspects of empirical legitimation research in regional and global settings – (1) the emergence and change of legitimation debates; (2) the differentiation of various legitimation arenas; (3) the role of the state as a reference point in legitimacy assessments; (4) the differentiation between various legitimation objects; (5) the actors that trigger legitimation change; and (6) the relationship between legitimation and polity development – in which EU-related academic work holds valuable lessons for global governance more broadly. The paper closes by formulating a set of desiderata for empirical research that applies to the study of legitimation both in the EU and elsewhere.

Legitimacy and legitimation: some conceptual clarifications

At its most basic, the idea of legitimacy refers to the rightfulness of political rule (Coicaud, 2002; Hurrelmann et al., 2007, pp. 3–9). In the language of Max Weber, it denotes a situation in which the exercise of rule 'enjoys the prestige of being considered binding' and is hence treated as requiring compliance, regardless of individual interests or expediency (Weber, 1968, p. 31). As Weber pointed out, the degree to which political rule and its components – political systems and institutions, rulers and governance arrangements, norms and operating principles, individual laws or policies – are legitimate may be evaluated based on criteria that vary across time and place. Regardless of this variation, the fact that legitimacy evaluations focus on the ideas of rightfulness and bindingness means that they represent normative validity claims of a generalizable character. This distinguishes legitimacy from broader concepts such as support or stability, which may as well be grounded in non-normative considerations, such as habitual obedience, fear of coercion and sanctions, or instrumental cost–benefit calculations (Barker, 1990, pp. 20–44; Pakulski, 1986).

The distinction that this article, along with much of the literature, makes between normative and empirical approaches to legitimacy research is not meant to deny this inescap-
able normativity of legitimacy. Instead, it points to the fact that social scientists can be
both authors and observers of legitimacy evaluations (Barker, 2001, pp. 1–29; Hurrelmann
et al., 2007, pp. 3–8). In the first case, social scientists perform these legitimacy evaluations
themselves, based on criteria of rightfulness that they consider appropriate and the application of these criteria to existing or imagined political systems. This approach results in
statements of a *normative* kind. In the second case, by contrast, social scientists
examine the legitimacy evaluations performed by other actors – for instance, political
elites or citizens. This approach results in statements of an *empirical* kind, which may
describe, for instance, the rightfulness of certain institutions as being more or less
widely accepted or certain legitimacy claims as being used more or less frequently.

This article, as indicated above, is interested only in the second, empirical approach to
research on legitimacy. In applying this approach, it makes a further distinction between
legitimacy as an attribute of governance arrangements and *legitimation* as the process in
which legitimacy is claimed/disputed or affirmed/withdrawn (Barker, 2001, pp. 1–29). As
Rodney Barker has pointed out, only the latter, legitimation, is directly accessible to empirical research. According to Barker (2001),

> 'legitimacy' does not exist as a feasible subject of empirical or historical inquiry, in the same
> sense that God does not exist as a possible subject for social scientific study. We need to
> speak of both legitimacy and God when describing the actions of people engaged in politics
> and religion, but when we do so, we are describing their actions and language, not any inde-
> pendent phenomenon. (p. 26)

In other words, all that can be empirically observed are processes of legitimation (including, of course, the possibility of de-legitimation), but in their analysis, we can draw inferences on the (empirical) legitimacy of the political systems or institutions to which these
processes relate.

Empirical legitimation, in this understanding, is a communicative phenomenon. This is
what links legitimation to the concept of justification examined in this Special Issue.
However, because legitimation refers to the ideas of rightfulness and bindingness of political rule, it must be understood as a *specific kind* of justification. As stressed in the Introduction to this Special Issue, justification as such is omnipresent in social life (Abulof &
Kornprobst, 2016; see also Boltanski & Thévenot, 2006). Yet the rightfulness and bindingness of political rule is explicitly brought up only in a small subset of justification processes.
This is true even if we restrict our analysis to *political* justification, focusing on processes of
collective decision-making. Most political activities and discourses deal with the content of
public policy, and never raise legitimacy-related questions. When a government defends
its policies, a Supreme Court gives reasons for its decisions, or protesters on the streets
demand a certain course of action, we are clearly dealing with instances of justification,
but legitimacy claims that explicitly refer to the rightfulness and bindingness of rule
come up only in exceptional cases.

Legitimation, in other words, is a subset of justification. Even public protest and criticism should not *prima facie* be interpreted as indicating legitimacy problems. Reus-Smit
(2007) is hence correct in putting the conceptual bar for the definition of 'legitimacy
crises' fairly high, by arguing that such crises only exist when:

the level of social recognition that [an actor or institution and] its identity, interests, practices, norms, or procedures are rightful declines to the point where the actor or institution must either adapt (by reconstituting the social bases of its legitimacy, or by investing more heavily in material practices of coercion or bribery) or face disempowerment. (p. 158)

This means that political actors or institutions may be subject to heavy criticism without their legitimacy being challenged.

For empirical research on legitimation, it is nevertheless beneficial to situate legitimation activities and discourses within the broader political justification processes that occur in a society. The understanding of legitimation proposed here implies that legitimation emerges from such processes: A social object (institution, norm, etc.) can only be legitimate or illegitimate once it has been politicized – meaning that it has become politically salient and controversial in collective decision-making processes (Zürn, 2014; Zürn et al., 2013) – and questions about its political justification have hence been raised. *Politicization*, and the justification processes that it entails, should hence be seen as a necessary, but not sufficient condition of legitimation: A political system or its constitutive components can be politically salient and controversial without being explicitly evaluated in terms of the rightfulness of political rule. On the other hand, if and when evaluations of legitimacy take place, these necessarily imply politicization. A political system that is not politicized cannot sensibly be described as legitimate or illegitimate in an empirical sense, rather it is simply 'a-legitimate' (Steffek, 2007, p. 190).

Based on these conceptual clarifications, the following sections of my review will examine six central aspects of empirical legitimation that have been examined in EU-related research. In line with the considerations above, I cast the net widely in identifying the relevant EU-related literature, and included research on broader politicization trends that constitute a necessary condition for legitimation to occur. The six aspects highlighted here have been identified in an inductive fashion, based on the frequency with which they are addressed in the examined literature. They are presented in an order that corresponds to an idealized legitimation sequence, beginning with the emergence of legitimation debates, continuing with their structure and content, and ending with their political consequences. For each of the six aspects, I will highlight the contributions, but also the conceptual and/or empirical weaknesses, of EU-related research, so that lessons can be drawn for studies on the empirical legitimacy of other global governance institutions.

How does legitimation emerge and change? The 'permissive consensus' and its abuses

Empirical research on the EU's legitimation can be dated back at least to the early 1970s, but it exploded in the 1990s, after the rejection of the Maastricht Treaty in the Danish referendum of 1991. Since then, the most important story told by the majority of contributions is one of seminal trend: from non-politicization – and hence 'a-legitimacy' – to increasingly more intensive politicization, including explicit challenges to the EU's legitimacy. '[In] the first three decades of integration', write Hooghe and Marks (2009) in one of the most widely cited recent contributions to the debate,

> the creation of a European legal system was driven by the demand for adjudication of economic disputes between firms. The implications for most people (except perhaps farmers) were

limited or not transparent. Public opinion was quiescent. These were the years of *permissive consensus*, of deals cut by insulated elites. The period since 1991 might be described, by contrast, as one of *constraining dissensus*. Elites, that is, party leaders in positions of authority, must look over their shoulders when negotiating European issues. What they see does not reassure them. (p. 5; emphasis in original)

Hooghe and Marks (2009) cite a long list of empirical studies to show that, indeed, European integration is now contested in member-states public discourse, and does resonate in public opinion (pp. 6–18). These findings have been emphatically affirmed by other authors, based on the secondary analysis of existing research (De Wilde & Zürn, 2012) or on original case studies of recent episodes in EU politics (Statham & Trenz, 2013). As far as the description of current realities is concerned, there are few reasons do doubt the accuracy of this research, whose main claims are confirmed by the 2016 'Brexit' referendum. Regarding the analysis of legitimation change over time, however, it often remains unsatisfactory. The reason is that many studies compare the EU's current state of contested legitimacy, for which empirical evidence is collected, with a constructed reference point that is not itself empirically validated: the 'permissive consensus' of the early integration years.

The concept of 'permissive consensus' was introduced to European integration research in the early 1970s by Leon Lindberg and Stuart Scheingold. However, Lindberg and Scheingold did not develop a systematic definition; rather they referred to the concept in a metaphorical fashion to describe a situation in which European integration is not in danger of being faced with widespread and focused popular opposition (Lindberg & Scheingold, 1970, p. 41). The European population, they argued, does not take much interest in the politics of European integration, but supports the broad goals of the unification project, and treats European institutions as 'an accepted part of the political landscape' (Lindberg & Scheingold, 1970, p. 62). Whether such a situation is adequately described as a 'consensus' is questionable, but this is not an issue that must concern us here. What mattered for Lindberg and Scheingold is that the mixture of a lack of detailed interest in European integration and generally positive inclinations towards constitutes a 'permissive' instrument for the functioning and further development of European institutions. This 'permissive consensus':

> provides relative assurance that the goals of the Community are widely shared and that normal operations of the community system will be accepted as authoritative and legitimate. And if these goals and these normal operations conduce to the progressive growth of the system, this too is likely to meet with general acceptance. (Lindberg & Scheingold, 1970, p. 121)

The ways in which the 'permissive consensus' concept is used in many recent discussions of the EU's legitimacy suggests that European integration before the early 1990s was virtually uncontested. But empirical evidence for this assertion is seldom provided. A few studies that take a broader historical perspective suggest that this view is inadequate. Schrag Sternberg (2013), for instance, in an impressive qualitative analysis of political and media discourses, shows that the history of discursive legitimation and de-legitimation of European integration can be traced back until at least the 1950s. Her analysis does not disprove the hypothesis of increasing political contestation about the EU's legitimacy, but it does show that the historical continuities in EU-related legitimation debates are as striking as the discontinuities. Studies that have used methods of quantitative discourse analysis to track politicization or legitimation processes over time, for instance in party manifestos (Green-Pedersen, 2012; Spoon, 2012) or media debates (Hutter & Grande, 2014), invite similar conclusions. While they do generally show longer-term trends of increasing political contestation, they also reveal that this trend does not start from a situation of complete 'a-legitimacy', that it does not unfold evenly over time, and that developments in various member states sometimes differ quite dramatically. Changes in the EU's empirical legitimation, therefore, should not be conceptualized as an unambiguous and unidirectional trend 'from permissive consensus to constraining dissensus', rather they are better approached as a development that proceeds in fits and starts, including slowdowns and outright reversals, and therefore must be studied using carefully conceptualized longitudinal research designs.

Where does legitimation occur? Unpacking the 'public sphere'

The definitions of legitimacy and legitimation developed above imply that the construction or deconstruction of legitimacy is a multifaceted phenomenon that involves multiple actors and consists of a variety of activities. Researchers in EU Studies have applied a large array of research approaches and methodological instruments to track evidence of legitimation (or politicization as its necessary condition). These include studies of political discourse such as government communication (Crespy & Schmidt, 2013), parliamentary debates (Wendler, 2014), party manifestos and positions (Benoit & Laver, 2006; Hutter & Grande, 2014; Spoon, 2012), and media reporting (Statham & Trenz, 2013), studies of protest (Imig, 2004) and public opinion (Hobolt & de Vries, 2016; McLaren, 2006; Thomassen, 2009), as well as studies based on qualitative methods such as focus groups (Duchesne, Frazer, Haegel, & Van Ingelgom, 2013; Van Ingelgom, 2014; White, 2011). The discipline of IR can surely learn from these diverse conceptual and methodological instruments. In interpreting research results, however, EU-related research has often fallen victim to a tendency of over-aggregation, driven by a desire to present diverse insights into the EU's legitimation as part of one comprehensive phenomenon, rather than allowing for internal differentiation.

The conceptual brace that is most frequently used to hold together such aggregated interpretations is the concept of the 'public sphere', which is understood as encompassing all of the above-mentioned sites of legitimation, regardless of whether they are populated by actors with a professional interest in the EU (such as politicians and media personnel) or citizens who discuss EU politics as laypeople. In the context of debates about a politicization of European integration, Statham and Trenz (2015) have expressed this idea as follows:

> [A] public sphere includes not only those who take an active part in the debate, but it presupposes that communication resonates among others, a 'public', for whom it is also relevant. This resonance of public communication between institutional actors and publics is carried primarily by mass-mediated political debates. This effectively 'brings the public back in' to European politics. (p. 292)

This conception allows Statham and Trenz to treat their own research results on EU-related debates in newspapers as relevant not only to the media, but to the EU citizenry as a whole. Existing evidence suggests, however, that debates about the EU and its legitimacy differ quite fundamentally depending on the discursive arena in which they take place. It makes sense to distinguish at least three kinds of such arenas (Hurrelmann, Gora, & Wagner, 2015): (a) *institutional arenas* at the core of the political system, which are populated by politicians (e.g. the European Parliament or national parliaments); (b) *intermediary arenas* linking political decision-making processes to the broader citizenry, which are dominated by participants with a professional interest in politics (political parties, interest groups, the media, etc.); and (c) *citizen arenas* in which laypeople communicate about politics (at the workplace, in discussions with friends, etc.).

Most empirical studies on politicization and legitimation in the EU have thus far dealt with the first two types of arena, often implicitly assuming that the findings could be generalized to the third. But research that has focused on citizen discourses indicates that European integration remains less explicitly contested in citizen arenas than in institutional and intermediary arenas (Duchesne et al., 2013; Van Ingelgom, 2014; White, 2011). What is more, only a selection of the legitimating arguments presented in institutional or intermediary arenas resonates with the citizens. In my own research, I have found that while media statements about the EU make use of a considerable range of pragmatic, moral, and identity-oriented arguments in favour of European integration (Hurrelmann, Gora, & Wagner, 2013), participants in focus groups with EU citizens tend to frame pro-EU arguments in a much narrower fashion, focusing primarily on direct effects of integration on their own personal lives, such as passport-free travel or the common currency (Hurrelmann et al., 2015). In seeking to assess the potential legitimation challenges, studies on the empirical legitimacy of the EU must not gloss over such differences by applying overly generalized concepts (such as that of the 'public sphere'), but should rather seek to differentiate carefully how the EU is legitimated (or de-legitimated) by various speakers and in various discursive arenas. This does not imply, of course, that these political arenas are closed off against each other. An analysis of inter-arena interactions, mapping whether (and how) certain legitimating or de-legitimating arguments spread from one arena to the next, also presupposes that these arenas are conceptually and empirically disentangled.

How is legitimacy related to the state? Different kinds of multilevel assessments

As the EU constitutes a relatively new and unfamiliar addition to the political landscape – an 'unidentified political object', as former European Commission President Delors (1985, p. 2) famously put it – the formation of legitimation discourses related to its institutions and activities does not necessarily follow established patterns. Unsurprisingly, more conventional political objects, especially the state and its procedures of representative democracy, often serve as a reference point for EU-related legitimation discourses. Many authors argue that, when assessed against the democratic institutions and principles that define the state, the EU will necessarily fall short, as its decision-making processes do not conform to state-based benchmarks of democratic legitimacy. Even if democratic accountability in the EU was expanded beyond the status quo, explains Philippe Schmitter, this problem would persist, as 'the nonstate European policy [would] have to come up with novel institutions in order to democratize itself', and as a result, politicians and citizens accustomed to state-based democracy 'would have considerable difficulty in recognizing these novel rules and practices as "democratic"' (Schmitter, 1999, p. 14).

The assumption that the state and its legitimacy, justified by democratic standards, constitutes the most important reference point for the EU is also at the core of many explicitly critical assessments of the legitimacy of the European integration process. Not only Thatcherite British Eurosceptics, such as Laughland (1998), but also academics with social democratic leanings, including Scharpf (1994, 2009), have interpreted the process of European integration as one in which high-legitimacy state institutions lose powers, whereas low-legitimacy EU bodies become politically more visible and influential, with a double-negative effect on overall legitimacy. Yet while this analysis may be defensible as a normative assessment, it should not be assumed that it also adequately represents the EU's empirical legitimacy. First, empirical legitimation research has shown that the normative criteria privileged in democratic theory do not represent the only, and often not even the dominant, criteria by which a state's legitimacy is assessed (Gilley, 2006; Hurrelmann, Krell-Laluhová, Nullmeier, Schneider, & Wiesner, 2009). Second, in real-world legitimation processes, member states of the EU are not everywhere assessed positively, nor is the EU always seen negatively. As a result, the relationships established between the EU and its member states are significantly more diverse than the zero-sum (or even negative-sum) models cited above, which assume that the traditional, non-internationalized state enjoys full legitimacy, and everything that diverges or moves away from this model will necessarily be perceived as deficient. Rather, there may be multiple constellations of state-related and EU-related legitimacy assessments. Based on public opinion data, Martinotti and Stefanizzi (1995) have distinguished 'integrated' citizen orientations (positive assessments of both the EU and one's member state) from orientations that are 'nation-statist' (negative assessment of the EU, positive assessment of one's member state), 'innovative/escapist' (positive assessment of the EU, negative assessment of one's member state), or 'alienated' (negative assessments of both the EU and one's member state). Martinotti and Stefanizzi show that all four types of orientation exist in the European population, and that their relative strength differs systematically between member states.

The typology by Martinotti and Stefanizzi does not tell us whether there is actually a connection between the legitimacy assessments of European and member-state institutions, or whether the respective assessments are performed independently. Yet more recent research, relying on both public opinion studies (Anderson, 1998; Hooghe & Marks, 2005; Kritzinger, 2003; Rohrschneider, 2002) and qualitative analysis of legitimation discourses (Hurrelmann, 2008; Hurrelmann et al., 2013), has established that perceptions of member-state legitimacy demonstrably influence how the legitimacy of the EU is assessed. These studies also show that there are different ways in which such multilevel legitimacy assessments are constructed. For instance, sometimes EU-related and member-state-related assessment do indeed stand in a zero-sum relationship to each other, meaning that perceived legitimacy problems of the EU are treated as an argument supporting the legitimacy of the member states, or vice versa. However, research has also found positive sum constructions, where the legitimacy of the EU and the member states are perceived as mutually supporting each other, or integrated assessments of Europe as a multilevel system in which the state- and the EU-level are no longer explicitly distinguished (Hurrelmann, 2008; Hurrelmann et al., 2013). This implies is that, while multilevel legitimacy assessments potentially matter a great deal for the EU's legitimacy, they prove too diverse empirically to just assume that one specific kind of assessment – affirming the state's traditional legitimacy and de-legitimating the EU in comparison – necessarily constitutes the most prevalent pattern. Empirical research will hence have to explicitly distinguish various constructions of multilevel legitimacy, to determine which of these constructions dominates in any given context.

What does legitimation address? Squaring contextualization and differentiation

This call for differentiation can also be extended to that various objects of legitimation *within* the EU. Thus far, most of the EU-related literature on politicization and legitimation treats 'the EU' (or 'European integration') as one unitary and homogeneous legitimation object. The advantage of this approach is that political debates about the EU can be compared to debates about other political issues, such as economic policy, migration, or the environment. Green-Pedersen (2012) has defended this research strategy, which he labels an agenda-setting perspective, as follows:

> [T]he question of the politicisation of European integration must be seen as relative. How is the issue ranked in the hierarchy of issues that constitutes the agenda[s] of political parties and the electorate? [...] Politicisation thus refers to an issue with a prominent position on both agendas. As outlined above, agenda-setting literature approaches the question by comparing across issues. (pp. 117, 121)

There are clear benefits to such attempts at contextualization, designed to prevent the drawing of far-reaching conclusions from what might ultimately be a relatively minor segment of political discourse. Yet at the same time, this approach introduces a bias: It defines European integration primarily in terms of fundamental questions of membership and institutional development, and distinguishes these from policy issues, which are treated as irrelevant to European integration. In doing so, it neglects how strongly policy making in EU member states has become Europeanized. As a result of this bias, many academic debates about the politicization and legitimation of European integration deal disproportionately with Eurosceptical political parties (Adam & Maier, 2011; Hooghe & Marks, 2009), which raise fundamental issues about European integration, but which have until fairly recently remained relatively marginal in most member states.

After six decades of European integration, the internal complexity of the European construction has grown to such an extent that it is very questionable whether 'the EU' can be treated as one homogeneous object of politicization or legitimation. Rather, it seems appropriate in empirical studies to distinguish five potential objects: (a) *European integration as an idea*, in other words, the basic principle of exercising political authority in a Europe-wide context; (b) *the EU as an organization*, including its basic organizational traits, one's country's membership, and the EU's geographical reach; (c) *the EU's constitutional structure,* including its institutions, objectives, and responsibilities, as well as decision-making procedures; (d) *specific policy issues* that are currently on the agenda of the EU's legislative, executive, or judiciary institutions; as well as (e) *domesticated issues,* that is, issues in member-state politics that emerge as an implication of membership, such as cuts to national budgets mandated by Eurozone requirements (for a similar distinction, see Hurrelmann et al., 2015). A categorization of this kind is particularly important to assess the implications of intensified political contestation: Other things being equal, we can assume that contestation about policy and domesticated issues, even if issues of legitimacy are raised, constitutes a less fundamental challenge to the EU than contestation about the idea of integration, the EU as an organization, or its institutions.

Debates in the context of the ongoing Eurozone crisis provide a good illustration of the value of such distinctions. There is little doubt that the crisis has led to increased contestation about EU issues, including explicit legitimacy challenges that question the appropriateness of the EU's crisis response (Schimmelfennig, 2014; Statham & Trenz, 2015). On the other hand, it is noteworthy that most of this contestation has occurred in domestic political arenas, in the context of member-state elections or decision-making processes; it has, in other words, politicized the European integration primarily as a domesticated issue (Baglioni & Hurrelmann, 2016; Genschel & Jachtenfuchs, 2014). This explains, in part, why the crisis-induced politicization, in spite of its EU-critical impetus, has not prevented the significant steps towards further supranational integration that were taken by the EU institutions in response to the crisis (Schimmelfennig, 2014). The example shows that, in research about the EU's politicization and legitimation, it is important to balance attempts at contextualization, which relate findings about 'the EU' to findings on comparable political objects, with an explicit differentiation of various European integration objects that captures the EU's institutional complexity.

What triggers legitimation change? Top-down and bottom-up processes

As is well known, European integration was initiated as an elite project whose main architects were not interested in – and at times actively sought to discourage – significant citizen mobilization (Majone, 2005). In research on the EU's politicization and legitimation, this (plausible) interpretation of the history of European integration has resulted in a tendency to view shifts towards the increasing contestation of EU-related issues exclusively as bottom-up processes forced by insurgent citizens on unwilling political decision makers, thus challenging the legitimacy of an elite-led integration project from the outside. Statham and Trenz (2015) have described this assumed trajectory as follows:

> As EU-level influence in decision making increases, a diffuse awareness by European citizens that the 'EU matters' drives a new polarization of opinions or interests, which then leads to an increase in public claims by collective actors that address policy formulation. (p. 292)

The EU's political elites, by contrast, are conceptualized as being interested only in de-politicization, trying to withdraw EU decision-making processes from public scrutiny and potential legitimation challenges (see also De Wilde & Zürn, 2012; Schimmelfennig, 2014).

There is ample evidence, not least from the Eurozone crisis, to show that such bottom-up trajectories are indeed a relevant feature of EU-related legitimation processes. It is important to recognize, however, that politicization and legitimation processes occur in a top-down fashion as well. Political leaders can be assumed to always be engaged in attempts to legitimate their own rule, even though the audience of such self-legitimation practices is not necessarily the whole citizenry. As Barker (2003) has suggested, the successive expansion of the audiences to which rulers' legitimation claims are directed is one way of conceptualizing the growth of the EU polity:

In this case, governors begin by legitimating themselves in their own eyes, then in those of their immediate 'cousins', and only when they actually begin governing, and hence creating, their citizens do they legitimate themselves in the eyes of their subjects. (p. 166)

The point here is not to suggest that the last stage in this top-down legitimation sequence has already been reached for all potential EU-related legitimation objects, but rather that it is important to realize that bottom-up politicization and legitimation processes interact with top-down processes. Many shifts in the EU's legitimation can only be understood if both types of processes are taken into account.

A particularly good illustration is the case of the proposed Constitutional Treaty, which failed in the French and Dutch referendums in 2005. The constitutional project was not the result of pressure for constitutionalization originating from the citizens; rather the project was devised by member-state governments in an attempt to bring the EU 'closer to its citizens' and to increase the EU's legitimacy (European Council, 2001). The constitutional debates between 2000 and 2005 provide plenty of evidence detailing that the proposed constitution was seen by many of its 'framers' as a device to bolster the citizens' attachment to the EU polity, *inter alia* through the inclusion of a large number of symbolic provisions, thus allowing for a shift from technocratic to more democratic legitimation strategies (Scicluna, 2012). This attempt at legitimation change through top-down politicization, however, resulted in failure, mainly because, in this particular instance, the (state-like) legitimacy claims contained in the constitution did not match most citizens' legitimacy evaluations of the EU (Hurrelmann, 2007; Moravcsik, 2006). The example of the Constitutional Treaty shows that politicization and legitimation dynamics in the EU can only be understood if both bottom-up and top-down processes are taken into account, and their interaction is analysed.

How does legitimation relate to polity development? The fallacies of functionalism

The debate about legitimation in the EU is strongly dominated by variants of functionalist regional integration theory. This becomes particularly clear if we examine politicization, which – as explained above – constitutes a necessary condition for legitimation to occur. The concept of politicization was first introduced into discussions of European integration by neo-functionalist theorists, who hypothesized that the growing contestation about regional issues would be one of the unintended consequences of the creation of regional institutions – a special case of 'spillover', as it were (Schmitter, 1969). A number of contemporary authors have built on this logic. De Wilde and Zürn (2012), while not using the term 'neo-functionalism', describe a similar process of increases in EU authority triggering politicization, a process that in their opinion is shaped by a number of intermediary factors (such as party and media strategies), but cannot be stopped or reversed as long as EU authority is not reduced. Hooghe and Marks (2009) have labelled their theory of politicization 'post-functionalism'; its main difference to neo-functionalism lies not in the explanation of how politicization comes about, but in the fact that politicization is explicitly conceptualized as a process that mobilizes national identity concerns against European integration, and hence functions as a constraint on further steps towards supranational institutional integration. In contrast to this account, Statham and Trenz (2015) have developed a theory they call 'democratic functionalism'; it assumes that politicization is not only the automatic effect of increased EU authority, but also unleashes a constant pressure towards the democratization of EU governance. All of these theoretical accounts have in common that politicization, and the legitimation debates that it may give rise to, are interpreted as standing in a quasi-deterministic relationship to the development of the EU polity: Politicization is interpreted as a necessary consequence of certain stages of polity development, and understood as having clearly defined implications for the polity's future – even though there is disagreement between the various authors about what exactly these implications might be.

However, the trajectories of past politicization processes give reason for doubt whether the coupling of politicization/legitimation and polity development is necessarily so tight. Research by Hutter and Grande (2014) on the politicization of European integration in electoral campaigns shows, for example, that in the UK, politicization levels receded between the 1970s and the early 21st century, regardless of the growth of EU powers in this period, a development that was only reversed in the 'Brexit' debate. In a similar vein, a study of my own on EU-related media debates between 2000 and 2009 reveals that the politicization that was intentionally triggered by political elites in the EU's constitutional debates was quite effectively contained by the same elites when the Lisbon Treaty was debated. Even though the Lisbon Treaty was largely identical to the Constitution, with the exception of the latter's symbolic provisions, media debates about it were less intensive, to a greater extent dominated by politicians, and more likely to affirm the EU's legitimacy (Hurrelmann et al., 2013). A final example is a recent study by Frank Schimmelfennig, who shows that in spite of the politicization triggered by the Eurozone crisis, political elites have been able to implement a number of far-reaching institutional reforms of EU governance, many of which strengthen technocratic supranational institutions (Schimmelfennig, 2014). In other words, the crisis-induced politicization did not prove 'constraining' on the EU's polity development, at least not in the sense of preventing further integration steps, nor did it push the EU into a more democratic direction.

These examples highlight that, when it comes to the EU's politicization and legitimation, theories of functionalist automaticity have to be approached with caution. The successive growth of EU competencies and supranational institutionalization clearly makes it more likely that EU governance is politicized, and becomes subject to legitimation debates, but processes of contestation will only be triggered if political actors – governing elites, political parties, interest groups, journalists, or civil society groups – explicitly raise EU issues as topics of collective decision-making, and find a receptive audience for their claims in public discourse. Such discursive dynamics will also determine the precise shape that politicization/legitimation takes – the aspects of the EU to which it relates (membership, institutions, policy, etc.), the kinds of arguments/legitimation standards that are advanced (economic prosperity, democracy, common values, etc.), the political cleavages that become apparent in the debates (member state vs. member state, left vs. right, winners vs. losers of integration, etc.), and so on. Patterns of legitimation are not necessarily stable either; like all public discourse, legitimation debates are subject to issue attention cycles that might see them disappear as topics of discussion as soon as they become 'old news' and new, more pressing issues of public debate come up (Hurrelmann et al., 2009). Finally, precisely because the EU is a creation of political elites, there is not necessarily a close relationship between its politicization/legitimation and institutional development. The future shape of European integration will depend on both institutional and political configurations, but these two aspects need not develop in sync.

Conclusion: desiderata for the empirical study of legitimacy in IR

Our survey of EU-related research has shown that there is a high density of studies on the legitimation and politicization of the EU, which provide important conceptual, methodological, and substantive insights for empirical legitimation research in IR. The discipline of IR is hence well advised to look to EU Studies when conceptualizing empirical research on the legitimation and politicization of global governance. Our analysis has also shown, however, that EU-related research suffers from a number of problems, rooted in conceptual fuzziness, untested assumptions, over-aggregation, or lack of empirical rigour, which research in IR should seek to avoid. By way of conclusion, we can summarize the results of our discussion by formulating six desiderata for the empirical study of legitimacy, which apply both to the EU and to global governance more widely:

1. *Legitimation analysis must study the emergence and change of legitimation debates using longitudinal research designs, rather than by comparing current realities to analytical constructs of the past.* While the concept of 'permissive consensus' is not widely used in IR, some of the existing discussions of legitimation of global governance proceed in a fashion not dissimilar to that identified in EU Studies: They assume that international politics before globalization was more or less completely 'a-legitimate', so that any evidence of politicization now can be treated as indicative of a general and unidirectional trend (Zürn et al., 2013). Our analysis above outlines the dangers of this approach; it highlights that assumptions of a shift from 'a-legitimacy' to more contested legitimation must always be empirically detailed.

2. *Legitimation analysis must differentiate various discursive arenas in which legitimation may occur, and must proceed cautiously when using aggregated conceptions of a public sphere.* The fact that the density of empirical research on legitimation is thus far thinner in IR than in EU Studies means that the incentives for over-aggregation might be particularly pronounced. This might lead to researchers making sweeping generalizations, for instance the claim (in an otherwise excellent article) that 'newspapers [...] are a good proxy for public debates about policies' (Rixen & Zangl, 2013, p. 373). The experience from EU Studies suggests that, rather than making such generalizations, researchers should carefully define the domain of what they are studying, to leave room for a differentiated analysis of various legitimation arenas. Only after evidence from various discursive settings has been obtained should researchers consider which forms of re-aggregation are appropriate.

3. *Legitimation analysis must not assume that positive assessments of the state constitute a universal benchmark for assessments of global governance, but should rather pay attention to diverse relationships of multilevel legitimacy.* In IR as well as EU Studies, it is tempting to treat the state, and its assumed democratic legitimacy, as a reference point for legitimacy assessments of non-state institutions. But while assessments of various political levels have indeed been shown to be related, this does not imply that the

traditional state is always legitimate, or even more legitimate than international organizations; it also does not mean that shifts of power from the state to global governance arrangements necessarily cause legitimacy problems (Scharpf, 2000). Rather, researchers have to observe empirically how the legitimacy of global governance is constructed, and which relationships to the state – and other political levels – are established in the process.

4. *Legitimation analysis must differentiate various aspects of global governance that may be politicized, rather than treating them as a unitary object of legitimation.* This rule might, at first sight, be considered less relevant for IR than for EU Studies, given that no International Organization is as complex institutionally as the EU. But many global governance institutions have of course reached considerable complexity. And even when analysing intergovernmental institutions that are weakly institutionalized, such as G7/G8, a legitimation analysis that does not distinguish between, say, the principle of intergovernmental cooperation, its processes, and concrete cooperation outputs, or between intergovernmental decision-making at a summit and domestic decision-making in preparation for the summit (Nonhoff, Gronau, Nullmeier, & Schneider, 2009), is necessarily incapable of capturing the full complexity of legitimation and politicization processes in the international sphere.

5. *Legitimation analysis must examine the interplay of top-down and bottom-up legitimation processes as triggers of legitimation change, rather than focussing exclusively on citizen mobilization and activism.* High-profile citizen mobilization against global governance institutions, such as the protests against the World Trade Organization in Seattle (1999) or against the G8 in Genoa (2001), are the most visible evidence of (de-)legitimation practices in matters of international politics. It is important, however, to complement the analysis of such bottom-up processes with research on top-down legitimation by political elites. The latter may involve attempts at de-politicization, seeking to withdrawing global governance from legitimation debates, but as the example of the EU has shown, elites may also attempt to (selectively) politicize some of their activities in order to shore up legitimation.

6. *Legitimation analysis must pay close attention to discursive and institutional dynamics, rather than assuming a necessary and unidirectional connection between legitimation and polity development.* Our discussion of the EU has pointed to the limits of various types of functionalist theories that assume a close conceptual connection between the development of EU institutions and the way in which European integration is politicized and/or legitimated in the population. In IR as well, attempts to forge such connections – for instance by claiming that non-transparent international institutions are more likely to face popular rejection than transparent ones (Zürn et al., 2013, p. 98), or that politicization will result in institutions becoming less prone to executive decision-making (Zürn, 2014, p. 59) – must be treated with caution. These might be useful research hypotheses, but they must always be verified through careful analysis of both institutional and discursive dynamics.

If empirical legitimation analysis in IR follows these rules, it will be able to avoid some of the pitfalls that have, at times, undermined the quality of legitimation research in EU Studies. The systematic and differentiated approach advocated here would also open the door for more comparative research on the legitimation of global or regional governance, which promises to augment our understanding of its facets, causes, and consequences. It is clear that, for pragmatic reasons (funding limitations, etc.), not each and every study will be able to conform to all of these rules. My own past research, most certainly, has violated a number of them. This does not, however, undermine their usefulness as a (tentative) guideline for how to conceptualize research on legitimation in IR.

Acknowledgements

Previous versions of this paper were presented at a workshop on 'Public Justification in World Politics' at Princeton University (March 2014), in the lecture series of the Bremen International Graduate School of Social Sciences (November 2014), and at the ECPR Joint Sessions of Workshops in Warsaw (March 2015). For useful comments, encouragement and constructive criticism, I am indebted to Uriel Abulof, Klaus Dingwerth, Matthias Ecker-Ehrhardt, Amitai Etzioni, Anna Geis, Jennifer Gronau, Tine Hanrieder, Sebastian Haunss, Monika Heupel, Markus Kornprobst, Ron Krebs, Ulrike Liebert, Gary Marks, Frank Nullmeier, Steffen Schneider, Henning Schmidtke, Arndt Wonka, Dominik Zaum, as well as two anonymous reviewers for *Contemporary Politics*.

Disclosure statement

No potential conflict of interest was reported by the author.

References

Abulof, U., & Kornprobst, M. (2016). Introduction: The politics of public justification. *Contemporary Politics, 22*(2).

Adam, S., & Maier, M. (2011). National parties as politicizers of EU integration? Party campaign communication in the run-up to the 2009 European Parliament election. *European Union Politics, 12*(3), 431–453.

Anderson, C. J. (1998). When in doubt, use proxies: Attitudes toward domestic politics and support for European integration. *Comparative Political Studies, 31*(5), 569–601.

Baglioni, S., & Hurrelmann, A. (2016). The Eurozone crisis and citizen engagement in EU affairs. *West European Politics, 39*(1), 104–124.

Barker, R. (1990). *Political legitimacy and the state*. Oxford: Clarendon Press.

Barker, R. (2001). *Legitimating identities: The self-presentations of rulers and subjects*. Cambridge: Cambridge University Press.

Barker, R. (2003). Legitimacy, legitimation, and the European Union: What crisis? In P. Craig & R. Rawlings (Eds.), *Law and administration in Europe* (pp. 157–174). Oxford: Oxford University Press.

Benoit, K., & Laver, M. (2006). *Party policy in modern democracies*. London: Routledge.

Bernstein, S., & Coleman, W. D. (Eds.). (2009). *Unsettled legitimacy: Political community, power, and authority in a global era*. Vancouver: UBC Press.

Boltanski, L., & Thévenot, L. (2006). *On justification: Economies of worth*. Princeton, NJ: Princeton University Press.

Buchanan, A., & Keohane, R. O. (2006). The legitimacy of global governance institutions. *Ethics & International Affairs, 20*(4), 405–437.

Clark, I. (2007). *International legitimacy and world society*. Oxford: Oxford University Press.

Clark, I., & Reus-Smit, C. (Eds.). (2007). Resolving international crises of legitimacy. *International Politics, 44*(2) (Special Issue), 153–339.

Coicaud, J. M. (2002). *Legitimacy and politics: A contribution to the study of political right and political responsibility*. Cambridge: Cambridge University Press.

Coicaud, J.-M., & Heiskanen, V. (Eds.). (2001). *The legitimacy of international organizations*. Tokyo: United Nations University Press.

Crespy, A., & Schmidt, V. (2013). The discursive double game of EMU reform: The clash of titans between French white knight and German iron lady. In B. de Witte, A. Héritier, & A. H. Trechsel (Eds.), *The Euro crisis and the state of European democracy: Contributions from the 2012 EUDO dissemination conference* (pp. 350–368). San Domenico di Fiesole: European University Institute.

De Wilde, P., & Zürn, M. (2012). Can the politicization of European integration be reversed? *Journal of Common Market Studies, 50*(S1), 137–153.

Dellmuth, L. M., & Tallberg, J. (2015). The social legitimacy of international organisations: Interest representation, institutional performance, and confidence extrapolation in the United Nations. *Review of International Studies, 41*(3), 451–475.

Delors, J. (1985, September 9). Speech at the first Intergovernmental Conference in Luxembourg. *Bulletin of the European Communities*, No 9. Retrieved from http://www.cvce.eu/obj/speech_by_jacques_delors_luxembourg_9_september_1985-en-423d6913-b4e2-4395-9157-fe70b3ca8521.html

Dingwerth, K., Lehmann, I., Reichel, E., Weise, T., & Witt, A. (2015). Many pipers, many tunes? Die Legitimationskommunikation internationaler Organisationen in komplexen Umwelten. *Politische Vierteljahresschrift*, Special Issue *49*, 186–212.

Duchesne, S., Frazer, E., Haegel, F., & Van Ingelgom, V. (2013). *Citizens' reactions to European integration compared: Overlooking Europe*. Basingstoke: Palgrave Macmillan.

Ecker-Ehrhardt, M. (2015). Soziale Legitimität globaler Organisationen unter den Bedingungen kosmopolitischer Politisierung: Eine Einstellungsanalyse. *Politische Vierteljahresschrift*, Special Issue *49*, 157–185.

European Council. (2001, December 14 and 15). *Presidency conclusions*. European Council meeting in Laeken. Document SN 300/1/01 REV 1. Retrieved from http://ec.europa.eu/smart-regulation/impact/background/docs/laeken_concl_en.pdf

Genschel, P., & Jachtenfuchs, M. (2014, March 14–16). *Vision vs. process: An institutionalist account of the Euro crisis*. Paper prepared for the Council for European Studies, 21st International Conference of Europeanists, Washington, DC.

Gilley, B. (2006). The meaning and measure of state legitimacy: Results for 72 countries. *European Journal of Political Research, 45*(3), 499–525.

Green-Pedersen, C. (2012). A giant fast asleep? Party incentives and the politicisation of European integration. *Political Studies, 60*(1), 115–130.

Hobolt, S. B., & de Vries, C. E. (2016). Public support for European integration. *Annual Review of Political Science, 19*, 413–432.

Hooghe, L., & Marks, G. (2005). Calculation, community and cues: Public opinion on European integration. *European Union Politics, 6*(4), 419–443.

Hooghe, L., & Marks, G. (2009). A postfunctionalist theory of European integration: From permissive consensus to constraining dissensus. *British Journal of Political Science, 39*(1), 1–23.

Hurrelmann, A. (2007). European democracy, the 'permissive consensus', and the collapse of the EU Constitution. *European Law Journal, 13*(3), 343–359.

Hurrelmann, A. (2008). Constructing multilevel legitimacy in the European Union: A study of British and German media discourse. *Comparative European Politics, 6*(2), 190–211.

Hurrelmann, A., Gora, A., & Wagner, A. (2013). The legitimation of the European Union in the news media: Three treaty reform debates. *Journal of European Public Policy, 20*(4), 515–534.

Hurrelmann, A., Gora, A., & Wagner, A. (2015). The politicization of European integration: More than an elite affair? *Political Studies, 63*(1), 43–59.

Hurrelmann, A., Krell-Laluhová, Z., Nullmeier, F., Schneider, S., & Wiesner, A. (2009). Why the demo-cratic nation-state is still legitimate: A study of media discourses. *European Journal of Political Research, 48*(4), 483–515.

Hurrelmann, A., Schneider, S., & Steffek, J. (Eds.). (2007). *Legitimacy in an age of global politics.* Basingstoke: Palgrave Macmillan.

Hutter, S., & Grande, E. (2014). Politicizing Europe in the national electoral arena: A comparative analysis of five West European countries. *Journal of Common Market Studies, 52*(5), 1002–1018.

Imig, D. (2004). Contestation in the streets: European protest and the emerging Euro-polity. In G. Marks & M. R. Steenbergen (Eds.), *European integration and political conflict* (pp. 216–234). Cambridge: Cambridge University Press.

Kritzinger, S. (2003). The influence of the nation-state on individual support for the European Union. *European Union Politics, 4*(2), 219–241.

Laughland, J. (1998). *The tainted source: The undemocratic origins of the European idea.* London: Warner.

Lindberg, L. N., & Scheingold, S. A. (1970). *Europe's would-be polity: Patterns of change in the European Community.* Englewood Cliffs, NJ: Prentice-Hall.

Majone, G. (2005). *Dilemmas of European integration: The ambiguities and pitfalls of integration by stealth.* Oxford: Oxford University Press.

Martinotti, G., & Stefanizzi, S. (1995). Europeans and the nation state. In O. Niedermayer & R. Sinnott (Eds.), *Public opinion and internationalized governance* (pp. 163–189). Oxford: Oxford University Press.

McLaren, L. (2006). *Identity, interests, and attitudes to European integration.* Basingstoke: Palgrave Macmillan.

Moravcsik, A. (2006). What can we learn from the collapse of the European constitutional project? *Politische Vierteljahresschrift, 47*(2), 219–241.

Nonhoff, M., Gronau, J., Nullmeier, F., & Schneider, S. (2009). Die Politisierung internationaler Institutionen: Der Fall G8. *Zeitschrift für Internationale Beziehungen, 16*(2), 237–267.

Nullmeier, F., Biegón, D., Gronau, J., Nonhoff, M., Schmidtke, H., & Schneider, S. (2010). *Prekäre Legitimitäten: Rechtfertigung von Herrschaft in der postnationalen Konstellation.* Frankfurt: Campus.

Pakulski, J. (1986). Legitimacy and mass compliance: Reflections on Max Weber and Soviet-type societies. *British Journal of Political Science, 16*(1), 35–56.

Reus-Smit, C. (2007). International crises of legitimacy. *International Politics, 44*(2), 157–174.

Rixen, T., & Zangl, B. (2013). The politicization of international economic institutions in US public debates. *The Review of International Organizations, 8*(3), 363–387.

Rohrschneider, R. (2002). The democracy deficit and mass support for an EU-wide government. *American Journal of Political Science, 46*(2), 463–475.

Scharpf, F. W. (1994). Community and autonomy: Multi-level policy-making in the European Union. *Journal of European Public Policy, 1*(2), 219–242.

Scharpf, F. W. (2000). Interdependence and democratic legitimation. In S. J. Pharr & R. D. Putnam (Eds.), *Disaffected democracies: What's troubling the trilateral countries?* (pp. 101–120). Princeton, NJ: Princeton University Press.

Scharpf, F. W. (2009). Legitimacy in the multilevel European polity. *European Political Science Review, 1*(2), 173–204.

Schimmelfennig, F. (2014). European integration in the Euro crisis: The limits of postfunctionalism. *Journal of European Integration, 36*(3), 321–337.

Schmitter, P. C. (1969). Three neo-functional hypotheses about international integration. *International Organization, 23*(1), 161–166.

Schmitter, P. C. (1999). *How to democratize the European Union ... and why bother?* Lanham, MD: Rowman & Littlefield.

Schrag Sternberg, C. (2013). *The struggle for EU legitimacy: Public contestation, 1950–2005.* Basingstoke: Palgrave Macmillan.

Scicluna, N. (2012). EU constitutionalism in flux: Is the Eurozone crisis precipitating centralization or diffusion? *European Law Journal, 18*(4), 489–503.

Spoon, J.-J. (2012). How salient is Europe? An analysis of European election manifestos, 1979–2004. *European Union Politics, 13*(4), 558–579.

Statham, P., & Trenz, H. J. (2013). *The politicization of Europe: Contesting the constitution in the mass media*. London: Routledge.

Statham, P., & Trenz, H. J. (2015). Understanding the mechanisms of EU politicization: Lessons from the Eurozone crisis. *Comparative European Politics, 13*(3), 287–306.

Steffek, J. (2003). The legitimation of international governance: A discourse approach. *European Journal of International Relations, 9*(2), 249–275.

Steffek, J. (2007). Legitimacy in International Relations: From state compliance to citizen consensus. In A. Hurrelmann, S. Schneider, & J. Steffek (Eds.), *Legitimacy in an age of global politics* (pp. 175–192). Basingstoke: Palgrave Macmillan.

Thomassen, J. (Ed.). (2009). *The legitimacy of European integration after enlargement*. Oxford: Oxford University Press.

Van Ingelgom, V. (2014). *Integrating indifference: A comparative, qualitative and quantitative approach to the legitimacy of European integration*. Colchester: ECPR Press.

Weber, M. (1968). *Economy and society: An outline of interpretive sociology*. Berkeley: University of California Press.

Wendler, F. (2014). Justification and political polarization in national parliamentary debates on EU treaty reform. *Journal of European Public Policy, 21*(4), 549–567.

White, J. (2011). *Political allegiance after European integration*. Basingstoke: Palgrave Macmillan.

Zaum, D. (Ed.). (2013). *Legitimating international organizations*. Oxford: Oxford University Press.

Zürn, M. (2014). The politicization of world politics and its effects: Eight propositions. *European Political Science Review, 6*(1), 47–71.

Zürn, M., Binder, M., & Ecker-Ehrhardt, M. (2013). International authority and its politicization. *International Theory, 4*(1), 69–106.

Zürn, M., & Ecker-Ehrhardt, M. (Eds.). (2013). *Die Politisierung der Weltpolitik*. Frankfurt: Suhrkamp.

The public valuation of religion in global health governance: spiritual health and the faith factor

Tine Hanrieder

ABSTRACT
This article explores how the role of religion is evaluated in global health institutions, focusing on policy debates in the World Health Organization (WHO) and the World Bank. Drawing on Luc Boltanski and Laurent Thévenot's pragmatist approach to justification, I suggest that religious values are creative and worldly performances. The public value of religion is established through a two-pronged justification process, combining generalizing arguments with particularizing empirical tests. To substantiate the claim that abstraction alone does not suffice to create religious values in global public health, I compare the futile attempts of the 1980s to add 'spiritual health' to the WHO's mandate with the more recent creation of a 'faith factor' in public health. While the vague reference to some 'Factor X' inhibited the acceptance of spiritual health in the first case, in the second case, 'compassion' became a measurable and recognized religious value.

1. Introduction

In the words of Peter Piot, former director of the United Nations Programme on AIDS, the relationship between the United Nations (UN) and faith-based organizations (FBOs) is a 'history of culture clashes' (as cited in Grills, 2009, p. 507). Multilateral health institutions such as the World Health Organization (WHO), the World Bank or the United Nations Children's Fund here embody a modern 'world culture' based on the enlightenment values of science, rationalization, and liberal individualism (Barnett & Finnemore, 2005; Boli & Thomas, 1999). Especially in the case of health politics, this secular culture is expressed in a belief in medical progress and technical cooperation beyond political and ideological cleavages (see Staples, 2006, p. 134). However, 'religious' or 'faith-based' actors have time and again challenged the policies of secular multilateral health organizations (MHOs) on religious grounds.

Such confrontations are most prominent in the politics of HIV/AIDS, due to the stigmatization and moralization that this disease has provoked not only, but especially in religious communities. Yet, the culture clash between secular and religious claims has emerged repeatedly over the history of global health governance.[1] For example, in the post-Second World War decades, population control was one such contested policy field. A transnational epistemic community in favour of population policy, sponsored by private philanthropists such as the Ford and the Rockefeller Foundations, met strong opposition from the Catholic Church, which was not willing to accept birth control research and policy (Connelly, 2010). This Catholic opposition meant that, for a long time, the WHO long refrained from engaging with 'human reproduction' at all (Finkle & Crane, 1976). Another prominent example of faith-based opposition to multilateral health governance was the popular opposition that a sectarian preacher in Niger mobilized against the WHO's polio eradication campaign in 2003 (Masquelier, 2012). At present, an antagonism between religious tradition and medical progress is being articulated in the Ebola epidemic that broke out in West Africa in late 2013. A faith-based insistence on church gatherings and burial rituals has clashed with biomedical attempts at halting the spread of the highly lethal Ebola virus (Abramowitz et al., 2015).

Nevertheless, multilateral organizations are increasingly seeking to integrate the specific contributions of religious groups and organizations. They do so in acknowledgement of the fact that in the context of worldwide liberalization and the retreat of the state, space has been created for faith-based service providers in public health. In African countries, for example, between 30% and 70% of health services are estimated to be provided by FBOs (Grills, 2009, p. 509; see Section 4). MHOs like the WHO and the World Bank therefore are displaying a growing sensitivity to religious actors, support them financially, or even engage in collaborative projects (Grills, 2009). Hence, like other domains of global politics, global health is developing 'post-secular' tendencies that blur the line between the 'public political' and the 'private religious' realms (Barbato & Kratochwil, 2009). Crossing the established boundary between the realms of religious faith and public policy has become a central challenge for global health governance. This makes it an important, but thus far neglected domain for exploring a more general problem of public justification in world politics: The question of how previously 'private' values gain acceptance as 'public' arguments. Due to its long-standing association with the non-political sphere of private belief, religion's recent inroads into the global health discourse make it a particularly fruitful case for observing how public reasons are created in global politics.

In this paper, I tackle this problem by exploring how religious values are made *valuable* in the global health discourse. For this purpose, I draw on sociological valuation theory, and in particular, on the pragmatist approach to justification advanced by Boltanski and Thévenot (1999, 2006). I maintain that the creation of public worth is a practical as much as a theoretical endeavour. This holds for all values for which actors want to gain public acceptance. They need to be *theoretically* connected to general principles, but must also be *practically* connected to the social world in which their validity is claimed. This requires that values – religious or secular – need to be performed in critical 'tests' with the help of shared evaluative tools (Boltanski & Thévenot, 2006, p. 40). Public justification, thus, is based on a two-pronged evaluative operation: The connection of (religious) values to a *general principle* of worth, and the *performance* of these values through manifest objects. I will compare two attempts at mainstreaming religious values into the WHO's policies: The promotion of 'spiritual health' as an extension of the WHO's mandate in the 1980s, and the construction of 'religious health assets' for the work of MHOs since the 2000s. We will see that the vagueness and ambiguity of 'spiritual health' made many states suspicious of the term, and that the failure to create performances of spiritual health inhibited its public recognition in the WHO. By contrast, the creation of manifest religious health assets as worldly performances of the generic principle of 'compassion' enabled their successful inclusion in the global health discourse. This comparison empha-sizes that abstraction alone is not sufficient for establishing religious norms, and shows how a focus on historical practice and devices can enhance a fuller understanding of post-secular normative dynamics. Inspired by sociological evaluation theory, I explore how de-contextualization and re-contextualization are intertwined when 'transcendent' values 'go public'.

The analysis in this paper is exploratory, reconstructing two major discursive terrains on which religious values have surfaced in global health institutions.[2] The paper mainly draws on public policy documents produced by and in association with MHOs: These include records of debates and resolutions of governing bodies, and research reports and policy papers that indicate the public contestation or endorsement of 'religious values' – that is, values which are put forward by religious actors and organizations, and which are pub-licly declared to be of religious origin. Organizational documents express collectively negotiated and thus publicly accepted policy standards (see Neumann, 2007). Hence, in this paper, I do not speculate about whether the public endorsement of a religious value reflects the true beliefs of the actors involved, but only focus on what is collectively agreed. Likewise, I do not contribute to attempts to provide context-free and substantivist definitions of 'religion' and 'religious values'. Rather, the cases explored in this paper show how religion itself is produced in public discourses, and thus a socially constructed and historically variable term (Hurd, 2008, p. 16). I thus adopt an institutional definition of reli-gion: If an institution, actor or value is publicly declared to be religious, it will be analysed as religious, and the challenge is in understanding how its moral status is ascertained in the policies of presumably secular, multilateral organizations.

The paper is divided into three main sections. The following section discusses in more detail the valuation theoretical approach to public justification and specifies how this approach builds on, but also differs from, Habermasian notions of post-secular 'translation' as universalization (Section 2). I then reconstruct the failed attempts of the 1980s to make 'spiritual health' an integral part of the WHO's policies – a failure which was also due to the lack of concrete tests of the vague idea of some religious 'Factor X' (Section 3). Next, I investigate recent and more successful attempts at establishing the 'faith factor' in global public health, which are based on a combination of generalization and empirical tests (Section 4). The concluding section summarizes the argument and discusses the role of non-verbal performances and regional variation of religious values in global health governance.

2. Global governance and the making of public religious values

The UN system has long sustained a liberal order, which is based on Western values like human rights, democracy, the rule of law, and scientific rationality (Barnett & Finnemore, 2005). This order is also referred to as 'secular', because religion is confined to the private sphere, and thus kept outside of multilateral institutions. However, this conception came under renewed scrutiny at the turn of the millennium, when several developments appar-ently questioned the secular core of global governance. These developments were in parts violent, as in the case of the 2001 Al-Qaeda attacks, which sparked new debates about reli-gious fundamentalism – and thus about religious conflicts in world politics. But there was also a more peaceful revival of religion in different domains of (global) social policy. In the

U.S.A, the state–church separation began to blur domestically with the Welfare Reform Act of 1996,[3] and subsequently in foreign aid through the rise to power of evangelical and Pentecostal Christians. Under George W. Bush's presidency (2001–2009), the US Agency for International Development was mandated to provide assistance for specifically religious institutions and purposes, and the President's Emergency Plan for AIDS Relief (PEPFAR) had a religiously motivated component of abstinence promotion (Clarke, 2007, pp. 82–83). Multilateral agencies like the World Bank as well developed partnerships with religious organizations (Belshaw, Calderisi, & Sudgen, 2001). Finally, faith promotion activities by non-Western states such as Saudi Arabia, and more generally, the rise of non-liberal powers seems to question the secular foundations of the global governance system (Clarke, 2007, pp. 83–84). Hence, the specific, post-Christian secularism of the West no longer seems to be taken for granted (Hurd, 2008).

These developments have led scholars of international norms to conceive of global institutions and the UN system as 'post-secular'. As Barbato and Kratochwil (2009) argue, liberal global governance institutions are moving toward a new order where religious claims are no longer excluded, but are entering and transforming the political discourse. The proponents of religious norms may be private faith-based groups and NGOs that participate in the UN (Haynes, 2013), but also state representatives who sponsor religious norms (Bettiza & Dionigi, 2015). These developments have fuelled scholarly interest in so-called intercultural dialogue in international politics, and in the dynamics through which religious norms are (becoming) part of the international normative order (Barnett, 2011). To make sense of this process, Bettiza and Dionigi have put forward the concept of institutional translation. Following Jürgen Habermas' reflections on post-secularism, they conceptualize post-secular translations as a filtering process through which religious claims are decontextualized to become globally acceptable (Bettiza & Dionigi, 2015). As I will discuss in the following, their idea of 'post-Western' institutional translation significantly widens the conceptual toolbox of International Relations (IR) norms research, yet its underlying 'subtractive' view of religion only provides a limited account of the translation process (2.1). Therefore, I bring in the French pragmatist approach to justification to point out the equally important thickening process involved in public evaluation: The creative construction of worldly tests for intangible ethical values (2.2).

2.1. Beyond a thin view of religious translation

It is only recently that IR scholars began to theorize how religious claims are debated in world politics. Constructivist norms research in IR has long focused on the spread of liberal values across the globe (e.g. Keck & Sikkink, 1998; Risse, Ropp, & Sikkink, 1999). The thrust of this research is universalistic. It is based on the assumption that the better argument is ultimately on the side of Western values (Deitelhoff, 2009). Arguing against this universalism, a host of contributions emphasized that the universal application of Western norms may be contested and that 'global' norms inevitably change when they are applied in different 'local' contexts (Acharya, 2004; Wiener, 2007). Nonetheless, such adaptation processes are mostly conceived of as instances of an overall diffusion story, according to which Western values remain the source of global normative change.

Against this backdrop, Bettiza and Dionigi (2015) have heralded a 'third generation' of norms research, which shifts attention to the norm-promotion activities of non-Western actors. They focus in particular on claims by religious actors, that is, claims which have traditionally been excluded from the liberal political discourse, but which are becoming increasingly relevant in a multipolar and post-Western world society (Bettiza & Dionigi, 2015, p. 2). Their analysis of the 'post-secular' entry of religious norms into previously secular debates is based on Habermas' (2006) concept of institutional translation. This concept suggests that, in order to be accepted in an official political discourse, a religious argument needs to leave some of its contextual normative luggage behind. It ought to 'transcend particularism' in order to be acceptable 'beyond the context in which it originated' (Bettiza & Dionigi, 2015, p. 3). This, in the authors' view, is achieved through a process of *abstraction*. In line with Habermas's (2006, p. 10) image of an argumentative 'filter' and also citing Walzer's (1994) metaphor of 'thin' versus 'thick' moral arguments, the authors theorize post-secular translations as argumentative 'thinning'. Hence, they propose that only religious arguments that are freed of idiosyncratic and particularistic legacies can have an impact on political discourses within 'secular global governance institutions' (Bettiza & Dionigi, 2015, p. 3). The idea of post-secular translation is thus imagined as a transition from a 'thickly' integrated community of faith where religious values are not questioned, to a normatively 'thinner' but more universal public domain, a domain where only those values that can be accepted across religions pass. However, this is not a one-way adaptation. The secular interlocutors also have to learn. Translation in the Habermasian sense is a dialogical process through which the parties converge on a mutually accepted reinterpretation of a religious claim. The outcome of this dialogue will differ from its context of origin, in that it is more abstract than the original norm. To be successful, it has to be marked by 'vagueness and malleability' (Bettiza & Dionigi, 2015, p. 3). Hence, to succeed, institutional translation must converge on very generic liberal values, values that can be more easily shared across cultures. This idea that vagueness is not an impediment but a condition of successful agreements has also been stressed by IR norms researchers who found that leaving some room for interpretation facilitates international agreements (see Steffek, 2005).

The concept of institutional translation extends IR norms research to the neglected terrain of dialogues about religious norms in global governance institutions, and sensitizes scholars to the complex and creative dialogue that post-Western engagements require. The focus on 'filtering' and 'thinning' processes, however, only allows for a limited view of how religious claims are publicly debated. I want to point out two significant limitations of the abstraction-centric view of translation. The *first* limitation is that the idea of thinning presupposes an asymmetry between a more general or 'universal' secular normative order on the one side, and more 'particularistic' and culturally situated religious claims on the other. Thinning implies that religious norms originate in a shared lifeworld of believers, which is marked by contextual, cultural features, but are purified through entering general political debates. Hence, Habermasian translations are based on a dichotomy between 'pure' and general public reason, and 'thick' additional religious concerns. This dichotomy resembles what Charles Taylor has described as 'subtraction stories' about religion: A view according to which the secular is what remains when religion is lifted (Taylor, 2007, p. 22; see Casanova, 2011, pp. 55–56). The secular then becomes a pre-set category that does not demand further investigation, or even sociological scrutiny. Yet, as Zwingel (2012) has elaborated in the context of the global women's rights discourse, 'global' norms translation is a multi-sited and not a teleological or linear process. From the normative pluralist perspective that she adopts, the seemingly decontextualized sphere of global institutions is itself a cultural context among others, and not the hierarchical sender or impartial arbiter of 'local' cultural values (Zwingel, 2012, p. 116). By thus provincializing the values of multilateral institutions, she highlights that the liberal institutions of global governance are themselves culturally thick and situated (classically Barnett & Finnemore, 2004), and thus suggests to scrutinize the concrete practices through which 'global' values are forged in multilateral institutions.

This also points to the *second* limitation of the concept of thinning, namely its neglect of the creative process of norms construction that is involved in each normative dialogue. Even though the creative construction of social values is a core claim of the constructivist research agenda, the thinning idea provides only a one-sided notion of social construction. It focuses on what is abandoned when (religious) norms travel, yet not on what is added in the process. Answering the question of how religious values are embedded in liberal institutions requires that we also analyse the 'thickening' operations that connect religious reasons to new (multilateral) contexts. If we take seriously the claim that the world is becoming multipolar and normatively pluralist, then we also need to focus our analysis on the innovative and creative component of religious arguments.

2.2. The public construction of religious values – from abstraction to devices

To understand the creative construction of religious values, the sociology of evaluation offers useful analytical tools. Evaluation studies focus not only on the theoretical reasoning, but also on the worldly performances that make public justification possible (cf. Lamont, 2012). This becomes evident in the pragmatist account of justification developed by Boltanski and Thévenot, which provides a decidedly empirical take on public justification as a creative social practice (Boltanski & Thévenot, 2006; see Barnes, 2001; Kornprobst, 2014). From this pragmatist perspective, normative agreement requires both an abstract generalizing principle, and a manifest 'critical test' through which the agreement can be socially stabilized. To stick with the authors' terminology, a public argument is based on a justificatory 'order of worth' as much as on a 'common world' of objects, roles, and evaluative instruments through which agreement is stabilized. This notion of the 'common world' thus forces us to look at the mundane and institutional means through which actors create shared normative understandings. Such an approach is particularly suitable for capturing how previously 'private' religious values 'go public' due to its dual emphasis on *context* and the need for *manifestation* of normative agreements.[4]

First, justification as a shared practice is contextual and situational. It does not demand a definite and universal answer to normative disputes, but contextually acceptable agreements (Boltanski & Thévenot, 1999). This context sensitivity is intrinsically tied to the insight of normative pluralism, that is, a worldview that does not presuppose that normative conflicts can be settled by recourse to one ultimate principle. Rather, critical actors can and do draw on a diverse set of principles, and it is their creative achievement to tie a specific general value to a particular justification problem (Boltanski & Thévenot, 2006, p. 33; see Kornprobst, 2011). In the multipolar and 'post-secular world' that IR scholars seek to understand today, it is crucial to understand how certain general principles are tied to specific contexts. Public justifications situate abstract values in concrete settings, thereby producing a contingent and particular answer to an abstract normative debate. This creative endeavour requires that 'thickening' operations and thus discursive contextualization be performed in addition to abstract debate. Contextualization is practically a routine operation in global norms development, used by both non-state norm advocates and by state diplomats. References to existing non-binding declarations like, for example, the 1978 Alma Ata Declaration on Primary Health Care, and binding norms such international human rights treaties, are commonplace in global debates. New normative claims are thereby connected to an evolving body of international norms and made historically concrete.

Second, in addition to discursive contextualization (see Payne, 2001), justification practices involve techniques of *manifestation* through which intangible values are made tangible.[5] Boltanski and Thévenot (2006, p. 33) describe public justification as the coordinated *performance* of critical 'tests'. Through the creation and performance of manifest tests, abstract ideas are transferred into a shared evaluative repertoire that stabilizes meaning and moral worth. In doing so, people involve worldly objects or 'things' in their arguments – artefacts such as technologies of visualization and measurement, symbols, or institutional roles – on which public agreement can rest (Boltanski & Thévenot, 2006, p. 40). This also applies to otherwise private and esoteric questions of faith and spirituality. As the authors elaborate with regard to the moral status derived from 'inspiration', the task of publicly evaluating what otherwise remains a private virtue is particularly challenging. To make this possible, specific symbols and role expectations are brought into play that allow for a person's publicly recognized status as 'inspired' (Boltanski & Thévenot, 2006, pp. 83–88; footnote 21). Hence, the practice view of public justification as social evaluation makes it clear that thinning and thickening are always intertwined in public discourse. Next to invoking a general principle on which agreement can be based, agents construct a practical test that performs a shared value in a specific context, or use historical analogies as shortcuts to make abstract values concrete. Devices and indicators are central to the construction of shared values that can be publicly accepted.[6] Evaluative devices are regularly used and produced in global politics. For example, the bureaucracies of international organizations, state agencies, or well-equipped non-state organizations develop assessment tools for measuring values such as political freedom, transparency, economic development or stability, and they increasingly use rankings that operationalize what are 'good' national health systems, 'creditworthy states' or 'environmentally sustainable' commodities (Cooley & Snyder, 2015; Dingwerth & Pattberg, 2009). They also develop new elaborate rituals such as the practice of 'truth telling' as a means to perform 'justice' and 'peace' (Renner, 2013). Thereby, 'universal' values such as peace, fairness or sustainability, which would otherwise remain thin and vague, take on manifest meanings that can be measured and drawn on in real-world interactions.

This operation of turning abstract values into social realities is of particular relevance to the global recognition of 'transcendent' religious norms. In the following, I will therefore use the dual lens of 'thin' abstraction plus 'thick' contextualization to reconstruct two attempts to translate religious values into global health institutions: The debate about adding 'spiritual health' to the mandate of the WHO, which took place in the 1980s (Section 3), and the attempt to establish faith as a determinant of health, which started in the new millennium (Section 4). In the first case, vagueness alone proved insufficient to make spiritual health acceptable. In the second, the manifest evaluative repertoire of 'religious health assets' elevated the moral status of faith in multilateral health institutions.

3. Spiritual health and the failure to mainstream 'Factor X'

During the first decades of its existence, the WHO did not explicitly endorse religious values. It followed a secular and modernist agenda that was formulated by medical and public health professionals (Staples, 2006, p. 134). The organization also upheld its abstention from religion when collaborating with religious actors, for example, in its work on the primary health care (PHC) agenda. PHC had become the WHO's main policy paradigm in the early 1970s, as the organization shifted its attention from high-tech biomedicine to basic, community-driven, and inter-sectoral health policies. Notably, the WHO designed this policy shift in close collaboration with a religious actor, namely the Christian Medical Commission of the World Council of Churches (Litsios, 2004). Furthermore, the WHO's director-general Halfdan Mahler propagated the PHC agenda and its slogan 'Health for All by the Year 2000' with 'missionary zeal' (Cueto, 2004, p. 1865). In retrospect, Mahler (2008) would consider the PHC movement and its legendary International Conference on Primary Health Care, which was held in Alma Ata in 1978, as an 'intellectual and spiritual awakening'. Still, he also stressed that 'spiritual' here was not to be understood 'in the religious sense [...] but in the sense that people wanted to accomplish something great' (Mahler, 2008). In fact, the PHC policies that were developed in the 1970s did not refer to questions of faith or religion. They encouraged the deployment of simply trained health workers, prevention and education measures, and community and rural development, and thus were designed as secular social policies.[7]

The secular approach of PHC was problematized, however, when a group of norm proponents of different religious backgrounds attempted to make 'spiritual health' an integral part of the PHC agenda as well. Yet, as we will see in the following, the advocacy for 'spiritual health' got lost in a process of abstraction. Its proponents failed to provide manifest tests of what was also called 'Factor X', and thus did not manage to establish spiritual health as a component of the PHC agenda.

3.1. The spiritual 'Factor X' and its interfaith alliance

The need for the WHO to address questions of spiritual health was first raised by the Indian delegate to the Executive Board in 1978, the year when the international PHC conference was to be held in Alma Ata, Kazakhstan. The delegate, Desh Bandu Bisht, suggested amending the definition of health provided by the WHO constitution, which reads that health is 'a state of complete physical, mental and social well-being and not merely the absence of disease or infirmity' (WHO, 2006). Drawing on 'Indian thinking through the ages', Bisht argued that the WHO definition of health should be enlarged to include the 'spiritual' dimension, because otherwise, there would be hardly any difference between the vitality of animals ('a pack of wolves') and the higher and 'more subtle' faculties of humans (Bisht, 1985, p. vii). Still, the delegate also conceded that the term 'spiritual' might not be equally acceptable across cultures. He therefore proposed that for the time being, the missing dimension should be referred to as a hypothetical 'Factor X' (Bisht, 1985, pp. 5–10). While this proposal was not taken up at the Board's 1978 session (Al Khayat, 1997, p. 224), it was followed up on by a larger group of countries who jointly sponsored a resolution at the 1983 World Health

Assembly (WHA), the WHO's annual member state meeting and supreme decision making body.

The draft resolution of 1983 was sponsored by a religiously diverse, though dominantly Islamic coalition of 22 countries.[8] It was entitled 'The spiritual dimension in health care programmes' and stated that a 'spiritual dimension' was not only implicit in the WHO definition of health, but also crucial for attaining the goals of PHC and Health for All (Al Khayat, 1997, pp. 221–222). The draft resolution therefore 'requested' that the director-general mainstream spiritual health in the PHC approach, that is, he was asked 'to take the spiritual dimension into consideration in the preparation and development of primary health care programmes aimed at the attainment of the goal of health for all by the year 2000' (Al Khayat, 1997, p. 222). This proposal thus amounted to extending the mandate of the WHO to the provision of spiritual health. It was first discussed in the WHA's Committee A, which is responsible for policy matters, and then brought to the plenary assembly. These discussions, however, were marked by confusion and disagreement about the meaning of 'spiritual health', an ambiguity that made many country delegations suspicious of the concept's value for policy-making. On the one side, delegates from the sponsoring countries such as Kuwait and Yemen emphasized that spiritual health was an important antidote to the 'materialism' of their times (Al Khayat, 1997, pp. 222, 223), and a delegate of the United Arab Emirates stressed that the resolution was relevant to individuals of any religious belief (Al Khayat, 1997, p. 223). On the other side, opposing delegations, for example from the Soviet countries, found any potential reference to 'religious aspects' unacceptable for countries where the state and the church had been deliberately separated (Al Khayat, 1997, p. 222). Prompted by the Indian delegate to give his opinion on the matter, the director-general proposed to refer the matter to the Executive Board to allow for an in-depth discussion and develop a consensus on the wording (Al Khayat, 1997, p. 224). Still, since a majority of the committee members voted in favour of the draft resolution, it was further debated in the plenary assembly.

In the WHA's plenary, however, the confusion and disagreement about the purpose of the resolution proved insurmountable. For example, a delegate from Mozambique pointed out that all the potential meanings of 'spiritual health' put forward in the discussions – among others 'mental health; medical ethics; respect for each people's culture; health education; and so on' – were already part of the PHC agenda (World Health Organization Regional Office for the Eastern Mediterranean [WHO ROEM], 1996, p. 270). By contrast, the specific value of 'spiritual' health had not yet been explicated, so that the concept was not 'mature enough' to be agreed upon (WHO ROEM, 1996, p. 270). Other delegates, for example from Italy and from Gabon, also held that further clarification was needed because at that point in time, the concept was hard to comprehend at all (WHO ROEM, 1996, p. 272). Hence, 'vagueness and malleability' (Bettiza & Dionigi, 2015, p. 3) turned out to be an obstacle to public consensus, and led to a postponement of the matter to next year's Executive Board (WHO ROEM, 1996, p. 274).[9]

3.2. Watering down and referring back to the periphery – the failure to globalize 'Factor X'

By the time the Executive Board reconsidered the spiritual health issue, the director-general had developed a compromise formula. In his three-page background paper,

'Global strategy for Health for All be the Year 2000: The spiritual dimension', the director-general (DG) elaborated on the concept 'spiritual', associating it with 'a *phenomenon that is not material in nature but belongs to the realm of ideas that have arisen in the minds of human beings, particularly ennobling ideas*' (WHO, 1998b, p. 1, emphasis in original). The paper suggested that political ideals could well lead to 'vast material changes', for example, the abolition of slavery – or the PHC-related strategy of Health for All, which was informed by 'such humane qualities as a sense of decency, empathy with the world's health [sic] underprivileged, compassion, and the desire for social justice regarding health' (WHO, 1998b, p. 2). The document avoided, however, proposing specific additional measures for furthering spiritual health through the PHC agenda. To the contrary, the DG emphasized that while 'the material component [of PHC] can be 'provided', the non-material or spiritual one cannot' (WHO, 1998b, p. 3). Thereby, the DG outright rejected the draft resolution's 'request' that he integrate spiritual values within the WHO's Primary Health Care strategies. The Executive Board endorsed this document without further public discussion and forwarded it to the 1984 Assembly (WHO, 1985, p. 5).

The 37th WHA adopted a resolution that followed the wording proposed by the secretariat, and that endorsed the points made in the DG's report. Instead of mainstreaming spiritual health in the WHO's policies, the resolution merely 'invite[d]' member states to 'consider including in their strategies for health for all a spiritual dimension [...] in accordance with their cultural and religious patterns' (WHO, 1985, pp. 5–6). Thereby, the spiritual dimension was effectively deflected by the WHO secretariat and referred back to the countries, which were free to follow up on the issue or not.

In summary, the fate of this initiative shows that despite support across religious denominations, the vague idea of some 'Factor X' proved too thin to successfully translate spirituality into the central organs of the WHO. Its vagueness and ambiguity did not make it easier to add spiritual health to the WHO mandate. To the contrary, it fuelled suspicion of the meaning and purpose of the term, and many states refused to support what looked like an open-ended and risky norm-creation process. In the years that followed, a few decentralized initiatives in two of the WHO's six regional organizations pursued the agenda of spiritual health further. In the South East Asian region, a workshop held in Bangalore in 1985 explored the health value of 'Factor X' from the perspective of different faiths. In the 1990s, the WHO's Eastern Mediterranean regional office launched a publication series entitled 'Health Education through Religion' (e.g. Al Khayat, 1997; Ottersen et al., 2014). The series was supported by the so-called Amman Declaration on 'Health Promotion through Islamic Lifestyles', which was jointly published by the regional office and the Islamic Educational, Scientific and Cultural Organization (WHO ROEM, 1996). The region also sponsored another attempt at extending the WHO definition of health to include a 'dynamic' and 'spiritual' dimension (WHO, 1998a, p. 2; see WHO, 1998b, pp. 40–43). Yet again, the initiative was not taken up, and the WHO definition of health has remained unchanged. Until today, the WHO headquarters and its central governing bodies have shied away from making spiritual health a part of WHO policy. Factor X has thus far not been up-streamed to the level of centralized policy-making.

It is, of course, only with the benefit of hindsight that we can see how a lack of specification and 'thickening' led to the dismissal of 'spiritual' health as part of the WHO's work. It remains a counterfactual question, whether more resourceful norm entrepreneurs would have come up with a more successful campaign than the diffuse promotion of 'Factor X'.[10]

We thus do not know whether it would have been possible at all to overcome the doubts of many member states through an interpretation of spiritual health that was acceptable to the sponsors and to the sceptics alike, and to build a sufficiently powerful coalition through a differently interpreted 'spiritual health' norm. Here, a first step can only consist of exploring the norm construction process in its specific historical context (see introduction to this special issue): Quite in line with Habermas' 'translation' proposition, the sceptical states were indeed suspicious that unwanted 'religious' baggage might travel with the unspecific concept of 'spiritual health' (WHO, 1985). Vagueness looked risky because it was too open for interpretation, not seeming like an opportunity to strike a 'cheap' and unspecific agreement that no one is against, and that hurts no one at the same time. Yet, from an interpretive viewpoint, what this debate about 'spiritual health' also reveals is that in order to convince the sceptics and diffuse their suspicions, a *particular* rather than a universal interpretation must be offered: An interpretation that rules out disputed content through disambiguation and a more concrete manifestation of the meaning of religious health values. Such an operation of making religious health values more specific and thus *particular* can be observed in the more recent agenda of evaluating the 'faith factor' in global health.

4. Tests of religion's health value: religious health assets and the faith factor

The 2000s saw the making of new concepts through which religious values could be acknowledged in global health policy. At a time of growing interest in the role of religion in world politics in general, and in development in particular, a range of formalized interfaith initiatives started contributing to the renewed translation effort. One important player here was the World Faith Development Dialogue (WFDD), founded in 1999 through a joint initiative of the Archbishop of Canterbury and World Bank President James D. Wolfensohn. Starting as an informal meeting between World Bank experts and representatives of nine major world religions, the WFDD quickly grew into a formal institution in which myriad religious organizations and development agencies were involved. Its governance was soon decoupled from the World Bank to ensure the independence of both institutions (Marshall, 2001, pp. 350–353). The WFDD serves as a forum for exchanging ideas about poverty, development or health, and about approaches to dealing with these issues by bringing in religious perspectives. In collaboration with the Tony Blair Faith Foundation, the WFDD has developed concepts for evaluating faith work in global health, particularly in Africa (WFDD, 2012). This endeavour has been joined by the Center for Interfaith Action on Global Poverty (see CIFA, 2010), and by the African Religious Health Assets Programme (ARHAP), which was created in 2002 and re-launched as the International Religious Health Assets Programme in 2012.[11]

These initiatives undertook studies and delivered reports to multilateral organizations such as the WHO (ARHAP, 2006), and to major Western philanthropists such as the Bill and Melinda Gates Foundation (Schmid, Thomas, Olivier, & Cochrane, 2008), in order to make religion valuable for multilateral organizations working on global health. They did so through a detailed mapping of tangible health services provided by religious entities

(Section 4.1), and by creating cognitive tools for testing the worth of the intangible 'faith factor' in public health (Section 4.2).

4.1. The public value of religious health assets

Attempts to revalue the worth of religion in global health have mostly been centred on the African continent, and especially the countries in sub-Saharan Africa. Donors and multilateral organizations have become interested in the health activities of religious entities,[12] because these apparently make up an important share of health services in these regions, and play an important part in the life worlds of 'the poor' (Narayan, 2000). Interfaith initiatives have strongly contributed to documenting the presence of health services provided by religious entities, by geographically mapping infrastructures and conducting surveys about the role of religion in the health concerns of individuals. For example, ARHAP provided a detailed study of so-called 'health-promoting religious assets' in Lesotho and Zambia, focusing in particular on HIV/AIDS programmes in these countries (ARHAP, 2006, p. 1). The focus on AIDS was an important move, because more than any other domains of health work, the HIV/AIDS pandemic had long been associated with religiously motivated stigmatization, denial, or the refusal of religious health agencies to distribute condoms.

The geographical mapping exercise of ARHAP focused on 'tangible' religious health assets or RHAs, meaning the physical 'infrastructures' provided by religious organizations, groups and individuals. These are, for example, not only hospitals, health centres and private practices, but also schools and other education providers and entities engaged in prevention and counselling (ARHAP, 2006, pp. 41–45). While containing caveats due to missing data and the need for further research, the study concluded that, on average, 40% of health services in sub-Saharan were provided by religious entities (ARHAP, 2006, p. 46) – a number that is in line with earlier studies of African countries, which came up with figures between 30% and 70%. ARHAP's detailed mapping exercise contributed to making visible the health work of religious actors, which is often not accounted for in public budgets due to their independent organization and funding. This mapping was endorsed in a 2008 WHO publication that stressed the importance of FBOs for PHC (WHO, 2008).[13]

Hence, the numbers and geographical maps helped to document the 'public value' of religious health work, especially in countries where governmental services were utterly deficient. The WHO secretariat endorsed this value by proposing policies on how local and national governments could systematically tap this public value and partner with religious actors to deliver PHC (WHO, 2008, pp. 19–22).[14] This recognition, though not reflected in an official WHA resolution, still goes far beyond the strictly secular stance that the WHO displayed in the debates about spiritual health outlined above. However, the focus on material infrastructures and services keeps a safe distance from religious ideologies and normative claims, and thus from what religious actors refer to as their 'intangible' RHAs. Recognizing material services provided by churches, thus, does not question the secular values on the basis of which this recognition is granted. Yet, the translation process went further, through the invention of specific devices for assessing religious worth in global health. For, in addition to the physical mapping, the RHA agenda has produced new evaluative tools through which the intangible value of religion for health is made visible in secular organizations.

4.2. Creating tests of the 'faith factor'

To assess the value of religious health services, an increasing number of studies have sought proof not only of their general effectiveness and functionality,[15] but also of religion's 'comparative advantage' vis-à-vis secular health services. These endeavours have been undertaken by interfaith agencies and WHO staff, but most importantly by World Bank staff, who have developed specific indicators and measurements of the faith factor (e.g. Coulombe & Wodon, 2013; Narayan, 2000; Olivier & Wodon, 2012). Their notion of the distinct added value of religious services here goes beyond the idea that they enhance the 'cultural sensitivity' (Schmid et al., 2008, p. 24) of medicine. Rather, the focus is on the so-called 'intangible' benefits of religions for health. A host of partially overlapping lists of such advantages has been put forward, which thereby aim to conceptualize the intangible health value of religion. The proposed assets here range from the values of 'prayer', 'commitment/sense of duty', or a 'sacred space in a polluted world' (Schmid et al., 2008, p. 23), to claims that religion provides a distinctly 'holistic perspective on human wellbeing' and that faith leaders enjoy a particular 'credibility and trust' in their communities (CIFA, 2010, p. 4; see also McGilvray, 1981). Hence, endeavours have intensified to estimate the value of the 'faith factor' for public health.

These attempts to translate the health value of religion for secular MHOs have involved parallel thinning and thickening operations. On the one hand, general concepts have been developed that serve as *abstractions* from specific faiths and particular denominations, thus proposing a generic notion of 'religion' that is believed to be applicable to different faiths and communities – and that distinguishes religion from secular, biomedical approaches to health. In particular, the general ideal of 'compassion' for the sick and vulnerable has been singled out as the generic value of religion for health – and as a value that faith-based actors display to an even greater extent than other medical or humanitarian professionals. For example, in the 2008 WHO document on religious actors and PHC, 'compassion' is identified as 'the universal attribute of faith' (WHO, 2008, p. 11). Each of the major religions, it is argued, 'recognizes the care of others as a divine calling' (WHO, 2008, p. 11). Evidently, such an altruistic inspiration is not tangible in itself, because is refers to inner motivations and spiritual attitudes. Thus, to enable a *public* valuation of religion's transcendent values, a range of studies have 'thickened' the concept through various indicators. In particular, two indicators have been emphasized in recent studies. First, these studies test faith-based compassion via the 'greater commitment' of health workers or volunteers in religious facilities (cf. WFDD, 2012, pp. 67–68; see WHO, 2008, p. 11). World Bank experts have, for example, compared the wages of health staff in religious and non-religious entities – and found preliminary evidence that at least in Ghana, religious commitment seems to be at work, because in religious facilities, staff were paid below the market wage. Nevertheless, and also despite the fact that the religious facilities also charged less for their services than other facilities, their health indicators were above average (Narayan, 2000). Hence, commitment is valued as a distinct 'faith factor' that demonstrably improves the quality of health services.[16]

A related second specification of the faith factor points out that compassion means caring for the poor. Hence, the 2003 World Bank study by Reinikka and Svensson stressed that religious service providers in Uganda provided more services to the poor, at lower prices, but without compromising on quality (Narayan, 2000). The idea that religious actors 'have special reach to the poor, rural, and other vulnerable groups' (WFDD, 2012, p. 66) has now become firmly established among global health and development actors. It informs the policies and self-presentations of agencies such as PEPFAR and World Vision (WFDD, 2012, p. 66), and underlies ongoing research efforts at measuring and quantifying the faith factor in global health (Coulombe & Wodon, 2013). While it is not predefined that an 'effect' of this factor will be demonstrated in each study of religious health assets, the existence of a manifest test of these assets helps to give them reality, and make religion a public value in global health.

Hence, through such measurements of the abstract ideal of compassion, the 'religious value' of compassion has become public and performable in global health. The idea that religious inspiration can improve health services has thereby become acceptable for MHOs, and it has begun to replace the ingrained suspicion of religion as an irrational factor that jeopardizes medical progress. This revaluation has been based on abstraction as much as on particularization. The creation of a generic, 'interfaith' concept of compassion as defining an entire 'faith sector' here has been as important as specific tests of this compassion in concrete health services. This public valuation of the faith factor in global health thus illustrates how thinning and thickening operations are intertwined in post-secular translations of religious values for global public policy.

5. Conclusion

This paper has investigated the public evaluation of religion in global health governance. I have analysed policy discourses in and around multilateral organizations through which the health value of religion has entered the secular domain of medicine and public health, focusing in particular on two such discourses: The debates about including the provision of 'spiritual health' in the mandate of the WHO since the 1980s, and debates about the value of the 'faith factor' in religious health services, which started in the new millennium. Combining the Habermasian idea of post-secular translation with pragmatist approaches to evaluative performances, I have argued that the public valuation of religion is a two-pronged process. On the one hand, it is based on the abstractions through which religious values are transformed into generic concepts that are compatible with secular discourses. On the other hand, it requires concretizations through which religious values become manifest and 'testable' in public debates. Only when the two operations of thinning and thickening are combined can previously *private* religious values become part of *public* justification. This also helps to understand why the abstract concept of spiritual health has gained far less traction than concrete assessments of the faith factor in public health. The previously vague 'Factor X' of the spiritual health debate has become a measurable and 'valu-able' concept through new measurements of the 'faith factor'.

The analysis provided here implies that post-secular valuations are eminently creative and potentially transformative processes. We have seen that to forge public understanding about religious values, new generic understandings of 'religion' as 'compassion' have been created, and new tests have been designed that specify the meaning of compassion and inspiration in global health. Hence, the concepts of religion and faith are themselves not fixed or primordial categories, but they gain their meaning and reality through ongoing justification efforts. In the words of practice theory, the value of religion in global (health) governance is a creative performance.

While this paper has centred on global policy debates as they unfolded in policy documents in and around multilateral organizations, future studies could extend this perspective to other sites, and to other performances of religions values. For example, the reconstruction of the spiritual health debate in the WHO has shown the inter-regional variation of this debate. While the WHO's regional offices in South East Asia and the Eastern Mediterranean have taken up the problem of spiritual health in regional contexts, other regions and the WHO's headquarters have abstained from engaging with the concept. Hence, different regional and institutional sites might produce different variations of religious themes in public policy, a dimension which has not been captured in this paper's focus on international organizations' metropolitan headquarters and centralized policy discourses. Given that public valuations are contextual and situated performances, exploring this variety can further contribute to understanding the careers of post-secular values in global health.

Likewise, future studies should explore performances other than textual performances and verbal constructions of critical tests of religious worth. Inter-religious and 'religion-development' dialogues are also tempo-spatial performances, for example, in globally broadcasted summits of faith and development leaders. These are publicly staged and entail ceremonies, rituals, and visual representations of what religion, health, or development entail. Visual analyses of these performances and their presentation through pictures or films can thus productively complement the text-based approach presented in this article. Such an approach can help us to identify how the location of religious and secular actors in public space and their physical association with value-laden symbols construct the public value of religion. An extension of the analysis to the visual dimension of public justification can generate insight into the ways in which physical performances support, complement, or maybe also counteract the creation of religious values on the global policy stage.

Notes

1. 'Global' health governance is usually distinguished from a presumably preceding world of 'international' health governance, to indicate the growing importance of non-state actors in addition to purely interstate institutions such as the WHO. In this contribution, I will use the more encompassing term 'global health governance' for the entire spectrum of cross-border health cooperation.
2. Other attempts to create religious health values might be found in biomedical circles, where, for example, the concept of 'religious coping' has gained considerable traction (see Pargament, Koenig, & Perez, 2000).
3. The Act allowed for welfare service delivery by faith-based organizations, and enabled them to receive government funding (Clarke, 2007, p. 82).
4. Evidently, the concepts of 'public' and 'private' are themselves not stable but take on different meanings in different contexts (cf. Casanova, 1994, pp. 40–66). In this article, I adopt an institutional perspective and consider that public values are those that are accepted in multilateral institutions.

5. See also Birnbaum (2015) on techniques of making religion measurable (or 'recognizable') in the case of postcolonial nation-building.
6. Of course, the use of devices can also fail and they do not automatically stabilize normative agreement. To borrow from Maria Birnbaum's terminology, they help to make values 'recognizable' (or acceptable), yet they do not guarantee their acceptance (Birnbaum, 2015).
7. On the origins and substance of PHC cf. Cueto (2004) and Litsios (2002).
8. The proponents of the resolution were Bahrain, Botswana, Chile, Democratic Yemen, Egypt, Kenya, Kuwait, Malawi, Mauritania, Morocco, Oman, Qatar, Saudi Arabia, Somalia, Sudan, Swaziland, Syrian Arab Republic, Tunisia, United Arab Emirates, Venezuela, Yemen, and Zambia (Al Khayat, 1997, p. 221). Curiously, India was not a co-sponsor, but participated in the WHA debates about the draft resolution, see below.
9. Of 113 members present and voting on the decision to postpone the matter, 80 voted for, 33 against, and 12 abstained (WHO ROEM, 1996, p. 274).
10. I thank an anonymous referee for raising this important question about the general prospects for a spiritual health campaign in the 1980s' constellation.
11. See http://www.irhap.uct.ac.za/about_history.php (retrieved 27 May 2015).
12. The term 'religious entities' refers not only to formal religious organizations, but also to self-organized groups and, in some cases, individuals (cf. ARHAP, 2006, p. 43).
13. This publication complemented the WHO's (2008) World Health Report *Primary health care – now more than ever* (Schmid et al., 2008), which sought to revive the PHC concept 40 years after the Alma Ata conference.
14. Among other assets, partnerships with FBOs were, for example, conceived as means to complement government services, bring in external donor money, or tap community resources and capacities (WHO, 2008, p. 19).
15. An overview of general effectiveness studies is provided in (WFDD, 2012, pp. 56–64).
16. Notably, this idea of using intrinsic motivation and commitment for public tests of religious values is similar to the tests of 'inspiration' that Boltanski and Thévenot (2006, p. 88) describe in their reflections on the inspired order of worth: Inspired actors here are those who do not strive for mundane rewards and not even 'recognition from others', but who pursue their ideals 'without concern for other people's opinion'. While the preparedness to work below market wage is not the same as renouncing any social recognition, it nevertheless points to a person's source of inspiration outside established remuneration schemes. In a sense, it refers to the 'spiritual health' of the health providers and their above-average altruism.

Acknowledgements

I thank Uriel Abulof, Markus Kornprobst, Rebecca Majewski and two anonymous reviewers for their helpful comments on previous versions of this paper, and Pavel Satra for research assistance.

Disclosure statement

No potential conflict of interest was reported by the author.

References

Abramowitz, S. A., Bardosh, K. L., Leach, M., Hewlett, B., Nichter, M., & Nguyen, V.-K. (2015). Social science intelligence in the global Ebola response. *The Lancet, 385*(9965), 330. doi:10.1016/S0140-6736(15)60119-2

Acharya, A. (2004). How ideas spread: Whose norms matter? Norm localization and institutional change in Asian regionalism. *International Organization, 58*(2), 239–275.

African Religious Health Assets Programme. (2006). *Appreciating assets: The contribution of religion to universal access in Africa. Report for the World Health Organization.* Cape Town: African Religious Health Assets Programme. Retrieved from http://www.irhap.uct.ac.za/downloads/ARHAPWHO_entire.pdf

Al Khayat, M. H. (1997). *Environmental health: An Islamic perspective* (The right path to health: Health education through religion). Alexandria: WHO Regional Office for the Eastern Mediterranean.

Barbato, M., & Kratochwil, F. (2009). Towards a post-secular political order? *European Political Science Review, 1*(3), 317. http://dx.doi.org/10.1017/S1755773909990166

Barnes, B. (2001). Practice as collective action. In T. R. Schatzki, K. Knorr Cetina, & E. von Savigny (Eds.), *The practice turn in contemporary theory* (pp. 25–35). New York, NY: Routledge.

Barnett, M. (2011). Another great awakening? Religion and international relations theory. In J. Snyder (Ed.), *Religion and international relations theory* (pp. 91–114). New York, NY: Columbia University Press.

Barnett, M., & Finnemore, M. (2004). *Rules for the world: International organizations in global politics* (1st print). Ithaca, NY: Cornell University Press.

Barnett, M., & Finnemore, M. (2005). The power of liberal international organizations. In M. Barnett & R. Duvall (Eds.), *Power in global governance* (pp. 161–184). Cambridge: Cambridge University Press.

Belshaw, D., Calderisi, R., & Sudgen, C. (Eds.) (2001). *Faith in development: Partnership between the World Bank and the churches of Africa.* Oxford: Regnum Books International.

Bettiza, G., & Dionigi, F. (2015). How do religious norms diffuse? Institutional translation and international change in a post-secular world. *European Journal of International Relations, 21*(3), 621–646.

Birnbaum, M. (2015). *Becoming recognizable: Postcolonial independence and the reification of religion* (Doctoral dissertation). European University Institute, Italy. Retrieved from http://hdl.handle.net/1814/35441

Bisht, D. B. (1985). *The spiritual dimension of health, including summary proceedings of the national workshop held at Bangalore in February 1985.* Delhi: Directorate General of Health Services, Government of India.

Boli, J., & Thomas, G. M. (Eds.). (1999). *Constructing world culture: International nongovernmental organizations since 1875.* Palo Alto, CA: Stanford University Press.

Boltanski, L., & Thévenot, L. (1999). The sociology of critical capacity. *European Journal of Social Theory, 2*(3), 359–377.

Boltanski, L., & Thévenot, L. (2006). *On justification: Economies of worth.* Princeton, NJ: Princeton University Press.

Casanova, J. (1994). *Public religions in the modern world.* Chicago, IL: The University of Chicago Press.

Casanova, J. (2011). The secular, secularizations, secularism. In C. Calhoun, M. Juergensmeyer, & J. van Antwerpen (Eds.), *Rethinking secularism* (pp. 54–74). Oxford: Oxford University Press.

CIFA. (2010). *Many faiths, common action: Increasing the impact of the faith sector on health and development.* Retrieved from http://www.partnershipforfaithanddevelopment.org/wp-content/uploads/2013/09/Many-Faiths-Common-Action-Report1.pdf

Clarke, G. (2007). Agents of transformation? Donors, faith-based organisations and international development. *Third World Quarterly, 28*(1), 77–96.

Connelly, M. (2010). *Fatal misconception: The struggle to control world population.* Cambridge, MA: Belknap Press of Harvard University Press.

Cooley, A., & Snyder, J. (2015). *Ranking the world: Grading states as a tool of global governance.* Cambridge: Cambridge University Press.

Coulombe, H., & Wodon, Q. (2013). Mapping religious health assets: Are faith-inspired facilities located in poor areas in Ghana? *Economic Bulletin, 33*(2), 1615–1631. Retrieved from http://www.accessecon.com/Pubs/EB/2013/Volume33/EB-13-V33-I2-P151.pdf

Cueto, M. (2004). The origins of primary health care and selective primary health care. *American Journal of Public Health, 94*(11), 1864–1874.

Deitelhoff, N. (2009). The discursive process of legalization: Charting Islands of Persuasion in the ICC case. *International Organization, 63*(1), 33–65.

Dingwerth, K., & Pattberg, P. (2009). World politics and organizational fields: The case of transnational sustainability governance. *European Journal of International Relations, 15*(4), 707–743.

Finkle, J. L., & Crane, B. B. (1976). The world health organization and the population issue: Organizational values in the United Nations. *Population and Development Review, 2*(3/4), 367–393.

Grills, N. (2009). The paradox of multilateral organizations engaging with faith-based organizations. *Global Governance, 15*(4), 505–520.

Habermas, J. (2006). Religion in the public sphere. *European Journal of Philosophy, 14*(1), 1–25.

Haynes, J. (2013). *Faith-based organisations at the United Nations.* EUI Working Paper, RSCAS 2013/70. Retrieved from http://cadmus.eui.eu/bitstream/handle/1814/28119/RSCAS_2013_70.pdf?sequence=1

Hurd, E. S. (2008). *The politics of secularism in international relations.* Princeton, NJ: Princeton University Press.

Keck, M., & Sikkink, K. (1998). *Activists beyond borders: Advocacy networks in international politics.* Ithaca, NY: Cornell University Press.

Kornprobst, M. (2011). The agent's logics of action: Defining and mapping political judgement. *International Theory, 3*(1), 70–104.

Kornprobst, M. (2014). From political judgments to public justifications (and vice versa): How communities generate reasons upon which to act. *European Journal of International Relations, 20*(1), 192–216.

Lamont, M. (2012). Toward a comparative sociology of valuation and evaluation. *Annual Review of Sociology, 38*, 201–221.

Litsios, S. (2002). The long and difficult road to Alma Ata: A personal reflection. *International Journal of Health Services, 32*(4), 709–732.

Litsios, S. (2004). The Christian medical commission and the development of the world health organization's primary health care approach. *American Journal of Public Health, 94*(11), 1884–1893.

Mahler, H. (2008). Primary health care comes full circle: An interview with Dr Halfdan Mahler. *Bulletin of the World Health Organization, 86*(10), 747–748.

Marshall, K. (2001). Development and religion: A different lens on development debates. *Peabody Journal of Education, 76*(3/4), 339–375.

Masquelier, A. (2012). Public health or public threat? Polio Eradication campaigns, Islamic revival, and the materialization of state power in Niger. In H. Dilger, A. Kane, & S. A. Langwick (Eds.), *Medicine, mobility, and power in global Africa: Transnational health and healing* (pp. 213–240). Indianapolis: Indiana University Press.

McGilvray, J. C. (1981). *The quest for health and wholeness.* Würzburg: German Institute for Medical Missions.

Narayan, D. (2000). *Voices of the poor: Can anyone hear us?* Oxford: Oxford University Press.

Neumann, I. B. (2007). "A speech that the entire ministry may stand for," or: Why diplomats never produce anything new. *International Political Sociology, 1*(2), 183–200. doi:10.1111/j.1749-5687.2007.00012.x

Olivier, J., & Wodon, Q. (2012). *Mapping, cost, and reach to the poor of faith-inspired health care providers in Sub-Saharan Africa. Strengthening the evidence for faith-inspired health engagement in Africa* (Vol. 3). Health, nutrition and population (HNP) discussion paper. Washington, DC: World Bank.

Ottersen, O. P., Dasgupta, J., Blouin, C., Buss, P., Chongsuvivatwonga, V., Frenk, J., … Scheel, I. B. (2014). The political origins of health inequity: Prospects for change. *The Lancet, 383*(9917), 630–667.

Pargament, K. I., Koenig, H. G., & Perez, L. M. (2000). The many methods of religious coping: Development and initial validation of the RCOPE. *Journal of Clinical Psychology, 56*(4), 519–543.

Payne, R. A. (2001). Persuasion, frames, and norm construction. *European Journal of International Relations, 7*(1), 37–61.

Renner, J. (2013). *Discourse, normative change and the quest for reconciliation in global politics.* Manchester: Manchester University Press.

Risse, T., Ropp, S. C., & Sikkink, K. (Eds.). (1999). *The power of human rights.* Cambridge, MA: Cambridge University Press.

Schmid, B., Thomas, E., Olivier, J., & Cochrane, J. R. (2008). *The contribution of religious entities to health in Sub-Saharan Africa: Study commissioned by Bill & Melinda Gates Foundation.* Cape Town: African Religious Health Assets Programme.

Staples, A. L. S. (2006). *The birth of development: How the World Bank, Food and Agriculture Organization, and World Health Organization changed the world, 1945–1965.* Kent, OH: The Kent State University Press.

Steffek, J. (2005). Incomplete agreements and the limits of Persuasion in international politics. *Journal of International Relations and Development, 8*(3), 229–256.

Taylor, C. (2007). *A secular age.* Cambridge, MA: Belknap Press of Harvard University Press.

Walzer, M. (1994). *Thick and thin: Moral arguments at home and abroad.* Notre Dame, IN: University of Notre Dame Press.

Wiener, A. (2007). Contested meanings of norms: A research framework. *Comparative European Politics, 5*(1), 1–17.

World Health Organization. (1985). *Handbook of resolutions and decisions of the world health assembly and the executive board. 26th to 37th world health assemblies, 51st to 74th sessions of the executive board.* Geneva: World Health Organization.

World Health Organization. (1998a). *Executive board. 101st session. Geneva, 19–27 January 1998. Resolutions and decisions. Annexes.* EB101/1998/REC/1. Geneva: World Health Organization.

World Health Organization. (1998b). *Executive board. 101st session. Geneva, 19–27 January 1998. Summary records.* EB101/1998/REC/2. Geneva: World Health Organization.

World Health Organization. (2006). *Constitution of the world health organization.* Supplement, Forty-fifth edition of 'Basic Documents'. Retrieved from www.who.int/governance/eb/who_constitution_en.pdf

World Health Organization. (2008). *Building from common foundations: The World Health Organization and faith-based organizations in primary health care.* Retrieved from http://apps.who.int/iris/bitstream/10665/43884/1/9789241596626_eng.pdf?ua=1

World Health Organization Regional Office for the Eastern Mediterranean. (1996). *Health promotion through Islamic lifestyles: The Amman declaration.* Alexandria: World Health Organization.

World Faiths Development Dialogue. (2012). *Global health and Africa: Assessing faith work and research priorities.* Washington, DC. Retrieved from http://repository.berkleycenter.georgetown.edu/GlobalHealthandAfricaWFDDEdition.pdf

Zwingel, S. (2012). How do norms travel? Theorizing international women's rights in transnational perspective. *International Studies Quarterly, 56*(1), 115–129.

Arguing deep ideational change

Markus Kornprobst and Martin Senn

ABSTRACT

How do actors come to contest previously uncontested background ideas? This is a difficult question to ask. On the one hand, deep backgrounds seem to be too foundational for actors to transform. Their political efficacy appears to end where ideas constitute their efficacy in the first place. On the other hand, ideas must not be reified. Even deeply taken-for-granted ideas do not always stay the same, and agents have a lot to do with these changes. In order to answer this question, we draw from social theory and rhetorical studies. We conceptualize the deep background as nomos, and the more easily accessible background as endoxa. We then proceed to identify three sets of conditions that make nomic change possible. These relate to opportunity, message, and messenger. Nomic change becomes possible when the need for something new has become widely established and a supply of new nomic ideas is easily available (opportunity); new nomic ideas are 'smuggled' into more orthodox and widely resonating arguments (message) as well as rhetorical encounters in which these arguments are made; and advocates are widely recognized as interlocutors (messenger). A plausibility probe of nomic contestation about nuclear governance provides evidence for this framework.

Introduction

How do agents change the deep background in which they are embedded? This is an important question to ask. Since the so-called Third Debate (Lapid, 1989), International Relations scholars have grown accustomed to addressing the background knowledge that scholars hold. Frequently, the discipline is understood as a field of competing paradigms. Scholars look at the social actors they study through different lenses (Herrmann, 1998; Hollis & Smith, 1990; Waever, 1996). Scholars, however, often shy away from inquiring into the lenses through which the social actors they study make sense of the world. For all the talk about ideas in the discipline, most students of global politics focus on knowledge that is situated in the foreground of social actors.

Research on norms, for instance, has proliferated in the last two decades. This literature made major contributions to our understandings of the salience of ideas as well as how they are reproduced and changed (Acharya, 2004; Finnemore & Sikkink, 1998; Kratochwil, 1989; Tannenwald, 2005; Wiener, 2007). But the bulk of the norms literature conceptualizes norms as standards of behaviour that are all out in the open. Actors experience little difficulty in spelling out in detail what these standards are. The deep background remains largely unaddressed. This is something akin to writing about the discipline of International Relations without inquiring into the meta-theoretical assumptions of scholarly perspectives that come so naturally to scholars that they hardly ever make them explicit and do not reflect upon them.

In this article, we develop a conceptual framework to address a particular kind of deep ideational change. How do decontested deep background ideas come to be contested? Our framework is eclectic, borrowing from research on communication conducted by social theorists and students of rhetoric. The former provide us with important clues for how to conceptualize the deep background while the latter put together a reservoir of insights on how to conceptualize change. We conceptualize the deep background as nomos and contend that three interrelated forces – rhetorical opportunities, the power of a message, and the authority of the messenger – explain how a decontested nomos comes to be contested.

Rhetorical opportunities are constituted by the widely shared understanding that the old ways of doing things cannot continue as well as by the supply of new nomic ideas in related fields of governance. The power of a message arises from familiarity. A message capable of carrying new nomic ideas to an audience is very familiar to the audience. Substantively new nomic ideas are 'smuggled' into familiar justifications of an already well-established idea. Procedurally new nomic ideas travel as rhetorical practices associated with powerful arguments. They remain implicit. Authority makes sure that a powerful message is heard.

We probe this theoretical framework by applying it to current contestation on nuclear governance. After decades of far-reaching agreement on the deep ideational background of this field of governance, disagreements pitting state security and human security as well as exclusive (state) governance and inclusive (state and non-state) governance against one another have developed. Inquiring into the processes through which this change from decontestation to contestation has become possible, this case study generates evidence for our theoretical framework.

Our argument unfolds in four steps. First, we review the literature on background ideas in International Relations and, more generally, the Social Sciences. Second, we outline our theoretical framework. Third, we present the findings of our case study on nuclear governance. Finally, we summarize our argument and propose an agenda for further research.

The analytical challenge: agency and deep ideational change

This section reviews the scholarly literatures on the deep ideational background and ideational change. The former conceptualizes the deep background in compelling fashion but struggles to explain change. The latter generates important insights on change but, focusing on foreground ideas, sidelines the deep background.

There are several conceptualizations about the deep background in the scholarly literature. The usage to some of these is more or less confined to a particular author. Gramsci, for instance, writes about 'conceptions of the world' (Gramsci in Murray & Worth, 2013, p. 731), Mehta (2011) about 'public philosophies', Culpepper (2008) about 'common knowledge', English (2000) about 'philosophical beliefs', Burke (1965) about a terministic screen, and Schmidt (2008) about 'background abilities'. May (1962) labels deeply seated ideas 'axiomatic'. Other conceptualizations have spread much further. They are widely used in the literature. This applies especially to paradigms, epistemes, and, more recently, also the nomos.

Hall (1993) introduced Kuhn's research on paradigms and scientific revolutions to the study of politics. Hall's agents are political actors rather than scientists. He makes a convincing argument that it is not just scientists who look at the world through a particular lens but political actors, too. Under normal circumstances, this lens is taken for granted. It is so deeply seated in the social background that there is no reflection about it. Following Kuhn, research on policy paradigms assumes that there is always one dominant paradigm at a time. Change is a shift from one paradigm to the next (Béland & Cox, 2013; Berman, 2013; Campbell, 2004, pp. 90–123; Hall, 1993). Research on policy paradigms is not all-encompassing. Instead, it focuses on issue areas and specifies the communities who hold the paradigms rather carefully. Hall's seminal research, for instance, is about the political economy paradigm in the pre-Thatcher United Kingdom (Keynesianism).

While Kuhn's work features very prominently in writings on policy paradigms, scholars addressing the episteme draw considerably from Foucault (1972, 1970). The episteme was introduced to the study of international politics by Ruggie (1975, 1983). In Ruggie's thought, too, there is only one dominant episteme at the time. Looking at the world through the episteme, the world becomes intelligible to us. Following Foucault, Ruggie's thought on the episteme is all-encompassing. The episteme explains how it was possible for actors to imagine an international order that was based on the sovereignty of nation-states. More recent research on the concept deals with somewhat more circumscribed dimensions of world politics, too. The epistemic community literature deals with taken-for-granted knowledge, in particular, issue areas, ranging from ozone depletion (Haas, 1992) to arms control (Adler, 1992). Legro (2000) writes about foreign policy epistemes in the United States, and Kornprobst (2005) on epistemes constituting national identities.

More recently, there has been a renewed scholarly interest in the concept of the nomos. This concept has been around for a long time. It originates with ancient rhetoric. To the Sophists, the nomos was an axiomatic ontological convention. It underpinned rhetorical encounters by delineating what is (Jarratt, 1991).[1] In today's social theory, this definition of nomos as ontological lens remains very much in place. Chopra (2003), for instance, defines the nomos as a 'meta-valuation system'. The concept is closely associated with the work of Bourdieu. He, too, defines the nomos is an underlying ontology (Bourdieu, 2001b, p. 51). Bourdieu links the nomos closely to other, somewhat less foundational kinds of taken-for-granted ideas. The former constitutes the latter (Bourdieu, 2000, 2001a, p. 32). The renewed scholarly interest in the concept keeps some of the linkages with Bourdieuan social theory but also moves again more closely to rhetorical studies (Epstein, 2008; Kornprobst & Senn, 2016). This is where Bourdieu borrowed the concept of nomos from in the first place.

Ideas must not be reified. The social world is a becoming and not a being (Adler, 1997). This puts the onus on scholars interested in ideas to explain how they change. But the literature on deep background ideas struggles to explain change. It remains unclear how actors, deeply embedded in social context, can still assert meaningful agency, including their ability to affect this deep background. Among the social theorists discussed above,

Bourdieu is among those that are still somewhat more agency-focused. Yet a standard criticism of Bourdieu is that his conceptualization of the deep background is too heavy as to allow for agents to change this background, especially the nomos (Battilana, 2006; Beckert, 2010, pp. 612–613; Friedland, 2009). This criticism is difficult to disperse.

There is a much more agency-focused literature on ideational change. It provides three clusters of clues for how to make sense of ideational change. First, the time has to be ripe for change. Rhetorical studies refer to this as *kairos* (De Certeau, 1984). The social movement literature uses the label of opportunity structure (Benford & Snow, 2000; Kriesi, 1995; Tarrow & Tollefson, 1994). *Kairos* can have material and/or ideational dimensions. When it comes to the former, many authors allude to the importance of exogenous shocks. These drive it home to actors that the old ways of doing things have become obsolete. Shocking events provide a 'cognitive punch' (Adler, 1991) that makes actors embark on something radically new. When it comes to the latter, a number of authors write about the supply of new but nevertheless familiar ideas. Willard (1989) makes this point very forcefully. Actors can import new ideas from one field of argumentation to a related one. Given the crisscrossing among orders, the ideas are familiar to the actors. But they are, nevertheless, new in the field to which they are imported. Some authors refer to this kind of importing as transposition (Mehta, 2011).

Second, the power of the word makes a difference. The framing literature writes about the power of frames (Farrell & Drezner, 2008; Snow, Rochford Jr, Worden, & Benford, 1986; Tarrow & Tollefson, 1994). Narrative theory identifies powerful modes of story-telling (Fisher, 1987; McGee & Nelson, 1985; Ringmar, 2006). Argumentation theory dissects arguments, providing important clues as to what kinds of messages resonate with what kinds of audiences and what kinds do not (Prakken, 2005; Walton & Sartor, 2013; Warnick & Kline, 1992). These perspectives diverge on how to study messages. Formal argument analysis (Alker, 1996), for instance, tends to do this more rigorously than narrative theory. But they also agree upon an important insight. Familiarity makes for a powerful message. To put this into the vocabulary of rhetorical theory, *loci* (*topoi*, commonplaces) are key components of powerful messages (Aristotle, 1995; Cicero, 2003; Quintilian, 1953).[2] In order for a message to resonate with an audience, it has to appear familiar to an audience. This still leaves room for agency. Not all elements composing an argument need to be familiar. But many have to. They need to be taken from a well-established repertoire.

Third, the authority of speakers makes a difference. Even arguments that emphasize the power of words allude to the importance of the status of advocates. Some actors are more entitled to be communicators than others (Crawford, 2002; Finnemore & Sikkink, 1998; Kornprobst, 2008). Some dimensions of this authority are more easily acquired than others. On the one hand, there are dimensions that are readily affected by the performance of a speaker in a rhetorical encounter. When Aristotle (1995) writes about *ethos*, for instance, he refers to furthering authority by finding the right words about one's expertize and trustworthiness as a speaker. On the other hand, there are also aspects of authority that are less malleable by performance. Actors enter rhetorical encounters with a particular standing. If they do not have any standing, they do not get access to the discourse. Their performance does not matter.[3]

These three clues are important. But they go only thus far in helping us to explain deep ideational change. Research on exogenous shocks is geared towards explaining deep change. But the change to be explained is a peculiar one. It is a shift, for instance a shift from one policy paradigm to another (Hall, 1993). The exogenous shock is less helpful in explaining evolutionary change. Yet deep ideational changes often occur through evolutionary processes (Carstensen, 2011a, 2011b). These kinds of changes are particularly pertinent for the research task at hand, that is, to explain how a decontested deep background comes to be contested. Research on transposition usually does not deal with deep ideational change. It focuses on foreground ideas, especially norms (Dimitrova & Rhinard, 2005; Toshkov, 2007). The same applies to research on the power of the word. This kind of research generates very important insights on how well-crafted messages can come to make a major difference. There are numerous studies on how advocacies strengthened particular human rights, for example (Risse, Ropp, & Sikkink, 1999, 2013). But deep ideational change remains sidelined. It also remains neglected in studies that address the standing of communicators. This standing tends to enter as an additional social force to explain how a message comes to resonate, alongside the power of the message itself. But where this standing comes from – how it waxes and wanes – is not systematically examined, especially not the kind of authority required to get access to a discourse in the first place.

A rhetorical framework for studying deep ideational change

This section develops an explanatory framework for studying the evolution from a decontested to a contested deep background. We draw heavily from social and rhetorical theory. This makes it distinctly eclectic. We first discuss how backgrounds, arguments, and rhetorical encounters are related. Then we identify three sets of social forces that foster deep ideational change from decontestation to contestation. These relate to opportunity, message, and messenger.

The social background in which actors are embedded consists of different layers. Some of these layers are more accessible to reflection than others. The deepest layer is so much taken for granted that it is hardly made explicit any more. It only appears in discourses explicitly in times of heightened contestation. In line with rhetorical theories and Bourdieu, we refer to this deepest level as nomos. The nomos is the ontological foundation of reasoning and communicating. Rigotti and Morasso (2010, p. 494) define this social ontology very well. It provides answers to 'questions concerning what entities exist or at what conditions they can be said to exist, and how such entities can be grouped, related within a hierarchy, and subdivided according to similarities and differences'.

Other layers are more easily accessible to actors. We refer to them as endoxa.[4] Ideas located at these layers are more frequently made explicit and they are also less abstract. References to certain rules and norms, for instance, or metaphors and historical analogies, are frequently found in arguments. The Munich analogy, for instance, is such a historical lesson. In debates on war and peace in the United Kingdom and the United States, this analogy often becomes a justification for war. Appeasement did not work in 1938. Appeasement never works. Not to intervene would amount to appeasement. Thus, intervention is necessary (Daddow, 2009; Kennedy-Pipe & Vickers, 2007). Endoxa are taken for granted, too. To stick with the appeasement illustration, the Munich analogy is deeply ingrained in the British and American identity narratives. But it is specific – about the resort to war – and tends to be made very explicit in debates about war and peace.[5]

Nomic and endoxic layers contain substantive and procedural ideas. The above illustration about appeasement is an example for a substantive endoxic idea. Whether to intervene into a conflict militarily or not is a substantive political question. Appeasement is an anchor that arguments dealing with this question can employ to figure out to do. Substantive ideas enable actors to compose their own arguments and evaluate the arguments put forward by others. Procedural ideas, by contrast, are clues that circumscribe the positioning of actors in rhetorical encounters. Some have access to the encounters while others do not. On matters of peace and war, to return to the above illustration, some actors have more access to political debates than others. Leaders of powerful states are much more likely to be heard than leaders of less powerful states or sub-state and non-state actors.

Arguments never feature the entire background. Actors select, partly habitually and partly reflectively, aspects of this background in order to cope with a given situation. They do so in order to make a situation intelligible to themselves (substantive ideas) and to distinguish those with authority to speak on this matter from those without (procedural ideas). The argument assembles substantive ideas. At a minimum, an argument consists of explicit commonplaces (*loci*), implicit commonplaces (*habitudines*), and an advocated idea (*conclusio*). The *loci* and *habitudines* justify the *conclusio* (Betz, 2012; Frazer & Hutchings, 2007; Wright, 2001). Implicit commonplaces are important (Green-Pedersen, 1987, p. 415; Purcell, 1987, p. 400; Rigotti & Morasso, 2010, p. 494). Not everything is made explicit in an argument. Some ideas remain implicit but, nevertheless, support the *conclusio*. These ideas have sunk so much in that they no longer require to be made explicit. The audience can, so to say, fill in the gaps (Aristotle, 1995, 1357a; Kienpointner, 1986, 340). When it comes to explicit commonplaces, some are more general (*loci communes*) and others more concrete (*loci prorii*). The same applies to implicit commonplaces. Some are more abstract (*habitudines communes*) and others more concrete (*habitudines prorii*). Actors select the more general commonplaces from the nomic layers and the more specific ones from the endoxic layers.

In addition to *loci* and *habitudines*, some arguments also feature ideas other than the *conclusio* that are not commonplaces (yet). Rhetorical theories are rather sceptical about their rhetorical force. Commonplaces, being familiar to actors, are seen as powerful justifications for advocated ideas. Less familiar ideas (*nulli loci*) are considered to weaken justifications (Aristotle, 1995; Cicero, 2003; Quintilian, 1953). Nevertheless, such less familiar ideas often feature in arguments. What may be familiar to the speaker, for instance, may not be familiar to the audience. Such *nulli loci* may be general or concrete. But, being *nulli loci*, they are not taken out of the widely shared context. They are non-commonplaces.

Rhetorical encounters are deeply relational. The relations among those who meet in these encounters are arranged in various horizontal or vertical shades. Habermas's counterfactual thought experiment of an ideal speech situation notwithstanding, equal relations are the exception (1991, p. 132). Hierarchy is the rule. Some participants of a communicative encounter have more authority than others. There are two different dimensions of authority. First, authorship reaches deeply. It is situated in the nomic layer. This is how Heinze (1925) interprets Cicero's concept of *auctoritas* (authority) and it comes close to Bourdieu's authorized spokesperson. Some categories of actors are entitled to speak whereas others are not. For instance, a Prime Minister is entitled to speak at general debates at the United Nations General Assembly. Authorship is the equivalent of *habitudines communes* in an argument. Understandings of who is entitled to be a speaker and who is not are so deeply ingrained in the background that they do not have to be made explicit.

Second, there is credibility. Rhetorical theory is full of insights about how actors can produce and reproduce their credibility. As Aristotle (1995) explains over and over, speakers use rhetorical tricks to augment their own personal authority. They reserve parts of their messages to drive it home to an audience that they are knowledgeable, of good character, and full of goodwill. Speakers have to appeal to these qualities. They have to make them explicit. When Aristotle writes about establishing *ethos*, he instructs the speakers to appeal to ideas about their credibility that are already somewhat familiar to the audience. In other words, Aristotle recommends them to reach into the endoxa, and reproduce and augment ideas about credibility that are already there. Having credibility in a rhetorical encounter is the equivalent to a *locus prorius* in an argument. It is explicit and specific. Note that credibility is more malleable than authorship. Credibility can be augmented by successful performance.[6] But producing credibility presupposes authorship. The latter is the foundation upon which the former can develop.

Under normal circumstances, the nomos is uncontested. Residing deeply in the background, it orders the interactions of actors with them hardly being aware of it. The nomos comes too natural to them as that it would allow for much reflection. There are circumstances, however, in which the nomos becomes contested. This destabilizes the order that the nomos constitutes. How does such a change from decontestation to contestation come about? In light of the above conceptualization of argumentation, it is possible to build upon the conditions for ideational change identified by the literature. These pertain to opportunity, message, and messenger.

Opportunity is about a particular endoxic idea and the supply of new nomic ideas. *The obsoleteness of the old ways of doing things has become a widely shared endoxic idea.* It is established that a given order has to change (De Certeau, 1984; Detienne & Vernant, 1974, pp. 295–296). At the same time, *related fields of orders have experienced nomic change.*[7] Actors can borrow from this nomic change and import it. To put this differently, the borderlands of orders are places that are important for ideational innovation. This is an insight that hermeneutic theorists have elaborated on in compelling fashion (Bakhtin, 1986, pp. 137–142; Bernstein, 1991, p. 65; Gadamer, 1972, p. 279).[8]

Compelling messages, capable of transforming nomoi, are composed in a particular fashion. New nomic ideas are not *conclusiones*. A new nomic idea cannot be justified by something else. It is too abstract and all-encompassing for such a straightforward advocacy.[9] But actors can advocate for a new – or, more precisely put, not that new – nomic idea more indirectly. They can 'smuggle' a new substantive nomic idea into a more orthodox argument. A nomic advocacy does not argue for a new *conclusio*. Instead it argues for a conclusio that is taken from the endoxa (*locus prorii*), supports this with other endoxa (*loci prorii*), and adds to this the new nomic idea, which fulfils the function of a *locus* communis in the argument. Thus, the novelty of the new substantive nomic idea is counterbalanced with the familiarity of the rest of the argument, including its *conclusio*. Furthermore, the new substantive nomic idea is actually not all that new. It is taken from a related field. Diplomats, for instance, routinely move back and forth between different fields, say environment and economics. It may be unexpected for them to encounter an idea that is foundational in the economics field in the environmental one (or vice versa). But the idea is not entirely new to them. It is merely transposed (Campbell, 1998).

Opportunity and compelling messages alone are not sufficient for nomic change. Such a change also requires actors with plenty of authority. Actors endowed with authorship and credibility – and the skills and talents required to augment this credibility further – need to be present from the very beginning of the process through which nomic decontestation moves to contestation. This ensures that the new substantive nomic ideas are heard by the audience. Successful advocacies can even develop a momentum that makes it possible for actors who entered an advocacy without widely recognized authorship to acquire such authorship, and, once they have done so, credibility as well. New procedural nomic ideas can travel with successful arguments. But these ideas, too, are, at second glance, not all that new. They are also transposed from a related field. New procedural nomic ideas, therefore, are 'smuggled' into a field from an adjacent or superordinate field as well. Furthermore, they are not smuggled into the argument. They can only be smuggled into a rhetorical encounter through rhetorical practice.[10] If such a foundational change through simply doing speaking differently happens, it provides additional momentum for contesting the old nomos. More advocates with the authority to be heard diffuse the successful argument.

Nuclear weapons: from nomic orthodoxy to nomic contestation

The remainder of this article puts this framework to use to explain the recent change from nomic decontestation to contestation in the nuclear weapons field. For decades, this field was based on a three-fold and uncontested nomos. (a) Nuclear weapons are immensely destructive (ordering imperative). (b) Nuclear order is about safeguarding the security of states. (c) The governors, in charge of making the rules for this safeguarding, are states. The first part of the nomos remains very much in place. It continues to be uncontested. The remaining ones, however, have become contested. The Humanitarian Initiative (HI) succeeded in countering state security with human security, and state governance with inclusive governance (state and non-state actors). How did this change from decontestation to contestation possible?

The focus on nuclear weapons makes for a difficult plausibility probe for the theoretical framework. It is often assumed that somewhat amorphous social forces such as rhetoric do not matter when it comes to the ultimate weapon. All that matters are material capabilities (Bracken, 1999; Powell, 1991; Waltz, 1990). Furthermore, the agreement on the orthodox three-fold nomos held for decades. The 1970 Nuclear Non-proliferation Treaty (NPT), for instance, is very much based on this nomos. So were the quinquennial Review Conferences (RevCons) and debates in the First Committee of the UN General Assembly. In the past, there were a host of debates, especially about disarmament, nonproliferation, and technological transfers for peaceful use. The debates often pitted nuclear weapons states (NWS) and non-nuclear weapons states (NNWS) against one another. When it comes to the latter, the Non-Aligned Movement (NAM) was a particularly outspoken grouping of critics. These debates could be very controversial, even making it impossible for the parties to agree on a Final Document of a Review Conference. But the nomos remained uncontested. This has changed in the last five years. Now, there are two competing lenses to look at nuclear weapons: the old nomic ideas of state security and state governance (embraced by NWS and allied states), and the new ones of human security and inclusive governance (embraced by most NNWS).[11] What has happened since 2010?

Our analysis starts in 1995, when the Review and Extension Conference of the NPT debated about the post-Cold War nuclear order and extends to today. We rely on a number of primary sources. These include the proceedings of Preparatory Committees (PrepComs) for RevCons, RevCons, First Committee debates (all 1995–2015), and the HI conferences in Oslo (2013), Nayarit and Vienna (both 2014). We participated in the latter, and conducted 12 interviews with proponents and opponents of HI in Vienna and New York.

Our argumentation analysis follows a key insight of Perelman's and Olbrechts-Tycea's *New rhetoric* (1958). We are not after assessing the logic of arguments according to stringent rules. We trace how actors come to assemble and diffuse arguments that are intelligible to them. Following our analytical framework, we put under scrutiny the opportunities for advocacies for new nomic ideas, dissect the contents of the arguments being exchanged by actors, and uncover the relationships among interlocutors and between interlocutors and audiences.[12]

Opportunity

There was an opening for new nomic ideas because of the endoxon that the old ways of doing things cannot continue and the supply of new nomic ideas was present due to post-Cold War moves to re-invent global order in related fields.

The end of the Cold War fuelled hopes that long-standing disagreements on nuclear governance could finally be resolved. For many NNWS, these hopes focused, first and foremost, on Article 6 of the NPT. With the Cold War being replaced by much more conciliatory relations among great powers, NWS would finally honour their disarmament obligations. They would disarm. At the 1995 Review and Extension Conference, the NPT was extended indefinitely. NNWS agreed to this step under the condition of a strengthened review process.[13] RevCon Final Documents would specify clear targets for implementing treaty provisions. The 1995 Final Document, for instance, contained a provision on the creation of the Comprehensive Test Ban Treaty Organization (CTBTO). The 2000 Final Document lists 13 steps towards nuclear disarmament to be honoured by NWS. The 2010 Final Documents extends this to 22 steps.

The envisaged disarmament, however, did not happen. This caused major frustration among many NNWS. As a senior European diplomat puts it, the NPT has 'lost credibility'. It has become mere 'occupational therapy' for states. 'The legitimacy of the regime is more and more questionable.' NWS make nothing but 'pro forma concessions', from which they withdraw again soon after the ink has dried on the final documents of review conferences.[14] The tone among protagonists of the NAM is even harsher. Seeming concessions made by the NWS, for instance the disarmament steps agreed in 2000 and 2010, amount to little more than 'blabla'. There is a 'serious implementation deficit'. There is a 'series of broken promises – that's all'. Future prognoses of the NPT regime are 'bleak'. 'I would not be surprised if, one day, the regime would fall.'[15] This is a very strong formulation. But the frustration about the perceived failure of NWS, sometimes expressed more diplomatically and sometimes less, to honour their disarmament obligations has become widely accepted. It is an endoxon that many NNWS share.

In the mid-1990s, two documents challenged nomic ideas on international politics. This challenge occurred not in the more narrowly confined nuclear field but in the adjacent and broader economics field as well as the superordinate diplomacy field. In 1994, the Human Development Report juxtaposed 'nuclear security' and 'human security'. Nuclear security was branded as old style security. During the Cold War, security was state security. States sought to safeguard their security by nuclear deterrence. Human security was identified as the new security concept for a new era. What really matters is that human beings are safe. They ought to be safe from internal and external threats. They also ought to be free from want (United Nations Development Program, 1994). A year later, the Commission on Global Governance (1995) issued its report entitled *Our global neighborhood*. This report was highly innovative as well. This report juxtaposed state governance and global governance. State governance was portrayed as the kind of governance of a bygone era. Addressing the challenges of the new era requires global governance, that is, the inclusion of multiple actors. States and their representatives (diplomats) are very much part of this multitude of actors. But so are non-state actors, sub-state actors, international as well as supranational organisations, and many more.

These two reports encapsulate important developments in international relations in the mid-1990s. Most importantly for the purpose at hand, they proposed alternative nomic ideas: human security and inclusive governance. From the mid-1990s onwards, these ideas left their mark in several policy fields, including arms control. The campaigns to ban landmines and cluster munition put human security to use. Seen through the lens of human security, these kinds of weapons are no longer tolerable. They may not threaten states. But they do threaten human beings. The campaigns also put inclusive governance to use. They very much practised it. The campaigns started with not-for-profit organizations. These aligned with groupings of states and, thus, were successful in making their ideas enter the diplomatic realm. Both campaigns were about prohibiting these kinds of weapons. They were concluded successfully. In 1997, the Anti-Personnel Mine Convention was signed in Ottawa. In 2008, the Convention on Cluster Munitions was signed in Dublin. Ratification levels for both agreements are good (with the Ottawa Convention doing somewhat better than the Dublin Treaty).

Message

HI made the most out of these opportunities. Its message is composed of a number of ideas taken from the social background. This includes the *conclusio*. The need for prohibiting nuclear weapons is an endoxon for the majority of parties to the NPT. But HI successfully 'smuggled' a substantive nomic idea into this argument, that is, human security. Delivering this message became a rhetorical practice. Through this practice, a new procedural nomic idea has sunk in with many actors as well, that is, inclusive governance.

The *conclusio* of the message is the prohibition of nuclear weapons. The demand for nuclear disarmament, sometimes even in the sharp formulations of 'prohibition' or 'ban', has been around since the beginning of the nuclear age. In the NPT, it is, albeit in somewhat ambiguous language, expressed in Article 6. HI formulations tend to reiterate the 2012 *Joint Statement on the Humanitarian Dimension of Nuclear Disarmament* of the original 16 participating states when they call for nuclear disarmament: 'All states must intensify to outlaw nuclear weapons and achieve a world free of nuclear weapons'

(2012b). The 2015 Humanitarian Pledge uses stronger language. It postulates 'effective measures to fill the legal gap for the prohibition and elimination of nuclear weapons'.[16]

This *conclusio* is justified in elaborate fashion. The destructiveness of nuclear weapons is a *locus communis*; in some formulations of the argument it is also a *habitudo communis*. Again, this linkage between the destructiveness of nuclear weapons and the need to get rid of them can be traced back to the dawn of the nuclear age and the development of the NPT, especially its Preamble. The linkage can be found in arguments presented by NWS, too. Obama's much celebrated Prague Speech, for instance, was all about the connection of the catastrophic consequences of nuclear weapons and the need for disarmament (Obama, 2009). There is also a *locus prorii* that had been well established before the advent of HI in 2010, that is, the failure of NWS to disarm. In other words, thus far, the argument looks rather orthodox.

The novelty is provided by the notion of human security. This notion fulfils the function of a *locus communis*, although – at least at the beginning of the advocacy – it had not assumed the taken-for-granted quality that makes it a *locus* yet. It was too new an idea for the nuclear field as that it would have been part of the social context already. At the beginning, human security was still a *locus nullius*. The ideas closely linked to this quasi-*locus communis*, however, were already very familiar to actors. They were *loci prorii* that had been used for discussing nuclear weapons for quite some time. A string of *loci* addresses the humanitarian catastrophes that nuclear weapons cause. These range from the terrible suffering of the civilian population in Hiroshima and Nagasaki to the consequences of nuclear testing for populations living nearby testing sites. Another string of *loci* is about international humanitarian law. While this body of international law is based on the distinction between combatants and non-combatants and vows to protect the latter, nuclear weapons simply cannot make this distinction.[17] As an interviewee puts this, '[i]f you are aiming at something with a 50 megaton bomb, you simply cannot differentiate between combatants and non-combatants'.[18]

The HI argumentation has become a rhetorical practice. It is remarkable how similarly the proponents of HI answered our interview questions and it is equally remarkable how strongly these answers mirror key statements. This includes the Kellenberger speech and the joint statements of the original 16 at the 2012 PrepCom (2012b), and 35 states at the First Committee of the General Assembly a few months later (2012a), both delivered by Switzerland. It includes the joint statement by 78 states at the 2013 PrepCom (2013b) delivered by South Africa, and 125 states at the First Committee again a few months later (2013a) delivered by New Zealand. The same country delivered the 2014 HI statement at the First Committee. Again the same overall argumentation is repeated. The Humanitarian Pledge (2015) echoed the broad consensus on the argumentation as well.

In procedural terms, the Humanitarian Conferences in Norway, Mexico, and Austria introduced new practices for debating nuclear disarmament. The conferences were organized in very similar ways. They first gave the word to victims of nuclear weapons attacks or nuclear testing, to scientists, layers, and representatives of not-for-profit organisations. State representatives were present. But they merely commented or asked questions. Only after these discussions did state representatives make more elaborate statements. Through these practices, these Humanitarian Conferences enlarged the group of interlocutors. Through practising authorship for previously marginalized non-state actors, HI came to endow these actors with authorship. Successful non-state actors include the

International Committee of the Red Cross (ICRC), Mayors for Peace, as well as, on a more general level, to the International Campaign to Abolish Nuclear Weapons (ICAN).

The substantive and procedural nomic novelty is imported. The proponents of HI are acutely aware of the successful campaigns to ban landmines and cluster munition.[19] Looking at these experiences taught them the importance of these nomic ideas. To HI advocates, nuclear governance is anachronistic. While global governance has moved towards human security and inclusive governance, nuclear governance still holds on to state security and state governance. Linking these new nomic ideas to established ideas made for a powerful argumentation. As one interview put it, 'what counts are good arguments [...] Nobody can tell us that we say something wrong; naïve perhaps but not wrong'.[20]

Messenger

For all the strengths of this message, it would have gotten nowhere without the backing of actors with plenty of authority in nuclear governance. Some entered with authorship, others acquired it through practice. Out of the former and latter group of actors, some played their cards more skilfully than others to augment their credibility.

In the mid-2000s, a number of precursors of HI can be identified. 2007 was a particularly important year. The New Agenda Coalition circulated a draft resolution in the First Committee. A year later, it introduced this draft resolution to the PrepCom for the 2010 RevCon.[21] The draft refers to human security. ICAN formed in 2007. Its arguments stressed human security from the beginning and it sought to practice inclusive governance from the start.[22]

On 20 April 2010, Jakob Kellenberger, President of the ICRC but also an experienced Swiss career diplomat, gave a speech to the diplomatic corps in Geneva (2010). This speech formulates the full argumentation as discussed in the previous section for the first time. Being a Swiss career diplomat, he was recognized as an author in the nuclear field who should be listened to. He made use of this recognition to practice authorship for the ICRC. Furthermore, he forcefully appealed to the ICRC's credibility. He dedicated no less than half of his speech to highlighting this credibility in the nuclear field. He emphasized that the ICRC does not have an interest to defend in this field, except for the humanitarian one. When it comes to the latter one, the ICRC has a lot of expertise. It is worth quoting him at length:

> The ICRC has a legitimate voice in this debate. In its 150-year history, the organization has witnessed immeasurable human suffering caused by war [...]. The ICRC also brings to the debate its own direct testimony to the consequences of the use nuclear weapons and their potential to render impossible the mission of humanitarian assistance that this organization exists to fulfil. Dr Marcel Junod, an ICRC delegate, was the first foreign doctor in Hiroshima to assess the effects of the atomic bombing and to assist its victims. (Kellenberger, 2010)

The Kellenberger speech inspired many diplomats in the audience. It 'gave us the final punch' to launch HI.[23] Sixteen states were part of the original HI: Austria, Chile, Costa Rica, Denmark, Holy See, Egypt, Indonesia, Ireland, Malaysia, Mexico, New Zealand, Nigeria, Norway, Philippines, South Africa, and Switzerland. Within this group, six states have been particularly active. Swiss diplomacy was the conveyer belt through which the

Kellenberger speech made it into the halls of traditional diplomacy. Diplomats from Austria, Mexico, New Zealand, Norway,[24] South Africa, and Switzerland were repeatedly the voice of HI, being very active advocates and delivering joint statements

Their advocacy frequently appeals to their 'in between status'. They occupy what Roman rhetoric labelled the *aurea mediocritas* (golden middle). These states emphasize that they have a history of positioning themselves in between radical NNWS, on the one hand, and the NPT, on the other. Instead of demarcating themselves from NWS due to the lack of meaningful progress on disarmament, they vow 'to work with them' towards nuclear disarmament. The words in between the quotation marks appeared twice in two independently conducted interviews.[25] This positioning in the middle lends credibility to these states. As a diplomat put it: 'We have legitimacy in this regard. We are concerned about the cause and nothing else, and others perceive us that way.'[26] Among these states, South Africa has a special status. Not only has post-Apartheid South Africa a history of positioning itself in the middle, but it is also one of the very few states ever to disarm. It is no coincidence that South African diplomats repeatedly read HI statements at multilateral fora.[27] This is a strategic move, trying to maximize credibility as much as possible.

Within three years, HI became the 'largest cross-national group of states ever to deliver a joint statement on a matter concerning the NPT' (Johnson, 2013). By now, 123 states have signed the Humanitarian Pledge, which is the outcome of the Vienna conference. More states are expected to join in the near future.[28] Thus, the advocacy has gained momentum, producing more and more persuadees and messengers. Even now, most of the states signing and advocating the Pledge are those with a history of situating themselves somewhere in the middle between radical critics of the NPT and outspoken defenders of the status quo. In their advocacy, they flag this middle position in their attempts to highlight their credibility. As an interviewee put it, 'we have legitimacy. It is clear that we have no selfish motives. This is how we are perceived'.[29] This helps to produce credibility.

Within HI, a number of non-state actors have secured authorship, and building on it, credibility. At the Vienna Humanitarian Conference, for instance, Setsuko Thurlow gave a very powerful speech on her experiences as a survivor of the nuclear attack on Hiroshima. Almost all her speech was about her shocking experiences. But there was also something about credibility. Hibakusha are dedicated to 'baring our souls with painful memories over the past 69 years to warn people about the hell on earth we experienced in Hiroshima and Nagasaki'.[30] This is a worthy cause, indeed. Sub-state actors such as Mayors for Peace echo this emphasis on credibility. Keeping the remembrance of Hiroshima and Nagasaki alive and advocating for taking the lessons from these disasters seriously, they are simply concerned about the 'safety and welfare of citizens' (Mayors for Peace, 2014). There are no ulterior motives, and they know very well what they are talking about. This makes for credibility.

Conclusion

This paper contends that changes from nomic decontestation to contestation come about through a communicative process involving rhetorical opportunities, compelling messages, and the authority of speakers. Endoxic ideas that the old ways of doing things cannot continue as well as a supply of new nomic ideas in related governance mechanisms make for rhetorical opportunities. Messages seize upon these opportunities by including these endoxic ideas as *loci prorii* and the imported substantive nomic ideas instead of *loci communes*. With the exception of the latter, they are composed of already taken-for-granted ideas, some being out in the open (*loci*) and others remaining implicit (*habitudines*). Even the *conclusio* is not a new advocated idea. It is already firmly established. New procedural nomic ideas, changing the recognition of authorship, travel as practices that are associated with successful arguments.

This contention makes at least two noteworthy contributions to the existing literature. First, it navigates a middle path between social theorists who put heavy emphasis on social context on the one hand and rhetorical theorists who tend to underline agency at the expense of context. It is difficult for agents to change the nomic layer of the social context. But there are rhetorical processes that make it possible. Second, our contention adds an interesting insight to literature on justification. Successful arguments cannot only bring new ideas into being if these ideas are actually argued for. In the case of nomic change, nomic ideas are, strictly speaking, not argued for. They are not *conclusiones*. Instead, they are 'smuggled' into an argument, fulfilling the function of a *locus communis* (substantive nomic novelty) and/or through rhetorical practices forming in association with such a successful argument (procedural nomic novelty).

Although our case study provided evidence for our theoretical framework, a lot of work remains to be done. Three areas of further research come immediately to mind. First, we only conducted a plausibility probe of a single case. More empirical research is required to reach firmer conclusions about the strengths and weaknesses of the theoretical framework. This should include cases in which nomic change is not confined to a move from nomic orthodoxy to contestation. It should, for instance, include cases in which one nomos came to replace another one. Second, it would be interesting to adapt this theoretical framework to the study of sudden nomic shifts. There are political situations in which many taken-for-granted ideas are put into question. European leaders faced such as situation after the Second World War, for instance. It made West European statesmen embark on a process of cooperation and integration. But how can they anchor their thinking in something that appears natural to them when so many formerly taken-for-granted ideas come to dismissed or at least questioned? Third, more research is required on how governance mechanisms are related to one another. There is crisscrossing, subordination, superordination, and so on. Field theory offers an intriguing avenue to conceptualize this. Fligstein and McAdam (2012), for instance, contend that fields are only semi-autonomous. The overlap of fields makes it possible to import new ideas from one field to the next. But further research is required to conceptualize the relationships across fields and how these relationships facilitate or hinder importing and exporting innovative ideas.

Exploring these research avenues amounts not only to an important theoretical endeavour. At a time when world politics seems to rush from crisis to crisis (intra-state conflicts, inter-state conflicts, sovereign debt, refugee flows) and established actors find it more and more difficult to manage these crises together, improving our understandings of how the deeply taken for granted comes to be disputed and hopefully re-invented in constructive fashion is particularly important.

Notes

1. For these strong ontological connotations, see also Bourdieu (2001b, p. 51) and McComiskey (1994).
2. *Locus* (pl. *loci*) is the Latin translation of the Greek *topos* (pl. *topoi*); we use the Latin term because we draw more from Roman than Greek rhetoric in this article (see also our conceptualisation of authority along the lines of *auctoritas* below).
3. Bourdieu's notions of symbolic power and the 'authorized spokesperson' (1991, p. 109) allude to this kind of constitution of communicative authority.
4. This is very close to Aristotle's use of the term (1995). See also Renon (1998) and Haskins (2004).
5. We developed a related distinction in Kornprobst and Senn (2016).
6. On the malleability of credibility, conceptualized as *ethos*, see also Oliensis (1998) and Goodwin (2001).
7. The nomos is usually uncontested. This status makes it possible for the nomos to constitute a field in the first place. Endoxa, by contrast, are much more contested in a field. There are many communities embracing different clusters of endoxa (Kornprobst & Senn, 2016).
8. On the porous boundaries of orders, see also Boltanski and Thévenot (2006) as well as Fligstein and McAdam (2012).
9. Even formal logicians hold that the foundations on which reasoning is based cannot be proven (Gödel, 1931).
10. On rhetorical practices, see De Certeau (1984). On practices more generally, see Adler and Pouliot (2011).
11. Judging by the signatories to the 2015 Humanitarian Pledge, there are more HI parties to the NPT than non-HI parties (about two-thirds versus one-third).
12. This resembles informal argumentation analyses as developed by Crawford (2002) and Kornprobst (2008).
13. Interview with a diplomat representing a North American state, conducted in Vienna, 6 March 2014; interview with a diplomat representing an East Asian state, conducted in Vienna, 21 February 2014.
14. Interview with a diplomat representing an EU member state, Vienna, 4 April 2013. Interview with a diplomat representing a European state, Vienna, 31 January 2014.
15. Interview with diplomat representing a lead NAM state, Vienna, 15 April 2013.
16. The Humanitarian Pledge (2015) originates with the 2015 HI Conference in Vienna, where it was introduced as Austrian Pledge.
17. All of these components featured in much detail at the 2014 HI Conferences in Nayarit (http://www.sre.gob.mx/en/index.php/humanimpact-nayarit-2014) and Vienna (Federal Ministry for Europe, Integration and Foreign Affairs, 2015).
18. Interview with Bernhard Schneider, Head of Department of the Legal Office, ICRC, Vienna, 4 February 2014.
19. Interview with a diplomat representing an EU member state, Vienna, 4 April 2013. Interview with a diplomat representing a European state, 31 January 2014.
20. Interview with a diplomat representing a European state, 31 January 2014.
21. NPT/CONF.2010/P.C.II/WP.26.
22. Interview with John Loretz, Program Director, IPPNW, New York, 3 March 2015.
23. Interview with Luis Alfonso de Alba, Permanent Representative of Mexico to the United Nations in Vienna, 6 March 2014.
24. Currently, there is a domestic battle in Norway, pitting the government against parliament, about whether Norway should sign the Humanitarian Pledge or not. The government, concerned about its NATO commitments, shies away from this step because the Pledge calls for a legal ban on nuclear weapons. This sharpening of the disarmament formulation made it a recalcitrant actor.
25. Interview with Luis Alfonso de Alba, Permanent Representative of Mexico to the United Nations in Vienna, 6 March 2014; interview with Alfredo Alejandro Labbe Villa, Permanent Representative of Chile to the United Nations, Vienna, 4 June 2013.

26. Interview with a diplomat representing an EU member state, Vienna, 4 April 2013.
27. For a detailed overview, see International Law and Policy Institute (2014, p. 188).
28. A list of the signatories can be found at http://www.icanw.org/pledge/ (accessed 13 February 2016).
29. Interview with a diplomat representing a European state, Vienna, 31 January 2014.
30. http://www.icanw.org/campaign-news/powerful-statement-of-setsuko-thurlow-in-vienna/.

Disclosure statement

No potential conflict of interest was reported by the authors.

References

Acharya, A. (2004). How ideas spread: Whose norms matter? *International Organization, 58*, 239–275.
Adler, E. (1991). Cognitive evolution: A dynamic approach for the study of international relations and their progress. In E. Adler & B. Crawford (Eds.), *Progress in postwar international relations* (pp. 43–88)). New York, NY: Columbia University Press.
Adler, E. (1992). The emergence of cooperation: National epistemic communities and the international evolution of the idea of nuclear arms control. *International Organization, 46*(1), 101–145.
Adler, E. (1997). Seizing the middle ground: Constructivism in world politics. *European Journal of International Relations, 3*(3), 319–363.
Adler, E., & Pouliot, V. (Eds.). (2011). *International practices*. Cambridge: Cambridge University Press.
Alker, H. R. (1996). *Rediscoveries and reformulations: Humanistic methodologies for International studies*. Cambridge: Cambridge University Press.
Aristotle. (1995). *Rhetorik* (Franz G. Sieveke, Trans.). Munich: Wilhelm Fink.
Bakhtin, M. (1986). *Speech genres and other late essays* (V.W. McGee, Trans.). Austin: University of Texas Press.
Battilana, J. (2006). Agency and institutions: The enabling role of individuals' social position. *Organization, 13*(5), 653–676.

Beckert, J. (2010). How do fields change? The interrelations of institutions, networks, and cognition in the dynamics of markets. *Organization Studies, 31*(5), 605–627.

Béland, D., & Cox, R. H. (2013). Introduction to special issue: The politics of policy paradigms. *Governance, 26*(2), 193–195.

Benford, R. D., & Snow, D. A. (2000). Framing processes and social movements: An overview and assessment. *Annual Review of Sociology, 26,* 611–639.

Berman, S. (2013). Ideational theorizing in the social sciences since 'policy paradigms, social learning, and the State'. *Governance, 26*(2), 217–237.

Bernstein, R. (1991). *The new constellation: The ethical-political horizons of modernity/postmodernity.* Cambridge: Polity.

Betz, G. (2012). On degrees of justification. *Erkenntnis, 77,* 237–272.

Boltanski, L., & Thévenot, L. (2006). *On justification: Economies of worth.* Princeton, NJ: Princeton University Press.

Bourdieu, P. (1991). *Language and symbolic power.* Cambridge, MA: Harvard University Press.

Bourdieu, P. (2000). *Pascallian meditations.* Cambridge: Polity Press.

Bourdieu, P. (2001a). Pierre Bourdieu im Gespräch mit Philippe Fritsch. In P. Bourdieu (Eds.), *Das politische Feld: Zur Kritik der politischen Vernunft* (pp. 29–40). Konstanz: UVK Verlagsgesellschaft.

Bourdieu, P. (2001b). Das politische Feld. In P. Bourdieu (Eds.), *Das politische Feld: Zur Kritik der politischen Vernunft* (pp. 41–66). Konstanz: UVK Verlagsgesellschaft.

Bracken, P. (1999). *Fire in the East: The rise of Asian military power and the second nuclear age.* New York, NY: HarperCollins.

Burke, K. (1965). Terministic screens. *Proceedings of the American Catholic Philosophical Association, 39,* 87–102.

Campbell, J. (1998). Institutional analysis and the role of ideas in political economy. *Theory and Society, 27*(3), 377–409.

Campbell, J. (2004). *Institutional change and globalization.* Princeton, NJ: Princeton University Press.

Carstensen, M. B. (2011a). Ideas are not as stable as political scientists want them to be: A theory of incremental ideational change. *Political Studies, 59,* 596–615.

Carstensen, M. B. (2011b). Paradigm man vs. the bricoleur: Bricolage as an alternative vision of agency in ideational change. *European Political Science Review, 3*(1), 147–167.

Chopra, R. (2003). Neoliberalism as doxa: Bourdieu's theory of the state and the contemporary Indian discourse on globalization and liberalization. *Cultural Studies, 17*(3–4), 419–444.

Cicero, M. T. (2003). *Topica.* Oxford: Oxford University Press.

Commission on Global Governance. (1995). *Our global neighborhood.* Oxford: Oxford University Press.

Crawford, N. (2002). *Argument and change in World politics: Ethics, decolonization, and humanitarian intervention.* Cambridge: Cambridge University Press.

Culpepper, P. D. (2008). The politics of common knowledge: Ideas and institutional change in wage bargaining. *International Organization, 62*(1), 1–33.

Daddow, O. (2009). 'Tony's war'? Blair, Kosovo and the interventionist impulse in British foreign policy. *International Affairs, 85*(3), 547–560.

De Certeau, Michel. 1984. *The practice of everyday life.* Berkeley: University of California Press.

Detienne, M., & Vernant, J. P. (1974). *Les ruses de l'intelligence: la me'tis des Grecs.* Paris: Flammarion.

Dimitrova, A., & Rhinard, M. (2005). The power of norms in the transposition of EU directives. *European Integration Online Papers, 9*(16). Retrieved from http://eiop.or.at/eiop/

Douglas, W., & Sartor, G. (2013). Teleological justification of argumentation schemes. *Argumentation, 27,* 111–142.

English, R. D. (2000). *Russia and the West: Gorbachev, intellectuals, and the end of the cold war.* New York, NY: Columbia University Press.

Epstein, C. (2008). *The power of words in international relations: Birth of anti-whaling discourse.* Cambridge, MA: MIT Press.

Farrell, H., & Drezner, D. W. (2008). The power and politics of blogs. *Public Choice, 134*(1–2), 15–30.

Federal Ministry for Europe, Integration and Foreign Affairs. (2015). *Vienna conference on the humanitarian impact of nuclear weapons: Conference report.* Vienna: Author.

Finnemore, M., & Sikkink, K. (1998). International norm dynamics and political change. *International Organization, 52*, 887–917.

Fisher, W. R. (1987). *Human communication as narration: Toward a philosophy of reason, value, and action*. Columbia: University of South Carolina Press.

Fligstein, N., & McAdam, D. (2012). *A theory of fields*. Oxford: Oxford University Press.

Foucault, M. (1970). *The order of things: An archaeology of the human sciences*. New York, NY: Pantheon Books.

Foucault, M. (1972). *The archeology of knowledge and the discourse on langauge*. New York, NY: Pantheon Books.

Frazer, E., & Hutchings, K. (2007). Argument and rhetoric in the justification of political violence. *European Journal of Political Theory, 6*(2), 180–199.

Friedland, R. (2009). The endless fields of Pierre Bourdieu. *Organization, 16*(6), 887–917.

Gadamer, H. G. (1972). *Wahrheit und Methode*. Tübingen: J.C.B. Mohr.

Gödel, K. (1931). Über formal unentscheidbare Sätze der Principia Mathematica und verwandter Systeme I. *Monatshefte für Mathematik und Physik, 38*, 173–198.

Goodwin, J. (2001). Cicero's authority. *Philosophy and rhetoric, 34*(1), 38–60.

Green-Pedersen, N. J. (1987). The topics in medieval logic. *Argumentation, 1*, 407–417.

Haas, P. M. (1992). Banning chlorofluorocarbons: Epistemic community efforts to protect stratospheric ozone. *International Organization, 46*(1), 187–224.

Habermas, J. (1991). *Erläuterungen zur Diskursethik*. Frankfurt am Main: Suhrkamp.

Hall, P. A. (1993). Policy paradigms, social learning, and the state: The case of economic policymaking in Britain. *Comparative Politics, 25*(3), 275–296.

Haskins, E. V. (2004). Endoxa, epistemological optimism, and Aristotle's rhetorical project. *Philosophy and Rhetoric, 37*(1), 1–20.

Heinze, R. (1925). Auctoritas. *Hermes, 60*(3), 348–366.

Herrmann, M. (1998). One field, many perspectives: Building the foundations for dialogue. *International Studies Quarterly, 42*(4), 605–624.

Hollis, M., & Smith, S. (1990). *Explaining and understanding international relations*. Oxford: Clarendon Press.

Humanitarian Pledge. (2015). Retrieved from http://www.icanw.org/wp-content/uploads/2015/03/HINW14vienna_Pledge_Document.pdf

International Law and Policy Institute. (2014). *Counting to zero: A statistical report on the interest and participation of United Nations Member States in the issue of nuclear disarmament*. Oslo: ILPI Nuclear Weapons Project.

Jarratt, S. C. (1991). *Rereading the sophists: Classical rhetoric refigured*. Carbondale: Southern Illiniois University.

Johnson, R. (2013, April 29). NPT and risks to human survival: The inside story. *openDemocracy*. Retrieved from http://www.opendemocracy.net/5050/rebecca-johnson/npt-and-risks-to-human-survival-inside-story

Joint Statement on the Humanitarian Dimension of Nuclear Disarmament. (2012a, October 22). 67th session of the United Nations General Assembly First Committee. Retrieved from http://www.reachingcriticalwill.org/images/documents/Disarmament-fora/1com/1com12/statements/22Oct_Switzerland.pdf

Joint Statement on the Humanitarian Dimension of Nuclear Disarmament. (2012b, May 2). First session of the preparatory committee for the 2015 review conference of the parties to the treaty on the non-proliferation of nuclear weapons. Retrieved from http://www.reachingcriticalwill.org/images/documents/Disarmament-fora/npt/prepcom12/statements/2May_IHL.pdf

Joint Statement on the Humanitarian Impact of Nuclear Weapons. (2013a, October 21). 68th session of the United Nations General Assembly First Committee. Retrieved from http://www.un.org/disarmament/special/meetings/firstcommittee/68/pdfs/TD_21-Oct_CL-1_New_Zealand-%28Joint_St%29

Joint Statement on the Humanitarian Impact of Nuclear Weapons. (2013b, April 24). Delivered by Ambassador Abdul Samad Minty, Permanent Representative of South Africa to the United Nations at Geneva. Retrieved from http://www.reachingcriticalwill.org/images/documents/Disarmament-fora/npt/prepcom13/statements/24April_SouthAfrica.pdf

Kellenberger, J. (2010, April 20). *Bringing the era of nuclear weapons to an end*. Statement to the Geneva Diplomatic Corps. Retrieved from http://www.icrc.org/eng/resources/documents/statement/nuclear-weapons-statement-200410.htm

Kennedy-Pipe, C., & Vickers, R. (2007). 'Blowback' for Britain?: Blair, Bush, and the war in Iraq. *Review of International Studies, 33*(2), 205–221.

Kienpointner, M. (1986). Topische Sequenzen in argumentativen Dialogen. *Zeitschrift für germanistische Linguistik, 14*(3), 321–355.

Kornprobst, M. (2005). Episteme, nation-builders and national identity: The re-construction of Irishness. *Nations and Nationalism, 11*(3), 403–421.

Kornprobst, M. (2008). *Irredentism in European politics: Argumentation, compromise and norms*. Cambridge: Cambridge University Press.

Kornprobst, M., & Senn, M. (in press). A rhetorical field theory: Background, communication, and change. *British Journal of Politics and International Relations, 18*(2), 300–317.

Kratochwil, F. (1989). *Rules, norms and decisions: On the conditions of practical and legal reasoning in international relations and domestic affairs*. Cambridge: Cambridge University Press.

Kriesi, H. (1995). The political opportunity structure of new social movements: Its impact on their mobilization. In J. C. Jenkins & B. Klandermans (Eds.), *The politics of social protest: Comparative perspectives on states and social movements* (pp. 167–198). Minneapolis: University of Minnesota Press.

Lapid, Y. (1989). The third debate: On the prospects of international theory in a post-positivist era. *International Studies Quarterly, 33*(3), 235–254.

Legro, J. W. (2000). Whence American internationalism. *International Organization, 54*(2), 253–289.

May, E. R. (1962). The nature of foreign policy: The calculated versus the axiomatic. *Daedalus, 91*(4), 653–667.

Mayors for Peace. (2014). *Statement at the 2nd conference of the humanitarian initiative*. Retrieved from http://www.sre.gob.mx/en/images/stories/cih/mayorsforpeaceremarks.pdf

McComiskey, B. (1994). Neo-sophistic rhetorical theory: Sophistic precendents for contemporary epistemic rhetoric. *Rhetorical Society Quarterly, 24*(3/4), 16–24.

McGee, M. C., & Nelson, J. S. (1985). Narrative reason in public argument. *Journal of Communication, 35*(4), 139–155.

Mehta, J. (2011). The varied roles of ideas in politics: From 'whether' to 'how'. In D. Béland & R. H. Cox (Eds.), *Ideas and politics in social science research* (pp. 28–63). Oxford: Oxford University Press.

Murray, K., & Worth, O. (2013). Building consent: Hegemony, 'conceptions of the world' and the role of evangelicals in global politics. *Political Studies, 61*, 731–747.

Obama, B. (2009). *Remarks by President Barack Obama*. Retrieved from http://www.whitehouse.gov/the_press_office/Remarks-By-President-Barack-Obama-In-Prague-As-Delivered

Oliensis, E. (1998). *Horace and the rhetoric of authority*. Cambridge: Cambridge University Press.

Perelman, C., & Olbrechts-Tyteca, L. (1958). *Traité de l'argumentation*. Paris: Presse universitaire de France.

Powell, R. (1991). Absolute and relative gains in international relations theory. *American Political Science Review, 85*(4), 1303–1320.

Prakken, H. (2005). AI & law, logic and argument schemes. *Argumentation, 19*(3), 303–320.

Purcell, W. M. (1987). Transsumptio: A rhetorical doctrine of the thirteenth century. *Rhetorica, 5*(4), 369–410.

Quintilian, M. F. (1953). *Institutio oratoria* (H.E. Butler, Trans.). Cambridge, MA: Cambridge University Press.

Renon, L. (1998). Aristotle's endoxa and plausible argumentation. *Argumentation, 12*(1), 95–113.

Rigotti, E., & Morasso, S. G. (2010). Comparing argumentum model of topics to other contemporary approaches to argument schemes: The procedural and material components. *Argumentation, 24*, 489–512.

Ringmar, E. (2006). Inter-textual relations: The quarrel over the Iraq War as a conflict between narrative types. *Cooperation and Conflict, 41*(4), 403–421.

Risse, T., Ropp, S. C., & Sikkink, K. (1999). *The power of human rights: International norms and domestic change*. Cambridge: Cambridge University Press.

Risse, T., Ropp, S. C., & Sikkink, K. (2013). *The persistent power of human rights: From commitment to compliance*. Cambridge: Cambridge University Press.

Ruggie, J. (1975). International responses to technology: Concepts and trends. *International Organization, 29*(3), 557–583.

Ruggie, J. (1983). International regimes, transaction and change: Embedded liberalism in the postwar economic order. In S. Krasner (Ed.), *International regimes* (pp. 195–232). Ithaca, NY: Cornell University Press.

Schmidt, V. A. (2008). Discursive institutionalism: The explanatory power of ideas and discourse. *Annual Review of Politcal Science, 11*, 303–326.

Snow, D. A., Rochford Jr, E. B., Worden, S. K., & Benford, R. D. (1986). Frame alignment processes, micromobilization, and movement participation. *American Sociological Review, 51*(4), 464–481.

Tannenwald, N. (2005). Stigmatizing the bomb: Origins of the nuclear taboo. *International Security, 29*, 4–49.

Tarrow, S., & Tollefson, J. (1994). *Power in movement: Social movements, collective action and politics*. Cambridge: Cambridge University Press.

Toshkov, D. (2007). Transposition of EU social policy in the new member states. *Journal of European Social Policy, 17*(4), 335–348.

United Nations Development Programme. (1994). *Human Development Report 1994*. New York, NY: Oxford University Press.

Waever, O. (1996). The rise and fall of the inter-paradigm debate. In S. Smith, K. Booth, & M. Zalewski (Eds.), *International theory: Positivism & beyond* (pp. 149–185). Cambridge: Cambridge University Press.

Walton, D., & Sartor, G. (2013). Teleological justification of argumentation schemes. *Argumentation, 27*(2), 111–142.

Waltz, K. N. (1990). Nuclear myths and political realities. *American Political Science Review, 84*(3), 730–745.

Warnick, B., & Kline, S. L. (1992). The new rhetoric's argument schemes: A rhetorical view of practical reasoning. *Argumentation and Advocacy, 29*(1), 1–15.

Wiener, A. (2007). Contested meanings of norms: A research framework. *Comparattive European Politics, 5*(1), 1–17.

Willard, C.A. (1989). *A theory of argumentation*. Tuscaloosa: Alabama University Press.

Wright, L. (2001). Justification, discovery, reason & argument. *Argumentation, 15*, 97–104.

Caveat: addressing public justification as an empirical phenomenon

Liah Greenfeld

ABSTRACT
Instead of a conclusion, this special issue ends with a discussion between Liah Greenfeld, on the one hand, and Uriel Abulof and Markus Kornprobst, on the other hand, about the merits of studying public justification and how best to do so. Greenfeld suggests that public justification is predicated on the autonomy of the political sphere, the importance ascribed to public views, and to the prevalence of justification. Seeing public justification as ultimately a cultural phenomenon, this caveat urges scholars to study it in only specific historical contexts, which are, for now, limited to predominantly 'Western liberal democracies'.

Several recent events, which momentarily attracted the attention of the media, contradicting 'expert' views of the societies in which they occurred, left some scholars groping for a new explanation and, as a result, produced a more lasting impression on these scholars than on the public at large, including, possibly, the participants in these events themselves. Among these events were the transient 'Arab Spring' and the protests in Israel and India, all involving mostly the 'middle class', relatively educated and articulate sectors in their respective societies, explicitly clamouring for the implementation of patently liberal values of political representation, social justice, and gender equality, non-controversial and generally accepted in leading Western democracies, such as the U.S.. These events led contributors to this special issue to focus on 'public justification' – articulated public reasoning for/advocacy of certain political desiderata – and at least some of them (see Introduction by Abulof and Kornprobst) to conclude that it is a key to the understanding of politics in general – not only politics in liberal democracies, not only modern politics, but also politics everywhere and throughout history since the Axial Age.

For an empirical student of politics (not a card-carrying representative of any particular discipline, guided by and dedicated to depicting reality in received categories, which distinguish one discipline from another, but a social scientist concerned with understanding what is), this is a problematic conclusion. Based on unexamined, though popular today, assumptions about human nature, it juxtaposes very distant past and very recent events, removed from it by 2500–3000 years, in effect denying the claim the historical framework in which it could be empirically tested. Empirical testing always involves comparisons of like relevant phenomena: if we make a claim about the nutritional importance of apples, we are limited to comparing apples in various diets; it would make no sense to compare apples and oranges. If we make a claim about the political importance of public justification, we must compare the role of public justification in politics within the historical period in which (a) societies are sufficiently differentiated to allow the observation of politics as an autonomous sphere – such societies would not become the rule for millennia after Axial Age; (b) there are publics, whose views matter, as distinguished from ruling elites, on the one hand, and the ruled population, required only to obey, on the other; and (c) there is justification – to establish which 'justification', to begin with, must be clearly defined. (It should go without saying that 'public justification', to be a meaningful addition to the discourse, should be considered as a particular case of legitimation and distinguished from legitimation in general, which, by definition, exists wherever there is any authority.) Assuming that all round fruit are apples would not allow us to understand (or prove) the nutritional value of apples. Similarly, assuming that all these conditions obtain by dint of universal human nature would not allow us to examine the importance of public justification in politics.

Two things are empirically (on the basis of relevant comparisons) warranted to be considered universal to humanity. The first of these is the constitution of our bodies. It is based on comparisons with other living bodies and establishes that human beings are animals. As animals, we differ from other animals quantitatively only, having more or less of the qualities that constitute an animal, without sharply separating us from others. The fact that, just like bodies of mice, horses, and so on, human bodies are in many respects like the bodies of other animals and in some minor respects species-specific, allows us to compare processes in our bodies, including the brain, with those in other animals of the same genus, family, and even class (mammals) to arrive at medical conclusions and even to extrapolate from experiments on animals (however morally detestable one may find this) onto humans.

The second characteristic empirical evidence (i.e. relevant comparisons) allows us to claim as universal to humanity is that, unlike all other animals, who transmit their ways of life genetically, we transmit our ways of life symbolically. We call such process of symbolic transmission *culture*, using the word which, from Cicero on, referred to phenomena superadded onto nature – like in agri*culture*. Indeed, culture is an *emergent* reality – that is, a reality superadded onto the level of reality which provides the necessary conditions for it without causing it, to which, therefore, it cannot be reduced, like the reality of life, for the most famous instance, which is a level of reality superadded onto the level of matter, which provides the necessary conditions for life but to which life cannot be reduced. Culture is *emergent* from the level of organic (living) reality. While emergent realities can exist only in the conditions provided by the level of reality underneath them, they are irreducible or self-causing, and the drastically changed nature of causality which operates within them sharply separates them from the level underneath, making such realities autonomous, which justifies, in fact necessitates, a separate science for their study, independent from the sciences studying the levels below – physics in the case of life, and biology in the case of culture.

Culture sharply separates humanity from the rest of the animal life and makes humanity a reality of its own kind, *sui generis*. The essential characteristic of culture is that it is symbolic. Symbols are arbitrary signs, whose meaning is determined by context, dependent on time and constantly changing. This means that culture is also, essentially, historical. This explains the extreme variability of human ways of life in distinction to virtual homogeneity of ways of life within every other animal species. Thus, while culture distinguishes humanity from all other animal species and, to be fully understood, must be studied in comparison with them, it, taken as a whole, cannot provide an empirical framework for the study of historically (or context-) specific elements of our transmissible ways of life; only specific historical contexts, that is, specific cultures, can provide such a framework.

Axial Age and 'Arab Spring', for example, belong to totally different frameworks and one can understand nothing about 'Arab Spring' by reference to Axial Age. Instead of painting history in such broad brushstrokes and connecting particular political events of yesterday to a vastly removed from them period when they could not be even imagined, one must place these events within the historical period (or context, specific culture) to which they belong. Each such specific culture will be defined by certain organizing symbolic principles, regulating the assignment of meaning to (i.e. interpretation, judgment of) specific symbols. For instance, in the framework of an aristocratic society, divided into legal estates, each with its own rights and duties, equality across collective identity lines had negative connotations and, still in the eighteenth century, one could talk exultantly about 'the glorious inequality of ranks'. In the context of contemporary U.S.A and its democratic culture, the notions of equality and inequality changed places, equality across collective identities becoming the shiniest of ideals and inequality a totally negative phenomenon, the main emblem of *unjust*, illegitimate social arrangement.

The organizing principles in each particular context reflect the way reality is imagined in it, that is, what is *believed to be not simply apparent but causally significant*. For example, in the eighteenth-century society, in which one praised 'the glorious inequality of ranks', reality was imagined as organized by God in a hierarchical order, in which each individual was assigned (called to serve in) a proper, unchangeable place. God was the causally significant, therefore central, element in this image, the final cause of everything, the source of all meaning, law, and truth, and every line of reasoning, value and instrumental, moral, philosophical, political, scientific, economic, aesthetic – whatever, stopped with Him. Social reality was constructed on the basis of this image and therefore confirmed and constantly reaffirmed it. While it functioned smoothly, there was no *public* in the aristocratic society, only the rulers and the ruled; spontaneous riots were quite common, but there was nothing one could call 'public justification'.

Today, in liberal democratic societies worshipping equality, reality is imagined as secular, ruled by laws of nature which assign sovereignty (i.e. absolute authority) over the world to the human species, endowed with a more capable brain than any other, while making all members of this species (with the exception of children under 18 or 21, depending on which liberal democracy we discuss, whose brain is presumably not sufficiently developed) fundamentally equal and partaking in this sovereignty. In the modern consciousness, Nature is the final arbiter in every dispute. This image of reality developed together with nationalism: secularism, fundamental egalitarianism of membership, and popular sovereignty are the principles of nationalism, and societies regarded by their members as nations are constructed on the basis of these principles. Nationalism was, in fact, the form in which modern inclusive democracy (as opposed to the democracy of ancient slave societies) first appeared, bringing in its train such concepts as civil society and public. Elites became fluid, political activism spread throughout the society. In Western liberal democracies, there is no identifiable stratum that can be called the governing class, and conversations between elected officials and the electorate is common and ongoing. It makes perfect sense, in such societies, to talk about 'public justification'. The principles of nationalism, however, are implemented in accordance with the type of nationalism that a society develops: such implementation would be dramatically different in individualistic civic nationalisms, which produce liberal democracy, and in collectivistic and, in particular, collectivistic ethnic, nationalisms, which produce modern forms of authoritarianism. As numerous recent events demonstrate (among others, in the lasting and scorching summer that succeeded the all-too-brief Arab 'spring'), 'public justification' has not replaced violence as the main instrument of conflict resolution/reaching agreements outside of liberal democracies.

Today, remarkably, of the three principles of nationalism, it is secularization that is most misunderstood. It is implicitly defined as the opposite of religion. As religion itself is never analysed by 'experts' in secularization, this definition is not particularly helpful. What is chiefly implied appears to be the existence of a personified transcendental force of creative intelligence – God – in religion, and its denial in secularized societies. Because God is assumed to be the source of all morals (distinctions between good and evil), the denial of God is equated with the absence of bases for morality. This, however, is a very narrow definition of religion, based exclusively on the experience of Western, that is, monotheistic, civilization; it disregards the great Eastern religions. Neither Buddha nor Confucius are transcendental forces, responsible for the creation of the world, and yet, no one would go so far as to deny that both China and India, with their combined billions of human beings, have lived at least as morally regulated lives as Jewish, Christian, and Islamic societies. The idea of religion based on the experience of one part of humanity to the exclusion of all others not unexpectedly results in a total misunderstanding of modern processes of secularization. Far from de-spiritualizing or 'disenchanting' the world (a phrase borrowed from Weber, whose *entzauberung*, incidentally, means de-magicalization, which occurs precisely with the spread of strict monotheism, specifically Protestantism, and not 'disenchantment'), nationalism's secularization imbues the mundane with spirit and enchants it. Nationalism brings heavens to earth, so to speak: this world of our experience becomes the sphere of the sacred, needing no transcendental help to imbue it with meaning.

Durkheim (1961), the great French sociologist, concluded in *The Elementary Forms of Religious Life*, that whatever name people give God, in fact God is Society – that is, we always worship those 'collective representations' by which our culture represents its organizing beliefs to us. Ironically, our image of reality (the image of reality in liberal democracies of today) is in some crucial respects remarkably similar to the image of reality characteristic of the rigidly stratified hierarchical society national democracies replaced. To start with, both are based on *beliefs* – knowledge which is untested, cannot be tested, and by and large goes unexamined. (There is no empirical evidence that we have more capable brains than other species and, if one considers this claim carefully, it, like the existence of God, can be neither proven nor refuted.) These beliefs are in both cases essentially *monotheistic*: in both cases, we imagine the world, despite the evident heterogeneity of phenomena in it, as one, a *universe*, consistently ordered, that is, logically organized, only in the first case, the creative intelligence, God, is behind it, while in the second –ours – Nature, it is immanent.

This leads us to the final point – the empirical sphere of the application of the 'justification' concept itself. Granted all cultures have principles in relation to which all actions within them can be assessed; whatever these principles are, they are, by definition, moral, allowing us to distinguish between right and wrong. Granted also that in complex differentiated societies, autonomous institutional spheres, such as politics, would be assessed, if not always explicitly, in relation to these moral principles. Granted, finally, that in modern societies, *nations*, constructed on the basis of three principles of nationalism, such assessment may take the form of a conversation between elected officials and the electorate or the *public*. What is meant by 'justification' and how useful is the phenomenon of 'public justification', necessarily based on this concept, in explaining – and facilitating resolution of conflicts in – contemporary politics?

Judging by such influential texts as *On Justification* by Boltanski and Thevenot (2006), 'justification', which is nowhere clearly defined, is used in the sense of logical reasoning from first principles. If the principles are assumed to be universal (as the principle *of common humanity* is assumed to be by B&T), that is, if we make the assumption of *moral minimalism*, then, logical connections between statements, sufficiently exposed, will necessarily lead to the *only* correct, *justified* – logical and just – conclusion, binding on both parties to the conflict, because, being in their right mind, they simply could not disagree with logic. In fact, it would be possible, based on articulate scenarios of various likely conflicts, to develop a technology for reaching agreements – B&T call this 'political grammar' – something like a diagnostic and therapeutic manual for political health, with exact prescriptions for common ailments. Turned backwards, this 'political grammar' would also provide the matrix for explanation of historical conflicts, which did not have the benefit of this technology.

The problem here is that the assumption of moral minimalism is empirically unwarranted (there are no universal moral principles and, as explained above, could not be, the symbolic nature of the cultural process mitigating against this) and that, moreover, logical reasoning is not a universal human endowment either and thus resonates in different cultures to vastly different degrees. It must be remembered that we, in Western civilization, based on monotheism, are exceptionally prone to make universalistic assumptions: we believe that the world is a consistently – logically! – ordered *universe*. Science itself is based on this monotheistic belief, without which (consider this for a minute) it would be impossible. Indeed, it is not coincidental that the famous transition from *mythos* to *logos*, the so-called *Greek miracle*, happened precisely when the first redaction of the Hebrew Bible (the first presentation of monotheism as a consistent system) was discussed in Babylon in the *lingua franca* of the region, Aramaeic. Logic of no contradiction was logically impossible in the polytheistic culture of Greek mythology: its heterogeneity could not be regarded in terms of contradiction. It was the Hebrew Bible that connected justice to logic, creating our Western concept of justice, as it created so many fundamental categories of our thought, our moral principles, which we consider universal, and our very mode of thinking. Unfortunately, this severely limits the applicability of the concept of 'public justification'.

Cultural relativism, stressed by both great theorists of sociology, Durkheim and Weber, is the core fact of human reality. It, as Weber argued explicitly, does not at all imply moral relativism. But it does mean that there is no substitute for empirical testing when it comes to theories which claim to help us in understanding, not to mention controlling, this reality.

Disclosure statement

No potential conflict of interest was reported by the author.

References

Durkheim, E. (1961). *The elementary forms of the religious life*. New York, NY: Collier Books.
Boltanski, L., & Thévenot, L. (2006). *On justification: Economies of worth*. Princeton, NJ: Princeton University Press.

COMMENTARY

Unpacking public justification

Uriel Abulof and Markus Kornprobst

ABSTRACT
This brief response to Greenfeld's caveat submits that public justification is not omnipresent, but can extend, and has extended, beyond the modern, liberal West. Subscribing to a thin, rather than thick, conceptualization of public justification, we chart the contested contours of public justification, and urge scholars of this emergent field to clarify their own take before advancing pertinent theories and case studies. We briefly expound the nature and historical roots of both 'justification' and 'the public', suggesting that their amalgam into public justification transcends the modern, liberal West.

Citizens: We will be satisfied; let us be satisfied.
Brutus: Then follow me, and give me audience, friends … And public reasons shall be rendered / of Caesar's death. (William Shakespeare, *Julius Caesar*, The Forum)

Liah Greenfeld's *caveat* provides a valuable opportunity to engage with some of the troubling aspects of public justification as both a concept and a research agenda. One quandary drives much of the discussion: What is the purview of public justification? Can it fit anytime, anywhere? Greenfeld forcefully argues against seeing public justification as 'a key to the understanding of politics in general – not only politics in liberal democracies, not only modern politics, but politics everywhere and throughout history since the Axial Age'. She suggests that public justification is predicated on (1) 'politics as an autonomous sphere', (2) the existence of 'publics, whose views matter' and (3) that 'there is justification'. Since public justification is ultimately a cultural phenomenon, it is essentially historical. Hence, we must not 'juxtapose very distant past and very recent events', and instead study it in 'only specific historical contexts'. For Greenfeld, viable contexts for public justification are limited to predominantly 'Western liberal democracies'.

We share Greenfeld's premises, but beg to differ with her conclusion. Although public justification is not omnipresent, we submit that it can extend, and has extended, beyond the modern, liberal West. Our take is partly driven by our subscribing to a thin, rather than thick, conceptualization of public justification. Below we briefly chart some of the contested contours of public justification, and urge scholars of this emergent field to clarify their own take before advancing pertinent theories and case studies. In what follows, we unpack public justification: we briefly expound the nature and historical roots of both 'justification' and 'the public', suggesting that their amalgam into public justification transcends the modern, liberal West.

Justification

Justification is about communicating reasons. We justify our past, present and prospective beliefs and actions when we explain to ourselves and to others *why* we take a certain stance rather than another one. We explain why something is right and another is wrong – factually, pragmatically or morally. Humans, and humans alone, have developed this trait that gradually became a predisposition. The relations between justification and culture are multifaceted. First, as Greenfeld accurately points out, justification is culturally embedded: whether or not we reason and communicate, and how we do so (in terms of both form and content) is shaped by – but also shaping – the socio-historical culture we inhabit. Second, culture is often the object of justification: we reason why our culture is good, perhaps even better than others. Third, justification itself can become a culture, a socio-historical creation and practice, so much so that we occasionally justify our very recourse to justification; we may even attempt to justify the very language we use for justification (Schieffelin, Woolard, & Kroskrity, 1998).

When we believe that the *is* and the *ought* are at odds, that the issue is important, and that the gap is troubling, we turn to justification to make amends, to propose a change. However, justification need not contest the status quo; it can also reaffirm, even sanctify, it. When we believe that the *is* and the *ought* coalesce, we justify why we ought to resist change. Thus, justification can in fact underpin Greenfeld's proposition, following Durkheim, that we worship our cultural 'collective representations'. Herein, however, lies a challenge, both theoretical and empirical: Why to reason the sacred? *Prima facie*, the divine needs no human explanation, let alone justification; it ought to simply be taken as is, a given to be followed, not a variable to grapple with. In practice, however, any *ought* can drive a *why*. On a collective level, this may be the result of worrying about the eventual emergence of internal dissention or of contact with external, divergent, cultures. On the individual level, it might be driven by the work of individual conscience; after all, 'humans are inevitably evaluative creatures' (Keane, 2015, p. 4). Either way, religion, whether turning to God, Nature or even People, not only allows for, but also often invites, justification. Ultimately, then, only utter hegemony precludes justification. Thus, studying *how* hegemony breaks is indispensable for grasping the social actors' turn to asking *why*, and for understanding why they succeed or fail at giving answers. As long as any belief or behaviour is potentially contestable, from within or without, justification kicks in.

Still, where justification kicks the *why*-can to is indeterminate. Justification is multi-layered, occasionally like an artichoke, leading to a core, other time like an onion, lacking it. Either way, peeling the justificatory layers is key to its analysis. We effectively follow the *why* through the chain of reasoning. We distinguish between beliefs that are *inferential, supporting, basic* and *absolute* (Abulof, 2015). Inferential beliefs are never used to justify other beliefs; conversely, absolute beliefs require no justification whatsoever, constituting maxims and taboos. In-between, the more common supporting and basic beliefs may both justify, and be justified by, other beliefs, with basic beliefs being more foundational.

For example, in the biblical scripture of the Ten Commandments, proscribing killing or stealing is not reasoned, constituting taboos; conversely, the command to 'honor thy father and thy mother' is reasoned on the consequentialist ground 'that thy days may be long upon the land', endowing life with an absolute value. Importantly, the Ten Commandments themselves include a preambular justification: 'I am the Lord thy God, which have brought thee out of the land of Egypt, out of the house of bondage'. God is the *cause sui*, bestowing Commandments upon the people, but even His authority seemingly requires justification through the people's memory of their servitude and the implicit absolute value of liberty. This exegesis reads the Ten Commandments, a prime and primordial example of divine ordinance, as involving public justification: God communicating his case, and his reasoning, to his people. For Voegelin (2000b, p. 19), this is the dawn of existential history:

> The order of history emerges from the history of order. Every society is burdened with the task, under its concrete conditions, of creating an order that will endow the fact of its existence with meaning in terms of ends divine and human.

This *nomization*, the justificatory creation of nomos out of chaos (see introduction), does not seem unique to modernity, but to human history, at least since the Axial Age. *Nomization* permeated antiquity, spanning China, India, Israel, Ancient Greece and Rome, and early Christianity (Harle, 1998). Yet more empirical evidence of *nomization* involves the early Middle Ages (Hen & Innes, 2000) onwards. For example, throughout the 'long fourteenth century', much scholarly thought was given to the legitimation of authority (Canning, 2011). Christianity, by purporting to 'know the truth', ironically opened the astronomical gate for secularization (Blumenberg, 1983), paving path for the rising existential authority of the individual in late medieval thought (Greenaway, 2012). Throughout the Middle Ages, order and dissent, in both idea and practice, fostered a creative tension that prepared the ground for the Enlightenment (Russell, 1992).

Yet modernity is a watershed in the chronicles of justification. Greenfeld rightly observes that 'the modern consciousness' is informed by secularism, fundamental egalitarianism, and popular sovereignty, the three principles of nationalism. These three national principles have indeed revolutionized political thought, and modes of political justification. However, nationalism transformed, not engendered, justification. Political justification need not be national, and subscribe to secularism, egalitarianism and popular sovereignty. What happens, however, when we append the 'public' adjective – would that not require confining justification to modernity alone?

Public

The modern emergence of the public stands at the crux of Greenfeld's caveat. Etymologically, the 'public', a Latin blend of *pubes* and *poplicus*, simply designates 'adult people'. Still, in modern scholarship, the public involves much more. Dewey and Habermas are two prominent thinkers who assign great importance to the public, and both entwine it with justification and legitimacy. Dewey (2012 [1927]) saw the public as the wellspring of creative inquiry into social problems and their resolution, Habermas (1999) as the source of democratic legitimacy. For Dewey, it would seem a vibrant public is the prime goal, democracy a means to promote it; for Habermas, democracy is the main aim, public deliberation a way to ground it.

The very existence of a public, however, is often presumed, not demonstrated. Founding a normative prescription on an unsubstantiated empirical description is a rather perilous move for political theory. After all, what does it take to register a group as a public – is every society, a polity-bounded population, also a public? Conversely, does (or should) public harbor cultural homogeneity, common fate, political awareness, substantial communication and collective action? Simply put, is the public perforce an agent? Granted, like all social phenomena we can treat 'the public' too, as a process, and in this regard an agent-in-the-making. But where do we draw the line – when does an aggregation of 'adult people' become a public?

Greenfeld's asserts that 'there was no *public* in the aristocratic society, only the rulers and the ruled'. This makes much sense if we predicate public on modern nationalism and its three principles (above). Accordingly, aristocratic society precludes the very idea, let alone the practice, of public, which can thus be only modern. Where, however, should we draw the line between the premodern rulers and ruled to the modern elite and public? In order to avoid anachronism and tautology, we need to conceptualize the public without attaching its meaning to modernity. We should also bear in mind that the ethos of equality informed discourses and practices both before and throughout modernity, often challenging the rulers. This ethos is neither wholly absent from pre-modernity (e.g. Servile Wars) nor hegemonic in modernity (e.g. Occupy Wall Street). In fact, terms such as 'public opinion' and 'public relations (PR)' were invented by modern elite partly to contain, even tame, the masses, 'engineering their consent' (Bernays, 1947) to an ostensibly benign hierarchical order, even in democracies.

We propose a more relaxed and inclusive conceptualization of public. Instead of adopting a binary either-or approach to the existence of public, we take a cue from Dewey and the situational theory of public to chart a scalar view of the public (Ni & Kim, 2009). Such a spectrum can, for example, span nonpublics (who face no common problem), latent publics (who have a problem), aware publics (who recognize their problem) and active publics (who respond to their problem) (Grunig & Hunt, 1984). Other scales can pertain to the extent to which people come together to participate in, and commemorate, events; or the extent to which they substantially communicate with each other, and designate themselves (and are designated by others) as a distinct collective.

Was Shakespeare right – does giving 'public reasons' in politics go back to antiquity? Bernays (1952, p. 12), the godfather of PR suggested as much: 'The three main elements of public relations are practically as old as society: informing people, persuading people, or integrating people with people'. And contemporary scholars, focusing on political PR follow suit: 'the practice of political public relations is probably as old as politics and society itself' (Strèombèack & Kiousis, 2011, p. 1). The annals of political thought, from Cicero to Machiavelli, abound counsels to heed public needs and sentiments. The important Greek concept of *doxa* (public beliefs) is a linguistic case in point. Whether or not the people actually listened to their rulers and prophets is, as Voegelin (2000a) recounts, a different matter.

The public seemed to matter in the Middle Ages too. A fascinating example is the Peace and Truce of God (*Pax Dei*), a Catholic movement that sought to limit violence. *Pax Dei*, 'by attaching sacred significance to privacy, helped create a space in which communal gatherings could take place and thus encouraged the reconstitution of public space at the village level' (Ariès & Duby, 1987, I, p. 27). The movement demonstrated 'the remarkable development of popular interest and cooperative public action' (Mackinney, 1930, p. 181; see also Head & Landes, 1992). On a more philosophical plane, *Pax Dei* resonates rather well with Nietzsche's (2007) thesis on the advent of 'herd morality'. In the late Middle Ages, we might also consider 'the introduction of public justice and the concepts of crime and punishment' in thirteenth-century Norway (Kangas, Korpiola, & Ainonen, 2013, p. 170) and the persistent preference of public reading in both Britain and France from the mid-fourteenth to the late-fifteenth century (Coleman, 2005). When it comes to inter-group relations, the Scottish Declaration of Arbroath (1320) is quite remarkable in justifying its demand for independence through the will of the people. Whether a proto-national document, presaging popular sovereignty, or a piece of propaganda (and probably both), the Declaration remains a public-based justification of politics.

Yet, even more than with justification, modernity underscored the importance *the public* in politics. The French Revolution married the once pejorative term 'opinion' with the 'public', thus bestowing upon it positive significance (Ozouf, 1988); the revolutionaries thus effectively deployed public opinion as an instrument of political legitimization and delegitimization (Cowans, 2001). In Britain too, terms like public opinion, the public spirit, the public mind, the public voice – all became ubiquitous in political discourse, catchphrases to be used and abused in justifying and criticizing politicians and their policies (Thompson, 2013). Ultimately, by the end of the eighteenth century, the socio-moral imagery of 'public opinion' had come to signify 'the authoritative judgment of a collective conscience, the ruling of a tribunal to which even the state was subject' (Vopa, 1992, p. 79). This did not dismantle the elites, or elitism, but made the public explicitly essential for the justification of politics.

In light of the above, we would like to propose that while public justification predates modernity, it has become increasingly prominent in modernity. To wit, public justification does not postulate that the *whole* public *constantly* engages in the reasoning of politics, but that parts of it occasionally do. It does not transpose reasoning from the elite or the private spheres onto the public; rather, it breaks the barrier between these realms. It focuses on how social actors come to assume a position that provides them with the authority to be agents and carriers of legitimating ideas, employing political reasoning in, by, and for the public. Public justification thus interweaves *reasoning* and *resonance*: it is about the emergence, adoption and adaptation of the reasons agents give, and the ways these reasons appeal to their carriers in the larger public sphere (Abulof, 2016). Importantly, speakers do not necessarily engage the public as a whole, and often target a specific public that they deem most pertinent to their cause, and reasoning.

Public justification may have become increasingly prominent in both domestic politics and global politics. The latter is less bounded by the borders of nation-states, and its justification is likewise less confined to the nation-state container. Growing need, and possibility, for public justification drive this trend. First, the nation-state is often ill equipped to meet single handedly its myriad challenges, let alone justify their handling. When a civil war rages in Syria, for instance, this is very much felt in Europe as well. States and a plethora of other actors ranging from civil society to international organizations have to figure out what to do together. This reckoning typically involves public justification.

Second, expanding channels of communication – from the CNN effect (Gilboa, 2005; Strobel, 1996) to new social media (Lynch, 2011; Bennett & Segerberg, 2011) – allow public justifications to flow more easily.

To be sure, more public justification does not promise better results in addressing pressing political issues. Publics engaging in justification often find it very difficult to communicate in meaningful fashion. Sometimes, they are part of different 'interpretive communities' (Fish, 1980), which, all too often, speak past one another. Yet there are examples for successful justificatory exchanges in global politics. The International Criminal Court (ICC), for instance, was justified into existence (Glasius, 2006; Schiff, 2008). Land mines and cluster munition were justified out of it (Carpenter, 2011; Docherty, 2009).

A final note on the content of public justification – is it, ought it be, only liberal, and culturally embedded in Western heritage? To this, we answer in the negative. Public justification can be applied to the liberal legitimation of gay marriage as it is to the Islamic State's vision of a global Caliphate. When people communicate their political reasoning in order to persuade many others to follow, public justification transpires. Hence, public justification need not, and indeed often does not, follow Habermasian deliberation, and be open, equal and peaceful. It also need not subscribe to universal, or even universalizable, principles of morality, although it occasionally does, and as Greenfeld accurately points out, this practice is especially prevalent in the West. This is why, again following Greenfeld, we cannot but fully endorse a research agenda that situate public justifications in their cultural context; we append this by calling for socio-historical comparison of such justificatory dynamics, acknowledging cultural uniqueness while avoiding the pitfalls of essentialism and determinism. If public justification does not apply to premodern, non-Western societies, let our research show it. Finally, and unfortunately, public justification is no panacea; communicating political reasons in public does not preclude bloodshed or tyranny. Indeed, often enough it facilitates them. 'Friends, Romans, countrymen, lend me your ears', asked Mark Antony in his funeral oration of Caesar, and they did.

Disclosure statement

No potential conflict of interest was reported by the authors.

References

Abulof, U. (2015). Normative concepts analysis: Unpacking the language of legitimation. *International Journal of Social Research Methodology, 18*(1), 73–89.

Abulof, U. (2016). Public political thought: Bridging the sociological–philosophical divide in the study of legitimacy. *The British Journal of Sociology, 67*(2), 371–391.

Ariès, P., & Duby, G. (1987). *A history of private life.* Cambridge, MA: Belknap Press of Harvard University Press.

Bennett, W. L. & Segerberg, A. (2011). Digital media and the personalization of collective action: Social technology and the organization of protests against the global economic crisis. *Information, Communication & Society, 14*(6), 770–799.

Bernays, E. (1947). The engineering of consent. *The Annals of the American Academy of Political and Social Science, 250*(1), 113–120.

Bernays, E. (1952). *Public relations* (1st ed.). Norman: University of Oklahoma Press.

Blumenberg, H. (1983). *The legitimacy of the modern age. Studies in contemporary German social thought.* Cambridge: MIT Press.

Canning, J. (2011). *Ideas of power in the late middle ages, 1296–1417.* Cambridge: Cambridge University Press.

Carpenter, R. C. (2011). Vetting the advocacy agenda: network centrality and the paradox of weapons norms. *International Organization, 65*(1), 69–102.

Coleman, J. (2005). *Public reading and the reading public in late Medieval England and France.* Cambridge: Cambridge University Press.

Cowans, J. (2001). *To speak for the people: Public opinion and the problem of legitimacy in the French Revolution.* New York: Routledge.

Dewey, J. ([1927] 2012). *The public and its problems: An essay in political inquiry.* University Park: Pennsylvania State University Press.

Docherty, B. (2009). Breaking new ground: The convention on cluster munitions and the evolution of international humanitarian law. *Human Rights Quarterly, 31*(4), 934–963.

Fish, S. (1980). *Is there a text in this class? The authority of interpretive communities.* Cambridge: Harvard University Press.

Gilboa, E. (2005). The CNN effect: The search for a communication theory of international relations. *Political Communication, 22*(1), 27–44.

Glasius, M. (2006). *The International Criminal Court: A global civil society achievement.* London: Routledge.

Greenaway, J. (2012). *The differentiation of authority: The medieval turn toward existence.* Washington, DC: Catholic University of America Press.

Grunig, J., & Hunt, T. (1984). *Managing public relations.* New York: Holt, Rinehart and Winston.

Habermas, J. (1999). *Moral consciousness and communicative action.* Cambridge: MIT Press.

Harle, V. (1998). *Ideas of social order in the ancient world.* Westport, CT: Greenwood Press.

Head, T., & Landes, R. (Eds.). (1992). *The peace of God: Social violence and religious response in France around the year 1000.* Ithaca, NY: Cornell University Press.

Hen, Y., & Innes, M. (Eds.). (2000). *The uses of the past in the early Middle Ages.* Cambridge: Cambridge University Press.

Kangas, S., Korpiola, M., & Ainonen, T. (Eds.). (2013). *Authorities in the Middle Ages: Influence, legitimacy, and power in Medieval Society.* Berlin: Walter de Gruyter.

Keane, W. (2015). *Ethical life: Its natural and social histories*. Princeton: Princeton University Press.

Lynch, M. (2011). After Egypt: The limits and promise of online challenges to the authoritarian Arab state. *Perspectives on Politics, 9*(2), 301–310.

Mackinney, L. (1930). The people and public opinion in the eleventh-century peace movement. *Speculum, 5*(2), 181–206.

Ni, L., & Kim, J.-N. (2009). Classifying publics: Communication behaviors and problem-solving characteristics in controversial issues. *International Journal of Strategic Communication, 3*(4), 217–241.

Nietzsche, F. (2007). *On the genealogy of morality*. Cambridge: Cambridge University Press.

Ozouf, M. (1988). "Public Opinion" at the end of the old regime. *The Journal of Modern History, 60*, S1–S21.

Russell, J. (1992). *Dissent and order in the Middle Ages: The search for legitimate authority*. New York: Twayne Publishers.

Schieffelin, B., Woolard, K., & Kroskrity, P. (Eds.). (1998). *Language ideologies: Practice and theory*. Oxford: Oxford University Press.

Schiff, B. (2008). *Building the international criminal court*. Cambridge: Cambridge University Press.

Strèombèack, J., & Kiousis, S. (Eds.). (2011). *Political public relations: Principles and applications*. New York: Routledge.

Strobel, W. P. (1996). The CNN effect. *American Journalism Review, 18*(4), 32–38.

Thompson, J. (2013). *British political culture and the idea of 'public opinion', 1867–1914*. Cambridge: Cambridge University Press.

Voegelin, E. (2000a). *Order and history*. Columbia: University of Missouri Press.

Voegelin, E. (2000b). *Order and history, Volume I: Israel and revelation*. Columbia: University of Missouri Press.

Vopa, A. (1992). Conceiving a public: Ideas and society in eighteenth-century Europe. *The Journal of Modern History, 64*(1), 79–116.

Index

Note: Page numbers followed by 'n' refer to notes

abduction research tradition 11
abortion rights 22
absolutism, moral 30–31
abstinence promotion 84
Abu-Lughod, L. 29
Abulof, U. 11–12, 13, 14, 34–52, 131; and Kornprobst, M. 1–18, 126–133
Academi 56
activism and citizen mobilization 76
actors: plurality 6; religious 85, 94; religious reasons 7; social 9, 127
adolescents, deception of parents/peers 27
Adorno, T. W. 36
advocacy networks 5
Afghanistan, US military troop levels 58
Africa, health and faith factor 92
African Religious Health Assets Programme (ARHAP) 91, 92
AIDS/HIV 84, 92
Alker, H. 7
Alma Ata Declaration on Primary Health Care (1978) 87
Alma Ata International Conference on Primary Health Care (1978) 88
America *see* United States of America (USA)
Amman Declaration on Health Promotion through Islamic Lifestyles (1996) 90
anthropological studies 29
Anti-Personnel Mine Convention (1997) 109
Antony, Mark 131
appeasement illustration 104, 105
Apple smartphone encryption 58
Arab Spring 3, 120, 122, 123
Arendt, H. 36, 39, 42
argumentation field 6
ARHAP (African Religious Health Assets Programme) 91, 92
aristocratic society 122, 129
Aristotle 25, 103, 106
artists, West/East German 7
Asch, S. E. 26
assumptions, universalistic 124

audience, message resonance 103
aurea mediocritas (golden middle) 112
authoritarian personality 36
authority: dimensions of 105–106; existential 128; Weber on 4–5
authorized spokesperson 103, 105, 114n3
Avant, D. 56
Axial Age 2, 3, 126, 128
Axial agents 2, 3
Axial separation 2, 8–9, 127

background knowledge 100
bad conscience 39, 46
bad faith 42
Barbato, M., and Kratochwil, F. 84
Barker, R. 65, 72–73
Beetham, D., and Lord, C. 9
behaviorism 20
beliefs: absolute 127; *doxa* (public) 129
Bellah, R. N. 2
Berger, P. L. 2
Bergson, H. 37
Berlin, I. 41
Bernays, E. 129
Bettiza, G., and Dionigi, F. 84–85
biblical scripture 128
Biersteker, T. J., and Hall, R. B. 55
Bill and Melinda Gates Foundation 91
Bill of Rights, American 54
birth control 81–82
Bisht, D. B. 88
Boltanski, L., and Thévenaut, L. 6, 7, 12, 82, 86, 87, 124
Bourdieu, P. 102, 103, 104, 105, 114n3
Bourdieuan social theory 102
Brexit debate 74
Burke, K. 101
Busch, N. E., and Givens, A. D. 55

Cairo, fieldwork by Wikan 29
Capitalist world-economy, The (Wallerstein) 4
Catholic Church, birth control 82

Center for Interfaith Action on Global Poverty 91
Chinese military, computer network hacking 56–57
Chopra, R. 102
Christian Medical Commission 88
Christianity 128
church and state separation 84, 89
Cicero, M. T. 105
citizen discourses, European integration 69
citizens: legitimacy evaluations 73; mobilization 76
Citizens United versus Election Commission (2010) 22
civil war, Syria 130
Claude, I. L. 9
cluster munitions ban 109, 111, 131
cognitive punch 103
collective perceptions 10
collective representations 123, 127
collectivistic cultures 22
Commission on Global Governance, *Our Global Neighborhood* (1995) 109
common good 40
Comparative Politics, materialist explanations 4
compassion, health and faith factor 93, 94
Comprehensive Test Ban Treaty Organization (CTBTO) 108
computer equipment and components 57
computer network hacking: Chinese military 56–57; private sector encryption 58
conclusio 105, 106, 109, 110, 113
conformism 9
conscientia, and *synderesis* 37, 41
conscientious objections, internal 40
conscientious politics 11–12
Constitutional Treaty (EU) 73
constructivist norms research 84
contraception 81–82
Convention on Cluster Munitions (2008) 109
cooperative public action 130
credibility, rhetorical theory 106, 114n6
Culpepper, P. D. 101
cultural orientations 29
cultural practices, societal norms 20
cultural relativism 124–125
culture, and justification 127
Cutler, A. C., Haufler, V. and Porter, T. 55
cyber security: encryption debates 57–58; private firms 56–57
cyber-espionage 57
cyberattacks 56–57, 58

De Wilde, P., and Zürn, M. 73
decision-making, social 25–26
decisions, political ramifications 26
defense contractors 56–57
Defense Department (US) 56, 57
Delors, EC President J. 69
democracy: inclusive 122–123; and public deliberation 129

democratic functionalism 74
democratic societies, liberal 122
democratic theory 70
determinism, and essentialism 42
Dewey, J. 128–129
dialogue: intercultural 84; silent 39
dilemmas 39, 46; moral 39, 46
DiMaggio, P. J. 4
Dionigi, F., and Bettiza, G. 84–85
discourse, citizen 69
discourse analysis modes 10–11
discursive field 6
divine ordinance 128
doublethink 41–42
doxa (public beliefs) 129
Druze Arab community, female inequality 28–29
Durkheim, E. 40, 43, 123, 124, 127

Ebola epidemic 82
economic life, amoral character 43
Egypt, Bedouin village 29
electric shock experiments 25–26
Elementary Forms of Religious Life, The (Durkheim) 123
elite society 123
elites, political 74–75
emotion, and reason 38–39
emotional dispositions 21
empirical legitimation analysis 63–77; communicative phenomenon 65; contextualization and differentiation 71–72; desiderata for study of legitimacy in IR 75–77; discursive arenas 69, 75; fallacies of functionalism 73–75; global governance 76; International Relations (IR) 63; legitimacy and legitimation 64–66; legitimacy and the state 69–71; legitimation change triggers 72–73; permissive consensus 66–68, 75; public sphere 68–69
empirical studies 71, 121
encryption debates, cyber security 57–58
endoxa 104, 106, 114n4
Englebert, P. 9
English, R. D. 101
equality: gender 3, 28–29; moral 24; of opportunity 27
Eshkol, Prime Minister L. 47
essentialism, and determinism 42
ethos 103, 106
Etzioni, A. 12, 53–62, 60
European integration: citizen discourses 69; citizen mobilization 72; electoral campaigns 74; legitimacy assessments 70; politicization 71, 73; public opinion 67
Eurosceptical political parties 71
Eurozone crisis 72, 74
existential authority 128
existentialism: dawn of 128; political 43
exogenous shocks 103, 104

faith, bad 42
faith factor *see* health and faith factor
faith-based organizations (FBOs): Africa 82; and multilateral health organization 81; and UN 81
family planning 81–82
female inequality, Druze Arab community 28–29
feminist scholarship 53
field theory 6, 13n2, 113
Financial Stability Oversight Council 57
Fligstein, N., and McAdam, D. 113
Foucault, M. 102
freedoms: closed/open 41–42; moral 35; women's covert actions 29
Freeman, A., and Mensch, E. 53
French Revolution 130
friends, deception of 27
functionalism, democratic 74
functionalist regional integration theory 73
fundamentalism, religious 83

gay marriage 22, 131
gay rights 23, 131
gender equality: Druze Arab community 28–29; India 3
Givens, A. D., and Busch, N. E. 55
global governance 12, 76, 84
global norms development 87
Global Strategy for Health for All by the Year (2000) 90
God: authority and justification 128; as creative intelligence 124; infallibility 41; reality organized by 122; as society 123; source of all morals 123
Golden Rule 49n2
Goldin, Hadar 46
governance: global 12, 76, 84
government: interference 53; surveillance 58
Government Accountability Office (US) 57
Graham, J., and Haidt, J. 22
grammar, political 124
Gramsci, A. 101
Grande, E., and Hutter, S. 74
Greek mythology 124
Green-Pedersen, C. 71
Greenfeld, L. 13, 120–125, 126, 127, 128, 129, 131
groups: inclusion/exclusion 25; inter-group relations 130
groupthink 9
gun ownership 22

Habermas, J. 6, 7, 84, 105
Habermasian deliberation 131
Habermasian translation 83, 85, 91, 94
habitudines 105
habitudo communis 110
Haidt, J. 38; *et al.* 21, 22; and Graham, J. 22
Hall, P. A. 102
Hall, R. B., and Biersteker, T. J. 55

Hamas 45, 46
Hannibal Directive 46
Hanrieder, T. 12, 81–99
hardwired instincts 36–37, 38
Haufler, V., Cutler, A. C. and Porter, T. 55
Havel, V. 42–43
health, WHO definition 88, 90
Health Education through Religion (WHO) 90
health and faith factor 81–96; Africa 92; compassion 93, 94; faith factor tests 93–94; global governance 83–87; norm construction process 91; religious health assets 91–94, 96n14; religious translation 84–86; religious values 83, 86–87, 95n2, 96n5; spiritual Factor X 88–91; staff wages and commitment 93, 96n16; thinning idea 85, 86
Heinze, R. 105
herd morality 130
heterogeneous orientations 30
Hiroshima nuclear attack 110, 112
HIV/AIDS 84, 92
homo conscientious 48
homo economicus 48
homo psychologicus 48
honesty 27
Hooghe, L., and Marks, G. 66–67, 73
Huckleberry Finn (Twain) 40
human beings: as animals 121; as justificatory animals 2–4
Human Development Report (1994) 109
human reproduction 81–82
human security: and inclusive governance 108, 109; notion of 110
human wellbeing 93
Humanitarian Initiative (HI) 107–109, 110, 111, 112, 114nn11,16&-24
Hurd, I. 5, 7, 9
Hurrelmann, A. 12, 63–80
Hutter, S., and Grande, E. 74

ICAN (International Campaign to Abolish Nuclear Weapons) 111
ICC (International Criminal Court) 131
ideal speech situation 6
ideal-types 10, 48
ideational change 100–114; analytical challenge 101–104; evolutionary processes 104; message 109–111; messenger 111–112; nuclear governance 107–112; opportunity 108–109; rhetorical framework for studying 104–107; rhetorical practice 107, 114n10; and South Africa 112
identity, national 73
IDF (Israel Defense Force) 46, 47
In the Penal Colony (Kafka) 40
inclusive democracy, and nationalism 122–123
inclusive governance, and human security 108, 109
India, gender equality 3

inequality, female 28–29
information technology systems 57
instincts, hardwired 36–37, 38
inter-group relations 130
intercultural dialogue 84
interest groups 55
intergovernmental institutions 76
interlocutors 7–8
Internal Revenue Service (IRS) 54
International Campaign to Abolish Nuclear
    Weapons (ICAN) 111
International Criminal Court (ICC) 131
international humanitarian law 110
International Religious Health Assets
    Programme 91
Iranian nuclear threat 47
Islamic State 131
Israel, mass demonstrations 3

Jaspers, K. 2
judgment, moral 10, 19, 20, 24, 25, 30
Junod, Dr M. 110
Justice not Charity, protesters' demand 45
justification 1–13; broader meaning 6, 13n3;
    communicating reasons 127–128;
    contextualizing claims 11; and culture 127;
    human beings 2–4; political 65; public
    engagement 131; public justification 7–11;
    and reason 2, 3; scholarly literature 4–7; social
    context 2, 7

Kafka, F. 40
kairos 103
Karamazov, I. 35
Kellenberger, J. 110, 111–112
Kellenberger speech 110, 111–112
Kihlstrom, J. H. 20
kinetic cyberattacks 57
knowledge, background 100
Kohlberg, L. 39–40
Kohlberg's dilemma 39–40
Kornprobst, M. 13, 14, 102, 115, 131–132; and
    Abulof, U. 1–18, 126–133; and Senn, M. 12–13,
    100–119
Kratochwil, F., and Barbato, M. 84
Kuhn, T. S. 102

land mine ban 109, 111, 131
language: communication access 6; elements
    and rules 2; games 42
Laughland, J. 70
legitimation crisis 2
Legro, J. W. 102
liberal democratic societies 122
liberalism: self-doubts 43; tradition of 23
liberty, positive/negative 41
Lindberg, L., and Scheingold, S. 67
Lisbon Treaty debates 74
loci 103, 105, 114n2

loci communes 113
loci prorii 110, 113
Lockheed Martin 57
locus communis 110, 113
locus nullius 110
locus prorii 110
locus prorius 106
logical reasoning 124
Lord, C., and Beetham, D. 9
Lowi, T., and Olson, M. 55

Maastricht Treaty, Danish rejection (1991) 66
McAdam, D., and Fligstein, N. 113
McConnell, G. 55
Mahler, H. 88
Majone, G. 9
Marks, G., and Hooghe, L. 66–67, 73
Martinotti, G., and Stefanizzi, S. 70
Marxism 43
Masada myth 46
Maslow, A. H. 37
May, E. R. 102
Mayors for Peace 112
Mehta, J. 101
Mensch, E., and Freeman, A. 53
MHOs (multilateral health organization) 81, 93
Microsoft XP operating system 57
Middle Ages 128
Middle-East, patriarchal cultures 28
Milgram, S. 25–26, 28
military: Chinese computer network hacking
    56–57; private sector support 58
Milton, J. 41
mobilization, citizen 76
monotheism 124
Moore, B. 4
moral absolutism 30–31
moral dilemmas 39, 46
moral equality 24
moral foundations 21
moral freedom 35
moral gap, man and other animals 38
moral judgment: children's 24; and culture 19,
    30; identifying 25; and justification 10; and
    reasoning 20, 23
moral learning process 37
moral meaning construction 35
moral minimalism 124
moral orientations 22
moral peer review 37
moral reasoning 34–48; character and
    circumstances 36–37; contours of conscience
    35–36; convenience and conventions 39–41;
    conviction and curiosity 41–43; counter-
    conventional 41; and culture 19; intuition and
    reflection 37–39; Israeli-Palestinian conflict
    46–48; time and interaction 36
moral relativism 40
moral residue 39

moral self-determination 42
moral self-knowledge 39
moral shock 39
moral skepticism 40
morals, God as source 123
Morasso, S. G., and Rigotti, E. 104
Moravcsik, A. 9
multilateral health organizations (MHOs) 81, 93
Munich analogy 104, 105
munitions, cluster 109, 111, 131
mythos to *logos* (*Greek miracle*) 124

NAM (Non-Aligned Movement) 107, 108
narrative theory 2, 5, 103
national behavior, observable aspects 9
national identity concerns 73
nationalism: modern 129; Taylor's critique 48n1
neo-functionalism 73
neo-functionalist theorists 73
Netanyahu, Prime Minister B. 45–46
networks, advocacy 5
New Agenda Coalition 111
New rhetoric (Perelman and Olbrechts-Tycea) 108
newspapers, proxy for public debates 75
Nietzsche, F. 130
NNWS (non-nuclear weapons states) 107, 108, 112
nomic changes 12–13
nomic ideas, new 101, 106, 113
nomization, and society 3
nomos: concept of 102; foundation of reasoning
    and communication 104; justificatory creation
    of 128; as meta-valuation system 102;
    uncontested 106, 107, 114n7
Non-Aligned Movement (NAM) 107, 108
non-nuclear weapons states (NNWS) 107, 108,
    112
nonconformist conscience 40
normative pluralism 86
norms: global 87; literature 100–101; religious
    83, 85; societal 20
Novak, W. J. 54–55
Nuclear Non-proliferation Treaty (NPT) 107, 108,
    109, 110, 112
nuclear testing 110
nulli loci 105
Nussbaum, M. C. 23, 24
NWS (nuclear weapons states) 107, 108, 110

Obama, President B.: administration 58–59;
    Prague Speech 110
obedience to authority experiments 25–26
Occupy Wall Street 41
Office of Personnel Management 57
Okin, S. M. 30
Olbrechts-Tycea, L., and Perelman, C. 108
Olson, M., and Lowi, T. 55
open society (Bergson) 37
Operation Protective Edge 46, 47
Orwell, G. 41–42

Our Global Neighborhood (Commission on
    Global Governance, 1995) 109

Palestinian–Israeli conflict 46–48
parents, deception of 27
PASSP (people are stupid school of psychology)
    11, 20–21
patriarchal cultures: Middle-East 28; research 30
Peace and Truce of God (*Pax Dei*) 129–130
PEPFAR (President's Emergency Plan for AIDS
    Relief) 84, 94
perception discrepancy 26
Perelman, C., and Olbrechts-Tycea, L. 108
permissive consensus 66–68, 75
personal choices 27
PHC (primary health care): and spiritual health
    88, 89, 90, 94; and WHO 88
Pinker, S. 49n2
Piot, P. 81
pluralism, normative 86
policing and criminal justice system, America 58
policy paradigms 102
polio eradication campaign 82
political elites 74–75
political existentialism 43
political grammar 124
political justification, collective decision-making 65
political power, internationalization 64
political realism 3
political rule, rightfulness 64, 66
political scientists 11
political theory 6, 8
political utterance 10
political views: conservative/liberal 20–22, 23,
    30; hardwired 36–37; public reasons 129
polygamy, unfair practice 29
Popper, K. R. 9–10, 37
Porter, T., Cutler, A. C. and Haufler, V. 55
post-functionalism 73
Powell, W. 4
power, political 64
power differences, relationships 27, 28
PR (public relations) 129
pragmadialectics 6
pragmatic reasons 7
Prague Speech (Obama, 2009) 110
President's Emergency Plan for AIDS Relief
    (PEPFAR) 84, 94
primary health care (PHC): and spiritual health
    88, 89, 90, 94; and WHO 88
prisoner's dilemma 46
privacy, sacred significance 130
private firms, cyber security 56–57
private–public divide 12
privatization, Israel 45
Protestantism 123
protesters, 'Justice, not Charity' demand 45
psychological perspective 19–29; cultural
    practices 28–29; liberalism 23; rights, social

inclusion, and honesty 26–27; social decision-making 25–26; social judgments 24; theoretical approach 20; thought, reasoning, and emotions 22–24
public: discrete meaning 12; etymology of term 128; presumed existence 129
public conscience 34
public deliberation and democracy 129
public health: faith-based service providers 82, *see also* health and faith factor
public justification, empirical phenomenon 120–125
public opinion: European integration 67; socio-moral imagery 130; surveys 27
public relations (PR) 129
public sphere: concept of 68; reconstruction at village level 130
public worth, creation 82

rational choice 4, 13n1
rationality, Weber 10, 13n5
Rawls, J. 45, 46
Reagan, President R. 21
realism, political 3
reality, organized by God 122
realpolitik, practicalities 47
reasoning: and emotion 38–39; as epiphenomenon 21; as human attribute 20; logical 124; and moral judgments 23; pre-conventional 40, *see also* moral reasoning
Reinikka, R., and Svensson, J. 94
relationships, power differences 27, 28
relativism: conscience 41; cultural 124–125; moral 40; and moral scepticism 40
religion: and health institutions 12; and secularization 128, *see also* God; health and faith factor
religious actors 85, 94
religious fundamentalism 83
religious health assets 82, 91–94, 96n14
religious norms 83, 85
religious reasons 7
religious values: and health 83, 95n2; private to public 86, 95n4; public construction 86–87, 96n5
representations, collective 123, 127
Reus-Smit, C. 65–66
Review Conferences (RevCons) 107, 108
rhetoric, ancient Greek 5
rights: abortion 22; gay 23, 131
Rigotti, E., and Morasso, S. G. 104
Roe versus Wade (1973) 22
Rokeach, M. 36
Rorty, R. 42
Ruggie, J. 102

Samson 46–47
Samson's option 47
Samurai's ritual suicide (*seppuku*) 40

Santorum, R. 22, 23
Scharpf, F. W. 70
Schattschneider, E. E. 55
Scheingold, S., and Lindberg, L. 67
Schimmelfennig, F. 74
Schmidt, V. A. 102
Schmitter, P. 69
scholarly literature, justification 4–7
scholarly perspectives 101
scholarship, feminist 53
Scott, W. R. 5
Scottish Declaration of Arbroath (1320) 130
secular conscience 37
secularization, and religion 128
self-doubts, liberalism 43
Sen, A. 23, 25
Senn, M. 115; and Kornprobst, M. 12–13, 100–119
Shakespeare, W. 129
Shalit, Gilad 45
silent dialogues 39
Singer, P. 38
situational contexts 26–27, 30
Skocpol, T. 4
smartphone encryption 58
Snowden leaks 56, 58, 59
social actions: interpreting subjective meaning 10; Weberian 9
social actors 9, 127
social conscience 34
social context 7, 8
social contract theory 48
social decision-making 25–26
social inclusion/exclusion 27
social intuitionism 38
social justice, historical struggles 23
social movements 5
social reality 87, 122
social science causality 9
social systems and conventions 24
social theorists 113
social theory 102
social values, creative construction 86
societal norms, cultural practices 20
society, nomization 3
sociological valuation theory 82, 83
Socrates 39
software, military use 57
Solomon's judgment 47–48
South Africa, and nuclear governance 112
speech: ideal situation 42; Kellenberger's 110, 111–112; Prague (Obama) 110
spokesperson, authorized 103, 105, 114n3
state: coercive power 56; and legitimacy 69–71
state-of-nature theory 48
Statham, P., and Trenz, H. J. 68, 72, 73–74
Stefanizzi, S., and Martinotti, G. 70
Sternberg, S. 67
Stewart, J. 22, 23

storytellers 2
Structural Realism 4
suicide (*seppuku*) 40
supranational institutionalization 64
Svensson, J., and Reinikka, R. 94
symbols and culture 122
synderesis, and *conscientia* 37, 41
Syria, civil war 130

Taylor, C. 48n1, 85
telecommunications revolution 1
Ten Commandments 128
Thatcherite British Eurosceptics 70
Theory of International Politics (Waltz) 4
Theory of Justice, A (Rawls) 45
Thévenaut, L., and Boltanski, L. 6, 7, 12, 82, 86, 87, 124
Third Debate 100
Thurlow, S. 112
Tony Blair Faith Foundation 91
topoi 5
totalitarianism 42–43
translation, Habermasian 83, 85, 91, 94
transmission culture 121–122
Trenz, H. J., and Statham, P. 68, 72, 73–74
trolley problem 46
truth telling 87
Turiel, E. 11, 19–33
Twain, M. 40

United Nations (UN): and faith-based organizations (FBOs) 81; General Assembly, First Committee 107, 110, 111
United States of America (USA): Afghanistan military troop levels 58; Agency for International Development 84; Bill of Rights 54; church and state separation 84; Constitution authority 21–22; Defense Department 56, 57; Government Accountability Office 57; policing and criminal justice system 58

values: dissonance 37; religious 83, 86–87, 95nn2&4, 96n5; social 86
van Creveld, M. 47
Vienna Humanitarian Conference 112
views, political 20–22, 23, 30, 36–37, 129
virtue ethics 37
Vlastos, G. 23
Voegelin, E. 128, 129

Wallerstein, I. 4
Waltz, K. 4
Walzer, M. 85
Weber, M. 3–5, 35, 36, 56, 64, 123, 124–125
Weberian social actions 9
Welfare Reform Act (1996) 84, 95n3
Western liberal democracies 126
why question 1, 4, 7
Wikan, U. 29, 30
Willard, C.A. 103
Winston (1984's protagonist) 41–42
Winter, Colonel Ofer 47
Wolfensohn, J. D. 91
World Bank 91, 94
World Council of Churches (WCC) 88
World Faith Development Dialogue (WFDD) 91
World Health Assembly (WHA, 1983) 88–89, 96nn8&9
World Health Organization (WHO): Executive Board 88, 89, 90; health definition 88, 90; Health Education through Religion 90; polio eradication campaign 82; primary health care (PHC) 88; and religious values 88, 95
World Vision 94
Wright Mills, C. 55

Yeats, W. B. 3

Zionism, secular 47
Zionist psyche 46
Zürn, M., and De Wilde, P. 73
Zwingel, S. 85–86